Rick Poy

Why Graphic Culture Matters

Essays, polemics and
proposals about art, design
and visual communication

Occasional Papers

Contents

3. Futures

Preface

Why Graphic Culture Matters gathers a selection of my essays about graphic design, visual communication and visual art written during the first two decades of the 21st century. Much of my writing since the 1980s has dealt with designers and designed objects. The pieces collected here concentrate on issues, tendencies, trends, prevailing ideas and fresh departures. They are discursive, opinionated and frequently polemical.

The book is divided into three sections, offering alternative angles of inquiry and perspectives on the field. The first, "Definitions", is a critical survey of the way design and graphic design have been annexed – if not so far taken over – by predatory forces and ways of thinking that limit the expressive possibilities of the medium. This is often presented as necessary or beneficial by those who see design primarily as a net for capturing consumers, but I am personally and professionally inclined to take a contrary view. The second section, "Tools", focuses on alternative ways of thinking about graphic communication as a practice and as a form of culture. These essays deal with topics such as design criticism, graphic design history, the relationship of word and image, design celebrity and the canon. The final section, "Futures", investigates where notable ideas and innovations in graphic communication have come from in recent years and where the practice might be heading.

It collects essays about authorship, critical graphic design and the relationship of art and design, and asks whether graphic design is even the right term for what graphic communicators do now.

Many of these essays (34 out of 46) first appeared in the American magazine *Print*, where I wrote a regular, two-page column from 2000 to 2017. They represent about a third of my *Print* pieces and I have chosen them to highlight interrelated themes that I pursued over time. They are unlikely to be familiar to non-American readers because the magazine was only patchily distributed outside the US – and barely at all in the UK – despite its venerable status, and this is one reason for republishing them. The introduction reworks and updates an unpublished essay about my practice as a writer commissioned by the designer and educator Andrew Howard. Other essays appeared in *Icon*, *I.D.*, *Creative Review*, *Tecknaren*, *Dutch Design Yearbook*, *Frame*, *Elephant* and *Eye*. The pieces are presented here as originally published; only the most minor editorial changes have been made for the purposes of clarity and consistency.

My heartfelt appreciation goes to Martin Fox, Joyce Rutter Kaye, Caitlin Dover, Judy Grover, Michael Silverberg, Melissa Mazzoleni and Zachary Petit, my editors at *Print*; the late Marcus Fairs (*Icon*); Julie Lasky (*I.D.*); Patrick Burgoyne and Mark Sinclair (*Creative Review*); Dick Schyberg (*Tecknaren*); Barbera van Kooij (NAi Publishers); Jane Szita (*Frame*); Marc Valli (*Elephant*); and my colleague and friend John Walters (*Eye*). Many thanks, too, to my publishers Sara De Bondt and Antony Hudek at Occasional Papers. I count myself exceptionally fortunate to have worked with so many wonderfully supportive editors. Good editors and thriving, imaginative publications make a life in design writing possible. They are the beating heart of the discipline.

Introduction

Writing about graphic culture

When I first imagined myself as a writer, growing up in suburbia, I knew nothing at all about design. The word barely figured in everyday English in the 1970s, let alone as a subject for writing. It was entirely feasible at school or university to imagine a future writing about music, literature, art or film. There were books aplenty on these subjects and articles and reviews in newspapers and magazines. I was fascinated by literary criticism and devoured the weekly music press. In 1976, while studying art history, I took out a subscription to *Sight and Sound*, the British Film Institute's quarterly film journal. I spent hours trawling through back issues in the University of Manchester's library.

The best music and film writers were forceful presences and there were lots of role models for an aspiring writer. The names of these critics and commentators became familiar and, returning regularly to their work, I absorbed the critical positions and aesthetic priorities they represented. They were granted a quantity of space to explore their ideas that seems incredible when measured against similar magazines today. The first issue of *Sight and Sound* to drop through my letterbox featured an article comparing the films *Seven Beauties* and *Taxi Driver* that runs to about 6,000 words. The writing was clearly seen as necessary by both editors and readers.

Design was another matter. There were no regular outlets for design coverage in any of the general newsstand magazines or papers I saw. It wasn't until 1979, when I took a routine job at a book production company, that I began to be aware of graphic design as a defined activity. I read Cal Swann's *Techniques of Typography* (1969) and bought the latest edition of *Hart's Rules for Compositors and Readers*. I learned how to use a Compugraphic EditWriter phototypesetting machine. Keyboarding a study of the Hollywood musical in a series style established by Richard Hollis (who would become a colleague years later), I relished the unusually large paragraph indents, the use of bold within the main text for film titles, and the American Typewriter Bold Condensed chapter titles.

As a music fan, I loved album cover art and around 1980 – the heyday of post-punk rock – record sleeves were spaces of boundless graphic invention. I threw together an amateur "new wave" single cover for a friend, using scissors, glue and a drawing I based on a found photo, and it was thrilling to find my efforts displayed on the wall at the Rough Trade record shop in Notting Hill, London. *The Face* magazine, self-consciously designed by Neville Brody, was essential reading and viewing in those years. In 1982, I landed a job in the in-house graphics department of an international computer consultancy in London, where I met expert typographers for the first time. I did some rudimentary design of overhead projection slides and simple company brochures, and signed up for an evening class in book design at the London College of Printing (now London College of Communication). I already knew the basics. In 1983, the revelatory first edition of Philip Meggs' *A History of Graphic Design* felt like a manual of deliciously arcane knowledge.

Although I had no formal training in graphic design, I had acquired a visual education and I knew how to analyse images. I discovered design magazines such as *Creative Review* and *Blueprint*, both launched in

the early 1980s, and the Design Council's long-running
Design. *Blueprint* was the first publication to show me
that design commentary could be handled with the same
historical awareness, intense personal commitment and
stylish prose found in the best film, music or art writing. In
1984, in thrall to the music and ideas of Brian Eno, I began
work on a visual book about him in collaboration with the
artist Russell Mills and the designer Malcolm Garrett. I
became a staff writer on one of the early personal computer
titles. By the time the Eno book, *More Dark Than Shark*,
came out in 1986, I wanted to change direction. I was a
visual person and design fascinated me. It was fashionable
and fast becoming a metropolitan obsession. I moved to
Designers' Journal, an interior design magazine published
by the Architectural Press in London. Then, in April 1988,
Blueprint's editor, Deyan Sudjic, took me on as his deputy,
with a brief to write about architecture, interiors, furniture,
industrial design and, once in a while, graphic design.

Those were years of discovery. The early *Blueprint*
was a writers' publication, despite the oversized pages
constructed around photographs arranged with a brilliant
eye. Yet the magazine's editorial priorities were rarely
mentioned. There were no directives from Sudjic or anyone
else about the writing's critical purpose. As a new arrival,
I was left to work it out for myself by observing the editor
and his contributors in action. I was free to choose my
subjects and approach them however I liked. *Blueprint*'s
undeniably exclusive commitment to an ideal of visual
perfection suited me fine. In the 1980s, like many young
people at the time, I was obsessed with matters of style
and this concern ran through all the areas of culture that
interested me, from writing to film.

In his afterword to *Lolita*, Vladimir Nabokov observes:
"For me a work of fiction exists only in so far as it affords
me what I shall bluntly call aesthetic bliss, that is a sense
of being somehow, somewhere, connected with other states
of being where art (curiosity, tenderness, kindness, ecstasy)
is the norm." I'm not sure I would have gone along with
Nabokov's "only", even then, or his rejection of didactic

purpose, but I certainly identified in every straining fibre with his desire for aesthetic bliss. Visual form supplied this kind of satisfaction and so did the process of writing: sifting words, fashioning sentences, trying to convey accurately my sensations as a viewer. While I would have pursued this pleasure regardless, my subject matter had turned out to be design.

Thinking like this gave me a sense of common purpose with many of the graphic designers I met on my travels and studio visits in those years. I shared their tastes and priorities, admired and disdained the same visual trends. If design could supply these experiences, then, for me at that point, this was its ultimate justification. Perhaps this sounds simplistic as a rationale – no doubt it was – but the process of learning about a subject, as well as discovering how to write about it, takes time and experience, so formal considerations came first. As a practice and source of aesthetic sensation, design often attracts people who might once have derived those satisfactions from art; this was true of my own shift in interest from art to design in the 1980s (art would become more important to me again a few years later).

I came to graphic design writing relatively late, in my early 30s, and I had no preconceptions about what it should be. My visual interests had been shaped in my youth by modern art, above all by Dada, Surrealism and Pop Art, my thinking influenced by a melange of ideas from existentialism, anarchism, the 1960s counterculture, rock music, feminism, literary criticism, and film theory. In the late 1970s, I read John Berger, Roland Barthes' *Mythologies* and Dick Hebdige's *Subculture: The Meaning of Style*, a key cultural studies text of the time. Susan Sontag's essays in *Against Interpretation*, *Styles of Radical Will* and *On Photography* offered an inspiring example of the writer as free-ranging cultural critic. In the early 1980s I became interested in deconstruction, though not with the same investment I felt in the movements and writers I discovered when younger. All these influences led me, as a design writer, to want design to be as intellectually stimulating as possible. At the same time, everything I had learned as a reader convinced me that design writing should be as sharp, involving and entertaining as the best writing about film or popular music, and it needed to be easily available – to anyone – through ordinary publishing.

For the aspiring design writer, though, there were obstacles. In the 1980s, most writing about graphic design in Britain was trade journalism. Its ambitions were set not much higher than providing information about the latest designers, projects and trends for a readership of practising designers. No matter how professional this coverage might be, it didn't allow writers to attempt more personal or critical investigations – the kind of writing found in *New Musical Express* or *Sight and Sound*. There was little sign that monthlies like *Creative Review* or *Direction* wanted this sort of article.

One encouraging exception was Robin Kinross' contributions about graphic design in *Blueprint*. Kinross tended to eschew direct reporting and journalism's reliance on quotation in favour of a more essayistic manner. His careful, inquiring and, when necessary, disapproving voice was unmistakably his own. He wrote with conviction and feeling from deep knowledge and his pieces found a natural home in *Blueprint*'s pages next to similarly reflective and argumentative articles about architecture by writers such as Martin Pawley, Janet Abrams and Rowan Moore. My hope, when *Blueprint*'s publisher launched *Eye*, a quarterly with the space to run longer features, was that it could develop into a more concentrated forum for this kind of writing – as the magazine's editor, I called it critical journalism. Kinross was a valued early contributor, although he never felt as engaged in *Eye*'s graphic design-focused pages as he had with *Blueprint*'s broad readership. This underscores one of the problems with writing about graphic design, which limits the activity even today. Almost all of this prose is aimed at designers, design students and design teachers and only a fraction is ever read by anyone else.

Publications dealing with art, music or film have never faced this constraint.

The question of audience is critical because there can be no viable writing without readers and their assumed concerns will determine the writing's scope, emphasis and tone. Some inherent limitations of graphic design as a subject for writing compound the problem and this helps to explain why it struggles to find a wider, non-specialised audience. One of these restrictions is that while graphic design is omnipresent in our visual culture, it isn't consumed in the same way as a novel, film or album. Graphic design isn't a product in itself, though it may be an essential part of a product, and it is unlikely to be the primary reason for buying something, even if it influences the decision to buy.

The elaborate forms of critical writing about books, films, cultural history and social issues found in quality newspapers, specialist magazines and essay collections function as more than consumer guides. Short journalistic reviews and round-ups already take care of the need for snappy assessment. Critical essays aimed at the general, non-academic reader take it for granted that sophisticated consumers of books, albums and films appreciate analysis and evaluation. An artistically ambitious film, consisting of thousands of images conveying an intricate narrative about some aspect of the human condition, can easily sustain a 2,000-word essay. A literary response on this scale doesn't feel out of proportion with the viewer's experience. Entire books are written about single films and albums.

Even if it were possible to spin a long essay from, say, a poster advertising a film, it is doubtful many viewers would be interested in a protracted critique. While ambiguity of meaning is fundamental to many complex artworks, the role of graphic design is usually to communicate more directly. Detailed critical interpretation of the outcome is simply not required. Unless it becomes a collectible item, or surfaces in a book, a film poster is an ephemeral message glimpsed in passing. There may be no correlation at all between its degree of interest as a piece of graphic communication and its attractiveness to the collector. Other factors, such as the fame and popularity of the film or its stars, are often more important to the viewer than the design. No branch of graphic activity, except for the undeveloped sphere of graphic authorship (see "Questions of Authorship", page 204), can be regarded as an end in its own right.

Viewers who would like to equate graphic design with other art forms might resist this conclusion, but the evidence is overwhelming. In contemporary design writing aimed at a non-academic readership (even a readership of designers) it is highly unusual to come across microscopic analysis of particular pieces of work. Instead, design writers who aspire to seriousness tend to focus on more general design matters, tacitly confirming that close-up description and analysis would expose the slightness of the designed object. Meanwhile, the paucity of close readings of actual designs is rarely commented upon by design people, even though it suggests some awkward limitations to graphic design as a potential subject for exploratory writing.

My way of handling this, when I started, was to look for designers whose bodies of work could sustain a more searching analysis because they demonstrated some continuity of outlook and method. The complexity of content required for criticism would come from the totality of a designer's output, as an expression of their ideas and intentions, if not from individual pieces. This seemed to present greater possibilities for a more concrete and textured form of writing sensitive to graphic communication's pervasive role in contemporary culture, and to viewers' everyday experiences. I believed that such an approach stood a chance of engaging readers – perhaps even readers approaching graphic design from outside the field. These "complex" designers interested me because they broke with restrictive norms and sent visual communication questing off in new directions.

I responded to images and messages that rewarded my attention and I wanted to find out more.

Although I still sometimes write about individual designers, my focus has altered since 2000 – the period covered by this book. After I left *Eye* in 1997, I concentrated on essays, columns and reviews, and then blogging. I had spent more than a decade interviewing designers, acquainting myself with the tenets, preoccupations and rituals of design practice. Extended observation had given me plenty of material for reflection. I was more interested now in design writing as a form of cultural criticism: with design's meanings, social uses and effects. My second and third collections of essays, *Obey the Giant* (2001) and *Designing Pornotopia* (2006), signalled this change of direction.

My column for *Print* magazine, initially named "Optic Nerve" and later retitled "Observer", was a remarkably generous gift from an American publication to a British writer based outside the country, although I had been a frequent visitor since the late 1980s and knew the American design scene. *Print*'s editors, then led by Martin Fox, gave me an entirely free hand, allowing me to write about any subject I chose, often without knowing in advance what I would deliver. Without *Print*, I wouldn't have had such a sustained opportunity to explore my own reactions and thinking, and some of this writing might not have appeared. ("Critique", my long-running column in *Eye*, which ran in parallel, focused on singular objects rather than themes.) The purpose of the *Print* essays wasn't to be exhaustive, but to make a concise intervention, to add another perspective to the conversation and, where appropriate, to provoke. If readers had agreed with everything I proposed, then I wouldn't have been doing much of a job. It's probably true to say that the *Print* essays provided foundations on which to build some of the other critical, polemical and speculative writing in these pages.

During those years, I continued to write mainly for a design audience, because this remained a consistently receptive readership. British newspapers showed only a sporadic and superficial interest in graphic design. My aim was always to be a full-time writer, like writers in other fields. To achieve this, the writing must pay. Related activities such as editing, lecturing and curating helped to make this line of work viable, but it was always a struggle. In the online era, it is harder to live a life that prioritises freelance design inquiry than it was in the print world of 30 years ago. Design writers who aren't also designers tend, over time, to quit the field. Most of the writing issuing from what used to be called the trade press – both in print and online – confines itself to professional agendas and goals. The writers who make a significant contribution to graphic design writing tend to be practising designers, or design educators, for whom writing is a secondary and occasional activity. There is often less urgency to this writing (in the sense of topicality) and it tends to be concerned with understanding and situating their own design practice.

In some crucial respects, the ambitions and perspectives of designer-writers are different from my own. My primary subject is best summarised as graphic culture. This is the part of contemporary visual culture formed by graphic communication and expression. My initial responses to this culture, as I have explained, were instinctive and unformed. Because graphic culture spoke to me, conveyed meaning and gave me pleasure, I felt that it mattered. Over the years, this conviction was repeatedly confirmed by my growing experience and knowledge of the subject. It amazed me that for so many otherwise perceptive and wide-ranging writers situated in the worlds of literature and criticism, this graphic reality barely seemed to exist as a potential subject matter.

Yet, consciously or not, we connect to graphic culture all the time. In its total effect, it forms a multifaceted, multimedia interface, a complex sensory environment through which we experience, mediate and navigate contemporary reality. We cannot escape from this realm; we depend on it. I wanted to say things about this graphic culture, in relation to our wider culture, that designers tend not to say because no matter how insightful they might be, they are inevitably preoccupied by the task and goal of being a designer – by their own processes and practice. While I understand these processes, for me, the outcome, the communication's meaning in the world, matters more. I don't believe it is possible to understand the graphic sphere fully without considering the intentions and actions of designers, their "studio culture", as it's been dubbed, but designer-writers are often reluctant to single out their colleagues as revealing examples. The critical tension in my writing comes from being both situated in the design world and immersed in graphic culture as a member of society, while remaining a semi-connected observer of the "design business". From that ambivalent vantage point, these essays zero in on prevailing ideas and tendencies, both positive and negative, airy and substantial, that struck me as salient, revealing or pressing. At root, this writing is about why we value what we value, using my own experiences of the graphic realm as a starting point and guide.

In the long run, I can see no reason why graphic culture – as a vital medium of communication and visual expression – shouldn't be absorbed into the lineage of commentary about popular visual culture written for a broad audience. The history of this kind of writing can be traced back to the essays of George Orwell and Robert Warshow (collected in *The Immediate Experience*) and books such as Barthes' *Mythologies*, Gilbert Adair's *Myths & Memories*, and Judith Williamson's *Consuming Passions*. Visual communication will continue to play a central role in every branch and level of society and writing that aims to illuminate our multidimensional graphic reality seems not only necessary but inevitable.

1. Definitions

The Soul of Design

The battle to define design

There is no better way to find out how people outside the design world view design than to check out books about the subject aimed at business readers. And, in the sphere of business gurudom, where a sought-after speaker can command $40,000 a lecture, there is no louder noise than Tom Peters, championed by *The Economist* as the "über-guru".

Peters has his own series, *Tom Peters Essentials* – "crucial guides for reinventing your business" – with the same little picture of him on the cover, the spine, the back and, in case you haven't quite taken it in, the back flap. The book on design (2005) begins with a startlingly bold claim that proves to be entirely typical of Peters' bombastic attempts to shock and awe aspiring captains of industry who come to him for enlightenment.

"I, not the Greek philosophers, have discovered the 'Seat of the Soul.' At least in enterprise," Peters writes. "And it is ... Great Design." He alone among the management gurus writes extensively about design, he claims. "Why? IT TURNS ME ON." (Peters' emphasis.) As with their leave-nothing-to-chance approach to the author's publicity photos, these books work by repetition. First you state something, then you state it again slightly differently, then you recap with a list of key points. Peters uses an entire page to drive home his amazing revelation about the soulfulness of design. "Design = Soul. Believe it."

Well, I would like to believe it, I really would, but the more that Peters shouts and brags about it, the less I want anything to do with this vision of design. I simply can't match my personal experience of design, as something you piece together for yourself because these are the things you value and want in your world, with all his exhortation and bluster. Peters' book would probably dumbfound any designer of any sensitivity who read it, though it isn't aimed at designers and that's why we should be concerned. As design becomes an increasingly public issue, with business leaders and politicians sprinkling the word around like magic dust, so its uses and meanings are being defined by narrowly commercial ways of thinking. Designers, who have rarely been given the chance to explain their work to the public on their own terms, find themselves reduced to an instrumental role, delivering design conceived only to satisfy business imperatives and marketing prescriptions.

By his own admission, Peters has been surprisingly slow to wake up to the power of a discipline that he now believes should be at the heart and soul of any business enterprise. He is not artistic, he says, and dropped out of architecture school to study civil engineering. He has been working as a management consultant since the mid-1970s and is now in his 60s, but it was only ten years ago, he reports, that he started to become more "design sensitive". What triggered this? "My secret: Waking up. Becoming alert," he reveals, with his usual modesty. As any wide-awake designer and quite a few business people could have told him, design was important for business long before the mid-1990s. One has to wonder what took him so long and why he now sees himself as an authority on design.

Peters' view of design is, in reality, utterly familiar. Design is about the difference between being cool and uncool. It's about creating awesome experiences and products with dreamlike power. It's about making an emotional connection. The book trots out all the usual role models: Nike, Virgin, Google, Armani ("We become

Armani"), Porsche ("I AM MY PORSCHE"). Mere physical presence won't cut it. Companies must create products with a metaphysical presence. Don't kid yourself that Starbucks sells coffee. What it sells is a whole Way of Life. "We must – all of us!" exclaims Peters, "come to grips, 'strategically,' with the fact that WINNERS IN THE NEW ECONOMY WILL BE … MASTERS OF THE DREAM BUSINESS." And, make no mistake, "winning" is what it's about. Peters enthuses about the billions of dollars at stake. He quotes a paean to tea from the founders of the American company Republic of Tea. "You might find all that to be a wheelbarrow load of crap," he says. "I think instead of wheelbarrows filled with gold."

Designers have been saying for years that they would like a place on the board and to be involved in companies' strategic thinking. So it's good that Peters urges his business readers to give designers a seat at the table, only he doesn't follow his own advice in the book. He includes interviews about design with three "cool friends" – a journalist, a general manager at the global design company IDEO and a former vice-president of marketing at Starbucks. Not one of them is a designer. Maybe designers don't have anything useful to say about the soul of design.

That's certainly the way some people who work with designers seem to see it. "Design is far too important to be left to designers," David Hepworth, publisher of *Word* magazine, suggested in *The Guardian*. The put-down appears to be catching on. Arnold Wasserman, chairman of the Idea Factory consultancy in San Francisco and Singapore, has used it, and so have others. Virginia Postrel, one of Tom Peters' cool friends, goes a step further in her book *The Substance of Style* (2003). "Aesthetics has become too important to be left to the aesthetes," she advises. "To succeed, hard-nosed engineers, real estate developers, and MBAs must take aesthetic communication, and aesthetic pleasure, seriously."

Postrel's book, which is heavily American in its examples and outlook, has received less attention in the UK, but it remains a significant marker – not for what

Apple Fifth Avenue
New York, 2019

it reveals about design, but for what it reveals about attitudes to design outside the design world. Postrel was an economics columnist for *The New York Times* and some designers were understandably thrilled that someone in her position should speak so positively about design and the rise of aesthetic value. If you don't know much about the subject you might feel, like Harvard psychology professor Steven Pinker, who wrote a blurb for the back of the book, that this is a "major new phenomenon": that people – gasp! – care deeply about the look of things.

The Substance of Style is lively, well argued (in the main) and a lot less irritating than Peters' over-amplified guide. Yet you still find yourself wondering where the author has been for the last 20 or 30 years. Postrel seems dazzled to find that sensory appeals are everywhere and becoming ever more prominent in our culture. She appears to think that it will come as news to learn that design provides pleasure and meaning as well as function. Meanwhile, the same old view of designers as somehow not to be trusted with design sometimes leaks out. At a conference, Postrel sees a venture capitalist addressing a crowd of graphic designers. "The role of design is to make life enjoyable," he tells them. "The designers generally agree," notes Postrel. This makes it sound like the designers needed the entrepreneur to set them straight, while her use of "generally" implies that there were some who disagreed with the proposition, unlikely as that sounds.

"Designers and other cultural opinion leaders used to believe that a single aesthetic standard was right – that style was a manifestation of truth, virtue, even sanity," writes Postrel. When was this exactly? Postrel makes it seem like the recent past. I have been writing about design since the mid-1980s and at no point during that time was this true in Britain. Nor, I would suggest, was it the case in the US. Of course, individual designers do have their sometimes dogmatic preferences, but these coexist within a marketplace that thrives on aesthetic diversity and a multiplicity of competing styles. Postmodern cultural analysis has explained all this, yet there is no entry for postmodernism in Postrel's index, though her worldview is shaped by a business-friendly version of some of this thinking – "We are constantly exposed to new aesthetic material, ripe for recombination" – and she makes an explicit passing reference to postmodern irony and camp.

The same mysteriously imprecise view of history occurs when Postrel says, "You no longer have to be a Medici to enjoy aesthetic abundance [...] Not only monuments but the humblest of objects increasingly embody fine design." Again, this makes it sound like something that has only happened in the last few years. Abundance is a relative term, but people in wealthy countries, not least the Americans, have been enjoying "aesthetic abundance" for many decades. Postrel makes no mention of American writer Thorstein Veblen's famous *Theory of the Leisure Class*, the book that gave us the term "conspicuous consumption" more than 100 years ago, even though she challenges the idea, first proposed by Veblen, that excessive consumption serves to signal social status. Veblen's well-heeled gentleman connoisseur spent his time cultivating his "aesthetic faculty", the better to learn "how to live a life of ostensible leisure in a becoming way."

It's no wonder that Tom Peters envies *The Substance of Style* because this deeply political book is an ode of joy to the way we live now that glides cheerfully past any problems of waste, sustainability or global fairness. The book can be interpreted as a clarion call to business to embrace design's profit-generating potential and as a green light for unlimited material production. According to Postrel, critics of consumption are misguided because they fail to see that people are not engaged in games of social one-upmanship when they buy luxury goods. They are simply indulging in a perfectly natural search for aesthetic pleasure.

The limitations of Postrel's analysis are most clearly exposed in her discussion of toilet brushes. She runs through some of the brushes available in the US: Michael

Graves' $8 brush from Target, a $14 Oxo brush, Philippe Starck's Excalibur at $32, an Alessi brush for $55. The options continue all the way up to $400 – for those with money to flush down the toilet. Postrel argues that such purchases cannot be explained as a desire to impress others (as clothes can, for instance) because few people will ever see our toilet brushes. Therefore, these highly designed items must be acquired simply on the basis of their sensory appeal. "We buy aesthetic models because we like what we see and feel," she says. That may be so but there are countless, better opportunities to satisfy our aesthetic inclinations.

If we feel dismayed at the possibility of having to throw a bare brush under the sink, then perhaps we have become a little too enmeshed in our role as good consumers. Step back and toilet brushes as the focus of aesthetic satisfaction just look frivolous. Is it even true that this has nothing to do with a person's sense of status? Postrel, like many design watchers, is preoccupied by design as an expression of personal identity. "Identity is the meaning of surface," she says. So when you buy a toilet brush as a design lover, you are confronted by a small dilemma of selfhood. Are you really going to let yourself down by buying something you know to be poorly designed? No point in spending all that money on the dining table and chairs if you are going to scupper the aesthetic effect in the bathroom. Visitors whose opinion you care about might see the offending item. People who take this to the limit and equip their homes with a brace of $400 toilet brushes are making a statement about who they think they are in the scheme of things. The brushes are simply less visible than their Armani outfits or Porsches.

Postrel acknowledges that people enjoy sensory appeals, while fearing manipulation. This is a key point, though it's not one that business advocates of design are disposed to explore with any openness. If aesthetic appeals engage us at a pre-rational level, then they offer a perfect way to encourage us to buy products and services. Again, there is nothing especially new about this insight. Advertising has understood for years that the way to influence consumers is by emotional stimulation rather than information or argument. "Everybody experiences far more than he understands," Marshall McLuhan observes in *Understanding Media* (1964). "Yet it is experience, rather than understanding, that influences behaviour, especially in collective matters of media and technology, where the individual is almost inevitably unaware of their effect upon him." This has become something of a mantra for exponents of "experience design", but they tend to leave out the cautionary words that follow "behaviour". What they like is the idea of experience as unconscious persuasion.

The more design is seen as a magic ingredient with the power to melt away customer resistance and win undying loyalty to the brand, the more it seems in danger of losing what consultants who dream of wheelbarrows laden with gold like to call its "soul". This will have profound consequences for the way we think about design and what we expect it to do for us, and this can already be seen in the views of design promoted at an institutional level. In the UK, the Design Council website has a series of texts introducing various kinds of design and one of these, under the heading "Emerging Issues", covers the field of experience design. The author, Ralph Ardill, who worked at design and branding agency Imagination for 12 years and runs the Brand Experience Consultancy, made his name beating the drum for a cross-disciplinary design approach also called everything from "experiential marketing" to "brand experience".

Call it what you will, experience design, as Ardill presents it, and as the Design Council apparently endorses it, sounds unashamedly manipulative. "For customers," Ardill explains, "all these moments of corporate experience combine to shape perceptions, motivate their brand commitment and influence the likelihood of repurchase in future ... the experiential designer must not only be concerned with the 'creation'

and 'content' of a particular experience. But also with
the 'context' within which it is to be staged, and the
planned 'consequences' – in terms of how it seeks to
encourage people to think, feel and behave after the
event." Unnecessary inverted commas aside, it could
hardly be plainer.

This kind of baloney must go down a treat with
clients. It might even sound acceptable when we are
talking about other people rather than ourselves. But
you only have to put yourself in the picture to see what's
wrong with it. No one with an independent point of view
and an ounce of self-respect wants to hear that his or
her thoughts, feelings and behaviour are being nudged
and even determined by other people who have gathered
in meeting rooms to research, plot and calibrate exactly
those desired responses. Yet this kind of motivation
and methodology is now taken for granted even by the
Design Council.

In practice, many of the experiential marketing
projects that Ardill mentions seem to be much the same
kind of thing – super-sized brand stores that offer an even
more concentrated blast of brand essence than a regular
shop. There's the Topshop flagship store on Oxford Street
in London, and the Apple Center, Prada Epicenter and
interactive Samsung Experience in New York, although
the latter is truly subtle – it's only for looking and you
have to buy the actual product elsewhere. Alongside the
predictable Disney World in Florida, Ardill includes an
Imagination project, the Guinness Storehouse in Dublin,
which expresses nothing less than the "Soul of Guinness",
according to Tom Peters. And, no, it's not just a pleasant
drink. It's all about community and "sharing stories".
It's a Way of Life.

Increasingly, design exists merely to serve the
needs of branding. The language of branding is now
so pervasive – some would say corrosive – it has
changed the way we think about design. Design's
economic importance is undeniable, but the trouble with
entrepreneurial diktats about the soul of design is that

they are anything but soulful. The business über-gurus and experiential branding consultants are desperate to find a way to bottle and sell us the miraculous elixir of design. The more they drone on about brands as powerful connecting experiences that transcend the product, the more bogus the enterprise starts to sound.

Down with Innovation

The business takeover of design

In the 1980s, when I began to write about design, its appeal seemed fairly obvious. Things that had received the attention of good designers tended to look better than their more routine counterparts. This improvement was layered with all kinds of meanings tied up with the question of how and why something looked better. Nor could visual appeal be dissociated from the function of an object, graphic, or interior design. If the designer's visual concerns got in the way of the design's intended use, then this was naturally a problem. But the crucial point was still that the designed object was attractive and provided a more pleasurable and engaging experience than undesigned or less-designed versions of the same experience.

Even then, some observers worried that designers saw their work as little more than decoration. Style was regularly denigrated for being superficial and empty-headed, usually by designers themselves. Yet the visual nature of design was not seriously challenged and designers continued to argue, as they had argued for decades, that "good design is good business". By improving the design quality of their products, companies would sell more than competitors that hadn't seen the light. Still, plenty of companies didn't seem to get it. In defiance of common sense, or maybe because their leaders lacked a visual education and just didn't know how to look at things, they really weren't comfortable with designers or design.

But designers were right. By the 1990s, almost everyone was getting the message. Design had turned out to be as important as designers always insisted, and it was the force of their commitment, imagination, and creativity, as an expression of public need and desire – designers are people, not a breed apart – that had made it so. Design is now so important, it seems, that designers can no longer be trusted with it, and to make it absolutely clear that control has moved into someone else's hands, design needs to be given a fancy new name. Call it *design thinking*. Call it *innovation*. "Everyone loves design but no one wants to call it design," *BusinessWeek*'s Bruce Nussbaum informed the readers of *Design Observer* in 2007. "Top CEOs and managers want to call design something else – innovation. Innovation: *that* they are comfortable with. Design, well, it's a little too wild and crazy for them." Roger Martin, dean of the Rotman School of Management at the University of Toronto, offers this prescription: "Businesspeople don't just need to understand designers better – they need to become designers."

The first step in the process of disempowering designers is to insinuate that, despite all that time at design school followed by years of doing the job, they have an incomplete grasp of design. They are so preoccupied with fussing over the details and their need to "make things pretty" – tantamount, it's always implied, to a character flaw – that the big picture passes them by. "Designers like the shiny-shiny," writes Peter Merholz, president of the US design and consulting firm Adaptive Path. "That's often why they got into design." Merholz has apparently spent his career "fighting small-minded design thought, particularly in the world of graphic design where the cool, novel, and stylish is lauded over the useful, usable, and truly engaging." Enough of those pesky design stars with an overinflated belief in their own creative vision! "Design is getting a lot more humble, and that is a very good thing," says Adam Greenfield, who teaches in the Interactive Telecommunications Program at New York University. "I take my inspiration from guys like Jasper Morrison or Naoto Fukasawa, who very consciously try to step out of the role of godhead or genius or expert." Never mind that Morrison, however mild his manner, has been a highly publicised design luminary for the better part of 20 years.

Having written off designers as mere stylists with insufferable egos, whose sole aim is to impose their impractical excesses on long-suffering consumers whom they never trouble to consult, the way is clear for a new breed of intermediary to step up and take business's hand. They might once have called themselves design consultants – the rhetoric is not so different – but today they are known as design thinkers and innovation experts. For these design-ovators, everything is subordinate to strategy. Design is one small cog in an elaborate analytical machine intended to dazzle prospective clients into believing that they are dealing with rigorous professionals who work with precise methodologies and defined, quantifiable outcomes. "The great news for designers about the rise of corporate interest in innovation is that it recognizes, more than ever before, the strategic contribution of design to product, service, information, and environmental offerings," says Larry Keeley, co-founder of the US "innovation strategy" firm Doblin. Doblin has an impressive chart detailing ten types of innovation it addresses in the areas of finance, process, offerings, and delivery. In the explanations of "business model", "networks and alliances", "product performance", "customer experience", and so on, the word "design" occurs just twice.

Design thinkers are masterly at weaving a dense web of plausible-sounding words around their analysis – just read their blogs – and this is where they win out against designers, who generally speak most eloquently through their work. But if we leave aside the self-serving patter aimed at building a would-be design thinker's reputation and wooing clients, what are the innovationists saying? Let's hear from Ziba, highly regarded in innovation circles, explaining its approach to experience design on its website: "Customers seek beautiful everyday experiences. To be moved. To grow. Laugh. Cry. Discover. Move beyond their basic needs. Surprise them – maybe throw in a bit of suspense [...] inspire, educate, involve and entertain. The right combination creates insane loyalty." Whether Ziba clients such as Pepsi, Dell, Black & Decker, Starbucks and Frito-Lay do any or all of this for you is a matter of taste (for me, it's a "'fraid not"). But let's be clear that the big conclusion about "insane loyalty" is pure marketing hogwash.

If a continuous cycle of vital innovation is going on, why do the mission statements sound so trite and patronising? And, actually, which is more patronising: to create something you believe in because you think other people might like it too, and just put it out there? (The old, design, way.) Or to study every facet of consumers' behaviour with the intention of filling them with feelings of "insane loyalty" for your client's products? (The new, innovation, way.) Lest there be any doubt about the ultimate goal of all this higher-grade design thinking, *Fast Company* magazine has the lowdown: "It's taken years of slogging through Design = High Style to bring us full circle to the simple truth about design thinking. That it is a most powerful tool and, when used effectively, can be the foundation for driving a brand or business forward." In other words, good design is still good business. While this view of design remains as limited as it ever was – what else might good design be? – it is becoming ever harder to keep sight of what is wrong with a culture mediated largely by commercial forces pursuing their own ends. But it comes down to this: is an encounter with an everyday brand – a bottle of soda, a power tool, a packet of snacks – the place to go if you want to be moved, to seek education, or to grow as a person, and aren't there better places to find those kinds of experiences?

This brings us back to design's visual qualities. It is hardly surprising that designers try to put as much distance as possible between themselves and the accusation that they are hung up on making things look pretty. Belittling language of this kind suggests that the visual is inherently trivial, easy to do, and beneath consideration, that form is not a powerful medium of expression and carries no meaning for the viewer. Design thinkers like to talk as though we have somehow passed beyond the stage where the way things look needs to be a primary concern, and designers, browbeaten and demoralised, half seem to believe them. They have been too ready to accept the caricature of themselves as airheaded stylists who care about insignificant niceties of no concern to anyone else. At the very point when designers most need to mount a spirited defence of the visual, many seem to have lost their nerve and fallen silent.

Yet the rhetorical reduction of design to frivolous prettification reveals a wilful blindness to the power of expressive form-making, if not a deep, philistine ignorance of the history of design and visual culture. The scale of the oversight is so colossal, and frankly baffling, one hardly knows where to start. Are the great cathedrals of Europe – Rheims, Lincoln, Chartres – merely pretty? Are the gardens of Kyoto? Is Alvar Aalto's Paimio armchair? Was Alexey Brodovitch's *Portfolio* magazine? How about Leica cameras? The patterns on Moorish ceramic tiles? Or the PowerBook and the iPod? There is surely no need to go on.

A moment ago I used the word "culture", a notoriously awkward concept. According to the critic Raymond Williams writing in *Keywords* (1983), his classic lexicon, culture is used in two crucial senses. In cultural anthropology – now there's a word the innovators love to bat around – it refers primarily to material production, while in history and cultural studies it refers primarily to signifying or symbolic systems. Combining these usages, we might conclude that culture is about things (which have a look) and meanings (conveyed by how they look). Whichever way you look at them – so long as you do actually look – these products of our culture tell us who we are. There is bound to be a relationship between impoverished ways of (design) thinking and impoverished visual form.

Design thinkers set great store by business targets, by driving the enterprise forward, because it is exactly what their clients want to hear and it gets them work. Seen from outside the cosy bond of service provider and client, this is a severely limited way of viewing design, and the total domination of current design discussion by this kind of commercial rhetoric is a worrying trend. Michael Bierut is one of the few designers to call out the design thinkers and question their nostrums, so I asked him whether design has a cultural value beyond its business uses and functional purposes. "The business use – the specific goal that motivated the client or sponsor to initially fund the work – often fades away, sometimes quickly," he says. "In some ways, you might argue that aesthetic value – for an enduring design, at least – is the only lasting value, since over time functional needs can change and business moves on to the next goal," Approaching heresy at a time when aesthetic quality is the last thing we are supposed to consider, Bierut goes so far as to modestly propose that "just making something look nicer" or "replacing something ugly with something not so ugly" is an admirable goal for designers.

That probably sounds woefully simplistic to design thinkers. Where is the system? Where are the charts and diagrams, the Capitalised Concepts, the new ways of thinking uniquely suited to market conditions today? To understand why it isn't at all simple, to appreciate how hard it is to create something special, of lasting quality, you need to know a little about design.

The problem that designers face now is the same problem they have faced all along: how to communicate with clients who lack a basic grounding in the visual arts and don't seem to think it matters. Business people don't need to become designers. They need to learn that there are types of awareness and understanding expressed through visual form that even a team of the finest poets would be hard-pressed to summarise as a list of handy PowerPoint bullets. Music, dance and the visual arts operate on a different plane from words. As Dori Tunstall, design teacher and anthropologist, says: "There is an inherent intelligence to beauty, which is about the depth and passion we feel for the world." Design thinkers like to wax lyrical about the elegance of their strategic thinking as a form of design in its own right, as though this could ever be a substitute. They can keep it – in the future, if there are museums then, no one will queue to see a strategy. Give me something tangible, something brilliant and extraordinary that illuminates our perception of what human life can be. For that, we still need designers.

Being Somewhere

The need for critical regionalism

I used to read quite a lot of writing by technology gurus and digital theorists. One thing that emerged clearly was a sense that this new electronic realm of the screen was so rich and wonderful – so extensive, if not infinite, in the territory it opened up – and so radical in its implications for identity and interaction that it would replace many aspects of the physical world.

These writers sounded completely intoxicated by this prospect. Judging from their enthusiastic prose, it seemed that they could hardly wait for it to happen. They were evangelists for what they saw as the inevitable and necessary next step for humanity. The more extreme among them regarded the body as "meat" – something useless, burdensome, rather repellent – and they even fantasised about a time when our minds would at last break loose from this prison of perishable flesh, and we would download our personal essence, like software, and merge with the machines in blissful union.

To this day, there are full-time futurologists with thriving careers based on sci-fi speculations of this kind. "Does Paris have something that telepresence cannot match?" asks architecture professor William J. Mitchell in his 1995 book *City of Bits*. It seems scarcely credible that anyone who has ever visited one of the world's great cities could pose such a ridiculous question. Whatever the body-denigrating, place-denying, virtual experience prophets might claim, there is no obvious universal wish in the 21st century to exchange the experience of physical reality for the immaterial satisfactions of "telepresence". Even something as banal as the constant stream of house makeovers and holiday programmes on TV reveals people's enthusiastic desire to appreciate, enhance and explore their surroundings – both near and far.

It must be obvious, too, that designers are implicated in all of these developments in a particularly deep way. Design is one of the disciplines that has been most caught up in, and most changed by, digital technology. A great deal of 1990s graphic design bore the mark of this transformation. It was constructed in the fluid inner realm of the computer and its layered visual form expressed the conditions of its making.

It was suddenly possible to generate accomplished-looking designs without doing any of the things that designers, as practical thinkers and makers, once did. Compared to the drawing board, the cutting mat and the actual desktop, the surface on which design was now created wasn't really a surface at all. It was more like a window – a window that looked onto nowhere. The ability to keep remixing and refining the screen image was seen as an advantage, and doubtless it was in many ways. But it led to a profound disconnection, fostering the illusion that the universe behind the screen was more vital, perfect, full of possibility and relevant to contemporary reality and experience than anything achieved with non-digital methods.

Twenty years ago, the architecture critic Kenneth Frampton grappled with the problem of "universalisation" – global civilisation's tendency to destroy traditional cultures and make every place look the same. We would probably now call this globalisation. How, he asked, could architecture avoid producing buildings that made no reference to the local cultures on which they were imposed, buildings that looked like they came from anywhere and nowhere? Frampton proposed "Critical Regionalism" as the basis for his "architecture of resistance".

"The fundamental strategy of Critical Regionalism," he writes, "is to mediate the impact of universal civilization with elements derived *indirectly* from the peculiarities of a particular place." As an instance of the specific architectural forms through which this might be achieved, he gives the example of windows, which have an innate capacity to endow architecture with the character of a region and hence to express the place in which a building is situated.

Another key point Frampton makes is the importance not just of the way architecture looks – the sense we need to prioritise – but how it literally feels to the touch. The liberating "importance of the tactile," he says, "resides in the fact that it can be decoded only in terms of *experience* itself: It cannot be reduced to mere information, to representation, or to the simple evocation of a simulacrum substituting for absent presences." And this, remember, was noted before the computer became an omnipresent design aid.

If we want to produce visual communication that is grounded in a sense of place, that feels like it comes from here, where we are, rather than some nebulous, universal nowhere-in-particular, then these two architectural ideas have obvious relevance to graphic design. Since the computer is perhaps the ultimate universalising tool, resisting the broader universalising tendencies of global culture will almost certainly mean that designers take a more questioning view of the technology upon which the design process has come to depend.

The good news is that many designers have reached this conclusion already. The return to handmade work, drawing and the use of handwriting seen in the past few years is a direct reaction to the formulaic effects and over-perfect finishes that have resulted from everyone using the same digital tools. A series of books has documented the trend: *The New Handmade Graphics: Beyond the Digital* (2002); *Hand to Eye: Contemporary Illustration* (2003); *Letterpress: The Allure of the Handmade* (2004); *Handwritten: Expressive Lettering*

Paul Elliman, *I will work at your destruction*, 2001.
Silkscreen print using objects from Elliman's Found Fount (c. 1989–ongoing).
Text from Mary Shelley's *Frankenstein*, 1818.

in the Digital Age (2004). Handmade design is more immediate, personal, unpredictable, and also riskier, because if it fails, there is no "undo" or "copy" function, and it may well have to be junked. The related interest in found objects – see Paul Elliman's prescient Found Fount typeface made out of cast-offs he finds in the street – and the creative use of accidents are part of the same impulse to valorise everyday materials and allow chance to mess things up.

After deluding ourselves for a while that tactility had no particular value, we once again appreciate its importance as a form of experience that binds us in the most intimate way, through our fingertips, to its source – the object of our interest. For the maker, the process of fashioning something three-dimensional using tangible materials, bounded by physical space, confers a feeling of actuality and, as a consequence, an element of authenticity that the depthless non-space of the computer screen cannot match. Constraints can often be a virtue, forcing the imagination to work harder. These qualities are communicated in the design and viewers pick up on them.

It's really no surprise, then, that in an era when "non-places" such as shopping malls, freeways, hotel lobbies and airports have become our dominant places, there is so much continuing interest in graffiti as a form of graphic expression. Every handmade mark is a sign that someone was actually there, on this spot, in that moment, committed to this location, sometimes at personal risk. How different this is from a communication that floats your way out of the electronic ether and often appears to have no precise, knowable point of origin, no context. The stencil has emerged, perhaps rather improbably, as one of the most urgent forms of contemporary visual expression, its crudity and simplicity a gesture of defiance against enervating digital slickness.

Designers undoubtedly have quite a job on their hands. The visual realm is not solely their responsibility, but as communication experts and image fabricators, they play a central role in defending a sense of place – of being somewhere, which is not elsewhere – that helps to give human experience and history continuity and meaning. None of this should be taken as a Luddite call to trash our screens and return to the scalpel and gluepot. I use digital technology, too. But it's certainly a plea for a sense of proportion. For as long as we continue to inhabit our bodies and navigate a path through the material world, no digital simulation will ever compare with the intense, unique, sensorial pleasure of being somewhere and making a mark.

Design as Dictator

Resisting the lure of digital control

I had arranged to meet a designer friend to go to an art opening. Neither of us had visited the gallery before and I had looked at a map to memorise its location. Within moments of setting off in the correct general direction from our meeting point, my companion pulled out his iPhone and started using a GPS app to map our route. So there we were, both of us with years of experience of finding our way around big cities, following the instructions issued by this handy little gadget.

Now, I recognise that many people would regard this as completely unremarkable. You have the phone. You have the app. Why wouldn't you use it to lead you to wherever you are going? We've already grown accustomed to doing this in cars – even cab drivers use GPS guidance now. But it's curious, isn't it, the way we so willingly give up small areas of responsibility, things we know how to do and always did perfectly well in the past, to this new technology? Of course, it was always possible to get lost without a map so a device that ensures you will never lose your way is a convenience. But is that really what it's about: eliminating the small effort involved in finding a destination, removing any potential risk of difficulty or digression along the way, and maximising our place-finding efficiency?

It would stretch credibility to say that we consciously want to hand over control to technology, though sometimes I wonder. Perhaps the explanation for the rapid normalisation of this behaviour is simply that we love the gadgets and can't resist opportunities to use them and show them off. Nevertheless, the effect of deploying the iPhone in this way is to surrender a small piece of personal decision-making to a machine, only one example of our burgeoning dependence on these tools.

There are two links here to design. The first comes from the fact that graphic design as a professional activity is now so heavily invested in technology, so utterly dependent on it at every level, that non-digital design is unthinkable. The designer has become an operator. (My designer friend was, in that sense, simply taking his work home with him.) The second link is that design, as a discipline based on the idea of planning, is itself a technique for imposing organisation, structure, regulation and control.

Typefaces are the most elementary example of this regulatory aspect of graphic design. By regularising the shapes of letterforms, typefaces make words easily transmissible, with enormous benefits for society. The grid is another example. By giving the page a regular underlying structure, grids allow the relatively simple creation of complex assemblages of data, rendered into clear and consistent form by typefaces. These are unarguable developments of enormous utility and value. As graphic design developed, the visual consistency it was capable of delivering began to be applied more widely. With the arrival of the corporate identity manual, an urge to impose control that goes beyond mere utility becomes apparent. The manual offers an idealised vision of reality: the company's image must be presented in this way and no other. Employees are charged with ensuring that the rules and guidelines laid down by the designers to maintain the company's visual identity are followed at all times.

When I first learned about the existence of corporate identity manuals in the mid-1980s, they fascinated me. They appealed to my own controlling tendencies. I worked as an editor, and editors are also engaged in ensuring that textual material conforms to precise editorial conventions. Historically, editing and graphic design, with their shared understanding of typography, evolved as two sides of the same process of communicating via print. There was something strangely satisfying about the idea of specifying in exhaustive detail all the ways that a company's logo, colours and other visible signs could be used on printed material, buildings and transportation. It seemed perfectly benign, nothing more than a reasonable demand for public and internal clarity, a kind of corporate good manners. I could also see why designers loved putting together identity manuals – the ultimate expression of their hopes for the project – and why they admired exceptional manuals designed by their colleagues.

That was a long time ago, though; a time before branding became the master narrative, talked up as the great new panacea for business by a legion of chancers and word-spinners who might once have been hawking snake oil. The more designers repositioned themselves as branding experts, the less sympathy I felt for their mission. Design was indisputably about control now – the control of audience perceptions, emotions and reactions – and this control began with the bondage of design itself.

These thoughts have been with me often of late, as I worked on an exhibition called "Uncanny: Surrealism and Graphic Design" (Moravian Gallery, Brno, 2010). The exhibition's premise is that a kind of alternative tradition influenced by Surrealism exists within graphic design, though it has never received much attention. This is a form of graphic design without limits, one which possesses the same power to involve and disturb us as art does, while remaining, unequivocally, graphic design. What you won't find in any of this work is an indication that it has been moderated by an intermediary professing to tell the designer, from some supposedly superior vantage point, what's most suitable for the viewer. The designers simply interpret the subject in their own way and then viewers are left to make up their minds. This process leaves everything to chance. People might not understand or like what they see. But if they get it, their responses are likely to be immeasurably stronger. They have the satisfaction of knowing that they have been addressed with honesty, intelligence and passion.

I'm not suggesting that all design could be like this. But I do argue that more of it could be and should be. Design has become much too closely aligned with interests that seek to neuter and control it for purely money-making purposes. Designers, by temperament obsessed with control, have been much too ready to comply. Within graphic design, there has always been a tension between its commercial applications and its cultural possibilities. Many designers have felt uneasy about the uses to which their work is put. The desire to resist, to configure design in alternative ways, can be seen in Tibor Kalman's subversive notion of "undesign"; in *Adbusters*' proclamations of "design anarchy"; in the Dutch design team Metahaven's concept of "uncorporate identity"; and in the periodic invocation of the term "anti-design" – first used in Italy in the late 1960s and most recently revived by Neville Brody, a designer prone to expressions of public ambivalence, for an "Anti Design Festival" in London in September 2010.

Technology is turning us into switchboard operators in the communication networks of our own lives. Far from encouraging a sense of freedom, graphic design is implicated every step of the way. Why does everything have to arrive through a screen? Does it really make life richer and more interesting? Why not try rejecting the templated experiences, the social media and the patronising attempts to involve us in prescribed interactions? Unplug, disconnect, wander at random for a while, submit to app-free chance, rely on your own unmediated instincts and non-digital perceptions, and see what comes along.

Immerse yourself in the blissful liberation of going off grid.

Adbusters, Adbusters Media Foundation, no. 37, September/October 2001.
Art direction: Jonathan Barnbrook. Design: Mike Simons.

Stuck in the Middle

Design's middlebrow tendencies

There is one thing in the design world that we rarely seem to admit. Perhaps it's because, here on the inside, we simply don't see it. Perhaps this quality is so pervasive and natural to designers that it seems no more noteworthy or problematic than water is to fish or air to the birds. Maybe we know it full well, but prefer not to talk about it openly. Isn't it the case, though, that in the way we think about professional design, discuss it and go about practising it, graphic design is repeatedly revealed to be an utterly middlebrow activity?

Even so, I can find only two descriptions of graphic design as being middlebrow. In the 1990s, Canadian design writer Joe Clark questioned attempts to impose grand theories on design. "I have tried it, been embarrassed at the results, and on reflection have given up," he wrote. "Rather, what could be described as middlebrow analysis is all graphic design can bear." He commended Philip Meggs' classic textbook *A History of Graphic Design* (1983) as a successful example of middlebrow design writing that dispensed with all the "hopelessly overblown theories". In 2004, CalArts MFA student Randy Nakamura noted in *Emigre* no. 67 that design was a "middlebrow cultural practice". He, too, was concerned about some designers' desire to raise design above its middlebrow status, and he found attempts to hook design to concepts borrowed from science, when the designer had no real understanding of the science, particularly misguided.

The whole point of middlebrow is that it exists in the centre between the two extremes of highbrow and lowbrow. These terms, which can be used as nouns or adjectives, first came into use around 100 years ago. A highbrow was a person with superior intellectual and cultural interests and tastes. A lowbrow was a person largely indifferent to such matters. The term middlebrow, meaning someone of conventional tastes and interests, first appeared in print in the 1920s. In an unsent letter, published posthumously in 1942, experimental novelist Virginia Woolf – a highbrow through and through – described middlebrows with evident distaste: "They are neither one thing nor the other. [...] The middlebrow is the man, or woman, of middlebred intelligence who ambles and saunters now on this side of the hedge, now on that, in pursuit of no single object, neither art itself or life itself, but both mixed indistinguishably, and rather nastily, with money, fame, power, or prestige."

To the avant-garde (when there still was an avant-garde), the middlebrow with his or her impure motives, lack of conviction and limited understanding was the enemy. Highbrows such as Woolf claimed to have far more sympathy for the lowbrow. Years later, you could see this in the tagline for Art Spiegelman's *Raw* magazine: "High culture for lowbrows." *The Modern Review*, an influential British magazine about popular culture, flipped the phrase to make: "Low culture for highbrows."

But there is another view of middlebrow as it flourished in the middle decades of the 20th century that is far more sympathetic. To this way of thinking, middlebrow culture provided ordinary people with an introduction to the less daunting books, plays, music and ideas created by highbrows. It made these experiences accessible, even to those who lived far away from the concert halls and museums found in metropolitan centres. By drawing attention to aspects of culture that any well-educated citizen ought to know about, middlebrow provided the basis for a common culture based on widely shared values. Avant-garde snobs might have scoffed, but there were obvious public benefits in this cohesion.

Champions of this view argue that, if the mid-century understanding of middlebrow is dying today, it's because of the proliferation of media and the vast increase in choice. Instead of three TV networks, there are hundreds of channels. The internet multiplies the fragmentation. Marketing thinks in terms of group lifestyles rather than taking a sweeping view of the entire population. As we pursue our individual paths, organising our cultural consumption to reflect our personal desires and agendas, any notion of a middlebrow common culture founded on shared expectations fades into the distance.

All that has happened, in reality, is that middlebrow has changed. Its brow might be set two or three notches lower than 50 years ago, but it is still right there smack in the centre. How else to describe the thriving cultural middle ground defined by *The Da Vinci Code*, or the *Harry Potter* books, or Oprah, or *Time* magazine? Meanwhile, journalism tends, as always, towards the middlebrow.

Then there is design. The bigger the audiences that design has to serve, the more likely it is to be middlebrow. The clients are middlebrow and designers who succeed in building studios and careers working for these clients are middlebrow, too. This is not to say that these designers are not smart. They are, but only up to a point. Their smartness goes into understanding what the client wants and knowing how to deliver it, and there it has to stop. The designer is not expected to challenge the fundamental basis of the client's activity unless it leads to some minor efficiency in the way the design work connects with the audience. Clearly, such limited horizons are unappealing to many designers. They opt for other sectors – publishing, music, fashion, the art world – which offer greater creative freedom but fewer financial rewards, or they avoid the problem altogether by working in education.

Designers who build careers in middlebrow client areas sometimes rationalise their choices by saying that they are trying to improve society by ensuring that all kinds of things – not just arty, exciting things – benefit from good design. This may be true, but it doesn't change the middlebrow nature of the outcome. Paul Rand is endlessly revered as a great designer. While I admire Rand's work, especially his early non-corporate designs – the book and magazine covers – he is the epitome of a worthy mid-century graphic middlebrow, whether you view that positively or not. As his writings repeatedly emphasise, he drew on the (highbrow) history of art and the visual languages of the 20th-century avant-garde to create corporate logos and packaging for the likes of Cummins, IBM and Westinghouse. Then he claimed, with a middlebrow's aspiration to lift himself up into more highbrow company, that these creations could also be viewed as art. In reality, they were just consummately well-turned commercial designs, limited by the same instrumental purpose as any such undertaking. The things that these visual expressions revealed about society, if that is one goal of critical art-making, were largely unintentional.

You can see Rand's middlebrow design legacy in British designer Michael Johnson's book *Problem Solved* (2004). Johnson, a member of the "big idea" school of design, is another smart fellow, highly accomplished at creating middlebrow designs for middlebrow viewers. His book was well received, a sure sign of design's persistent middlebrow leanings. Even design students submit to the tendency. Johnson takes some awkward graphic phenomena – Ben Shahn's poster about Nazi brutality (1942); Hipgnosis' text-filled, anti-design record cover for XTC's *Go 2* (1978); Makoto Saitō's haunting graphic enigmas – and mashes them down into a smooth, flavourless paste. Nothing is allowed to remain knotty and intractable. As Johnson presents it, any kind of design, whatever its motivations and frames of reference, can be absorbed into the eager middlebrow design professional's stock of solutions and fixes, ready for future application.

Where does this leave us? My own ambivalence towards middlebrow must be obvious. Middlebrow design isn't all bad. It is often very good – of its kind. But when it becomes the prevailing mood and the summit of our social, intellectual and aesthetic ambitions, we really do have a problem that needs to be solved. In the 1990s, some designers and design educators tried to elevate design through theory, experimentation and a commitment to critical thinking. Whatever their shortcomings on occasion, these were necessary tasks. We need this kind of ambition today as much as ever.

The trouble with design's monopolistic middlebrow is that by constantly marginalising the highbrow, it reduces the possibility of more complex kinds of feeling and meaning. The public graphic culture that results is unnecessarily narrow, complacent and too often trite. Highbrow's demands and difficulties, like lowbrow's vulgarities, are a lot more stimulating to come to grips with.

Raging Bullshit

Truthfulness in practice

On the *Design Observer* blog, my colleague Michael Bierut asked what turned out to be a surprisingly provocative question: "What is the relationship of bullshit and design?" Bierut was inspired by the astonishing success of *On Bullshit* (2005), a slender little volume by Princeton University philosopher Harry G. Frankfurt. Public enthusiasm for the book, which was first presented as a lecture 20 years ago, suggests that the quantity of bullshit in our culture is an issue that preoccupies many people.

Bierut had some startling confessions for anyone nursing the idea that a bullshitter is not the most positive thing to be. "Early in my life as a designer," he said, referring to his student days, "I acquired a reputation as a good bullshitter." The Pentagram partner expressed the view that every client presentation was "inevitably, at least in part, an exercise in bullshit". It was clear, even in these opening remarks (the online discussion, in which I participated, ran on and on) that Bierut was using the word "bullshit" in a particular way. "The design process," he noted, "always combines the pursuit of functional goals with countless intuitive, even irrational decisions." Bullshit was the kind of explanation offered to clients to explain these intuitions. Simply admitting, "I don't know, I just like it that way," would be unlikely to do the job because most clients need to hear something that sounds like a rational justification.

This struck a chord with many designers who responded to Bierut's post. "Bullshit is one essential part of the selling process, particularly at the stage where we are trying to sell the idea to the client," ran a typical remark. A design educator, Greg Hay, said he tried to make his students realise that "the best artists are not necessarily the ones with the best talent or work ... they are invariably the ones who bullshit the best."

The odd thing about the way people kept using the word was that they seemed to disregard the basic dictionary definition. *Merriam-Webster* defines the noun as "nonsense" or "foolish insolent talk". As a verb, to bullshit means "to talk nonsense especially with the intention of deceiving or misleading". There is no dispute among lexicographers about the meaning of bullshit. Robert Chapman's *New Dictionary of American Slang* has: "nonsense; pretentious talk; bold and deceitful absurdities".

This is all rather damning, but the collective view of design bullshit, as it emerged on *Design Observer*, was much more tolerant and forgiving. "Bullshit is not necessarily bad and can function quite well in the design process until someone decides to call it," Bierut said as the argument unfolded. I began to suspect that my own distaste for bullshit, grounded in the dictionary definition, was more severe than that of many designers, especially those who had come to regard a degree of bullshit as an inescapable part of dealing with clients. Bierut pointed out that "charlatans have long been viewed with something verging on affection in American culture" and someone else mentioned the snake-oil salesman as a quintessential American character.

Whichever way you look at it, though, a too-ready acceptance of the idea of bullshit spells problems for design. From the way the word was bandied about, it seemed that any explanation dealing with the intangible aesthetic aspects of designing ran the risk of being written off as bullshit. Using the word as a lazy synonym for rationalisation does intellectual damage to design,

suggesting that "fancy talk" offered in support of a design decision will always be suspect, no matter how apt or well-intentioned.

In fact, the meaning of bullshit is much more specific. The bullshitter speaks purely for effect. He cares only about the way his words influence the listener. For this reason, Frankfurt writes, bullshit is a greater enemy of the truth than an outright lie. The liar knows and accepts the truth but chooses to deny it. The bullshitter couldn't care less whether what he says is true or not.

Referring to the use of so-called bullshit in client meetings, Bierut notes the "desire to conceal one's private intentions in the service of the larger goal: getting your client to do it the way you like." But is this really bullshit? What, after all, is being concealed? It must be obvious to the client that the designer is trying to win acceptance for the design proposal. That's a given. It must further be obvious that anything the designer says, any rationale offered, has this aim in view. Designers would be guilty of misleading the client – of bullshitting – only if they knew that their preferences would not serve the project's purpose and might even harm it, but they chose to hide this and make a case for them anyway.

It's quite possible that this happens all the time, though not a single person owned up to such irresponsible behaviour in the *Design Observer* discussion. However, if a designer sincerely believes that their preferences will serve a project's aims, then bullshit is the wrong word to describe any rationale used to support them. Moreover, it is inevitable, given the subjective component of so much design, that designers will sometimes realise only later why their intuitions were appropriate. "If you made something red because 'it felt right' and later realized that it evokes worker solidarity or sexual abandon or fire trucks or hot sauce," writes design educator Gunnar Swanson, "it is neither lying nor abandoning truth to say 'the color red does *X*.'" Exactly.

What tended to be overlooked in this discussion was the far more serious problem of the pervasiveness of bullshit in our culture. If designers can accept bullshit as part of their working experience, as a selling technique they might legitimately use on clients, then how scrupulous are they about having a hand in communications that contribute to the avalanche of bullshit in advertising, commercial promotion and the media? Frankfurt certainly believes that there is a connection between the two phenomena.

"The realms of advertising and of public relations, and the nowadays closely related realm of politics, are replete with instances of bullshit so unmitigated that they can serve among the most indisputable and classic paradigms of the concept," he writes. Frankfurt points out that these areas are staffed by "exquisitely sophisticated" craftspeople – designers, art directors, photographers, copywriters – who work tirelessly to perfect every word and image. If people are drawn to Frankfurt's unlikely bestseller, it's because contemporary life splatters them with bullshit and they want to know why. Bierut asked the right question: what is the relationship between design and bullshit? But by taking a purely professional view, he approached the issue from the less significant side.

Any sign of tolerance for bullshit in public life should concern us. The last thing we can afford is to view the bullshitter indulgently as a source of amusement. In communication, as in all our social relationships, there has to be a basis for trust, and trust is grounded in a sense of what is real or unreal, reliable or unreliable, true or false. Those who aim to create an effect on the listener or viewer without regard for the truth of what they say contribute to a climate of vagueness and confusion that eats into everything. The willingness to switch off our bullshit detectors and go with the flow of verbiage, nonsense, dubious claims and even falsehoods shows that the bullshit habit is dulling our critical faculties and blunting our instinctive sense of why honesty and accuracy matter. Lost in a haze of wishful thinking, we can have no sensible basis for action, no way of making a rational choice. Bullshit leads only to even more bullshit.

When words become overfamiliar, it's easy to take them for granted. This seems to have happened to bullshit, especially when it's reduced to the milder-sounding "BS". So imagine yourself in a field where cattle are grazing. You trip over a clod of earth and fall headlong into a deposit on the ground. This is our subject. There is nothing sweet-smelling about it.

Empty Buzzwords

Designers as would-be "storytellers"

In the summer of 2014, an internet row blew up over remarks made by Stefan Sagmeister about the way that some designers describe themselves as "storytellers". A brief interview with Sagmeister appeared on Vimeo, the video hosting platform, filmed while he was taking part in FITC Toronto, a conference about technology and creativity, and many viewers took exception to his words. Some quickly concluded that the whole episode was a storm in a teacup. However, it did succeed in raising an important issue to do with the use of language – although plenty seemed to ignore this.

Sagmeister began gently enough by saying that he was "quite critical" of the way the term "storyteller" is used. He moved on to describe an interview he'd read with a roller coaster designer, who referred to himself as a storyteller. "No, fuckhead," Sagmeister said, "you are not a storyteller. You are a roller coaster designer and that's fantastic and more power to you, but why would you want to be a storyteller if you design roller coasters? Or, if you are storytelling, then the story that you tell is bullshit." He continued in the same scornful vein for several seconds.

Then he suggested that the "true" storytellers, people who write novels or make feature films, don't see themselves as storytellers. By this he obviously meant not that they are unaware that they are producing stories, but that they would never use the term storyteller to describe what they do. They would say: I'm a novelist or a playwright or a screenplay writer or a film director. The listener would then understand the story-creation part as a matter of course without any need to spell it out so pretentiously.

"It's all the people who are not storytellers who, for strange reasons – because it's in the air – suddenly want to be storytellers," Sagmeister continued. "I think by now, in our space, meaning the space of design, it sort of took on the mantle of bullshit. You know, now everybody's a storyteller."

Here we come to the crucial point. Sagmeister's meaning is plain to anyone paying attention, but it needed more development than it could receive in the format in which it was presented. The two-minute clip, an off-the-cuff response, consisting of not much more than 250 words, was taken from a longer interview dealing with other topics. No doubt the FITC organisers couldn't believe their good fortune when their design-star speaker sounded off so candidly and with such strong feelings. This kind of outspokenness doesn't happen much these days in the ultra-cautious, public image-conscious realm of professional design (more's the pity, some might say), so why wouldn't FITC put it online? But the inevitable result was that some took offence at both the message and the manner of delivery.

"That's outrageously narrow-minded [...] hate to break it to you FITC, Sagmeister's old-school generalization-rant may indeed warrant the word 'philistine'," wrote Molly Willows in the Vimeo comments. Others defended the use of the term, claiming that it expressed what they do. "It's impossible to sell creative [work] or communicate a product without a story. *Why do you need this item? Tell me about your needs? OK, this is how it will solve your need* [...] is a multiple story," added Steve Hodges on the thread.

Inadvertently, though, the protesters only confirmed Sagmeister's observation. The term is rife. Storytelling has become so ingrained in the lexicon of branding, marketing and now design, that it can seem "freakishly traditionalist", as one of Sagmeister's critics put it, to question its prevalence. Once a term is in the air, it becomes difficult to resist it.

Constant repetition introduces clients to the new concept and its use becomes a benchmark of contemporary thinking and relevance. In the early days, when a term still feels fresh and exciting, it is especially seductive, and that's how buzzwords spread so fast – even when they are just fancy new labels for old, familiar stock. Clients expect their design advisers to talk about stories as a means of connecting with people and distilling the essence of the brand. It takes a lot of confidence to shun these buzzwords when a potential commissioner could construe this as lack of know-how.

Eventually, as Sagmeister points out, everyone comes to feel that they should be conceptualising and promoting what they do as storytelling. The term has a ring of meaningfulness and authenticity, a vibe of almost anthropological depth and truth. Since human beings began to talk, we've loved to tell each other stories.

The burden of Sagmeister's complaint lies in the word "bullshit", which he says has come to cloak the activity of design. Nearly a decade ago on *Design Observer*, Michael Bierut initiated a discussion about the use of bullshit as (in his view) a valid rhetorical tool when communicating to design clients (see page 55). If Sagmeister is correct, then the problem of design bullshit hasn't gone away and may be more tenacious than ever.

What does Sagmeister feel about the negative response to his criticisms? He concedes that he probably shouldn't have been so emotional. "I can get quite worked up about casual dishonesty in the language of numerous fields," he says, pointing to architecture and contemporary art as two other areas notable for their own kinds of bullshit. He mentions earlier clichés of creative parlance, such as "thinking outside the box" and "the importance of failure", as well as designers who talk grandly about creating an experience, when the "experience" is nothing bigger than a banner ad. The vogue for storytelling is in much the same vein. "This terminology loses its meaning through overuse and misuse," he says.

In any field that purports to be about communication, loss of meaning is a serious matter and a cause for concern. Accuracy of language is vital. Without it, there can be no accuracy of communication. Vague language reflects vague thinking and the vaguer our thinking becomes, the less clearly we're able to see the world. This is dangerous and it makes us highly suggestible and exploitable.

The problem with the marketing mentality, from a communication point of view, is that its priority is at root always to sell something – a product, a service, or whatever it might be. Marketing language is consequently prone to inflation, hyperbole, distortion and spin. Those involved in the field will say that this is perfectly reasonable to achieve their clients' goals. But if a rational, thinking population is what our society wants, then it's vital that we maintain scepticism and detachment when assessing all forms of commercial speech. This freedom from market-determined thought is especially important in public life. Precision in the use of language and rejection of all forms of bullshit are essential for critical thinking and, ultimately, for a healthy society.

The arts offer a public space where we expect to find honesty and vitality in the use of words as a form of resistance to debased promotional speech. That's one reason why the "storyteller" self-designation, when it's made for commercial purposes, looks so suspect – because it claims a seriousness and status that it most likely doesn't merit.

It comes down to how designers perceive what they do and how they wish to position themselves. Are they salespeople working alongside advertising and marketing, and essentially no different? Or are they rigorous communicators engaged in a task that can be bracketed with the work of the best writers, journalists and filmmakers? The storyteller meme may not be the worst example, but its use is symptomatic of a creeping linguistic malaise that committed communicators should challenge and reject.

"For the work that our studio is creating," Sagmeister says, "I've found that 'graphic design' covers it rather well." Is that old-school irrelevance, or an eminently sane, much-needed blast of realism and clarity?

Ontwerp: Total Design by Kees Broos, Reflex, Utrecht, 1983.
Design: Total Design.

Agency or Studio?

What these designations signify

In 1983, on a visit to Amsterdam, I saw a remarkable book in a bookshop on Leidsestraat. Its shape was completely irregular. I understood a certain amount about typography and graphic design by then. I knew it fascinated me, but had yet to engage much with the history of the subject. The book, *Ontwerp: Total Design* by Kees Broos, had just come out and I bought it with great excitement, knowing it was unlikely to be available back home. In 1987, Total Design founder Wim Crouwel was the first graphic designer I interviewed for a magazine.

I begin an essay about Dutch graphic design in such a personal way because the subject is so close to me that it is impossible to disentangle these early encounters from my subsequent commitment to the discipline. It is hardly news to a Dutch audience that Dutch graphic design went through an extraordinarily inventive phase in the 1980s, but perhaps an outsider's view can still shed some light on the degree of impact the country's graphic design enjoyed overseas in those years. There is a well-worn line about the Netherlands appearing to be some kind of heaven for graphic designers. The cliché holds true because that's exactly how it seemed. Total Design, Studio Dumbar, Jan van Toorn, Anthon Beeke, Hard Werken, Wild Plakken, to name only the most obvious, were titanic figures able – as it seemed from afar – to seduce or even bend clients to their will, unless (remarkable thought) the clients actually sought such challenging work. In the 1980s, Studio Dumbar, the most emblematic Dutch designers for the British, entered project after project into the D&AD awards in London and won again and again. We had nothing to compare with this awe-inspiring level of graphic sophistication, originality and swaggering self-belief. Visits to the Netherlands, further meetings with Dutch graphic designers, and a growing knowledge of the Dutch design tradition powerfully underwrote my sense, in the late 1980s, that graphic design had much to offer and was worth writing about.

It is reasonable to ask, though, what exactly it was we were so enraptured by in Dutch graphic design: what were we celebrating? It was the brilliance of its graphic and typographic form. By degrees, since then, we have moved towards a situation where many of the assumptions about advanced graphic design's inherent value as visual culture that were taken for granted among designers before the 1980s, during that decade's design boom, and on into the 1990s, are now seen as misguided and no longer relevant to our circumstances today. As the century ended, the sticking point for many disillusioned design-watchers became form itself – the very attribute for which Dutch graphic design was once so highly prized. The repudiation of form as a valid pursuit in its own right wasn't a specifically Dutch development. Nevertheless, Carel Kuitenbrouwer's article "The New Sobriety", published in *Eye* in 1995, was early to note a profound quietening down in Dutch graphic design after the turmoil of the 1980s.

After slow beginnings in the Netherlands and Britain (among other places), this yearning for formal sobriety became an international phenomenon within forward-thinking graphic design, a heartfelt reaction against the coercive visual overload of an increasingly spectacular global culture. Graphic excess had precipitated visual burn-out and elaborate kinds of formal expression could no longer signal anything trustworthy or meaningful. As Jop van Bennekom observed in *HD: Holland Design New Graphics* (2001): "Form is so worn out in the nineties." That curious book, styled like a chunky, throwaway, airport bestseller, remains a revealing document of its moment, but compared to Dutch graphic design's glory days, when the work was often distinguished by what Gert Dumbar liked to call "stylistic durability", a decade later *HD* contains few images to set your attention on fire and little worth lingering over. Dutch graphic design, I felt then and still feel today, appeared to have thrown its beautiful graphic baby out with the decade's excessively soapy bath water.

However well intentioned the motivations that underpinned some designers' embrace of the new visual simplicity, it soon became just another fashionable style ripe for commercial exploitation. There was a time when much Dutch graphic design looked unequivocally Dutch because it came out of a Dutch modernist tradition of typography and montage to which it continually referred, even as it introduced new devices and directions. This tradition was still apparent in the 1980s within the postmodernism of Jan van Toorn or Studio Dumbar. Today, Dutch graphic design is much less obviously Dutch. Instead, its habitual graphic routines and styles of address are determined by international conventions of advertising, marketing, branding, fashion and popular culture. The most renowned Dutch "design" company of the last 15 years, KesselsKramer, is in reality an advertising agency, and co-founder Erik Kessels is regularly invited to speak about KK's irreverent and humorous campaigns at international design conferences. Another way of saying this is that Dutch graphic design, once so vividly defined as an aspect of national visual culture, now feels much like everyone else's graphic design. Most Dutch graphic design no longer leads the world in purely graphic terms because it has been obliged to fall into line with the imperatives of a globalised economy. Like graphic design everywhere else, Dutch graphic design mostly exists now to serve the market and the market's needs must come first.

Studio Dumbar, where strategy director Tom Dorresteijn has been a 50 per cent partner since 2005, exemplifies these changes. Dorresteijn's concept of "visual branding" is explained in the "Vision" section of the Studio Dumbar website (the term also has a whole website of its own), where it is followed by a brief section titled, with heartbreaking poignancy, "Free spirit". In this other, apparently rather recherché kind of design, we learn that "the designer has only one challenge: to see how far his or her creativity can go." The new statutes of graphic design could hardly be made any plainer. Most of the time the designers are reined in, their creativity apportioned and constrained by the branding task. Once in a while, a benevolent client in the culture sector happens along and allows them to run around free and do what they want, like in the old days.

Somewhat anachronistically, Studio Dumbar still describes itself as a "studio". This is a word that immediately implies a connection to art, conjuring an image of a small atelier where a creative person or group undertakes work of personal significance. Many Dutch design companies, like those in other countries, now prefer the term "agency". De Designpolitie, a design team that fully embodies the contemporary ethos of Dutch graphic design, describes itself as a "graphic design agency". Lava, named "European design agency of 2010", also uses the term, explaining that it "belongs to a generation that has positioned itself between the traditional design agency and an advertising agency." This is the point, of course: graphic design is ever more closely entwined with advertising, an activity whose commercial exploitation of the public sphere many graphic designers used to resist as a matter of principle. "Agency" is a service-orientated, marketing-friendly word. It makes designers sound more biddable.

The website rhetoric that contemporary Dutch designers use to explain their methods to prospective clients is just as revealing. "Thonik's style is attractive and effective. Clear concepts are conveyed with a minimum of means." (Thonik) "A lot of our work is concentrated, stripped to the bare essence." (De Designpolitie) "Design is not art. We have no specific visual style. We always try to find a unique design solution." (Lava) These statements are noteworthy not because they are inherently unsound but because they are absolutely standard rationales for a design company to offer. I have been hearing sentiments like these from British designers for the last 25 years. They originate from the "idea-based" design espoused by American and British designers in the late 1950s and 1960s, which was rejected in these countries in the 1980s and 1990s by younger designers, who argued that these shop-worn and often patronising methods of public address were no longer adequate to deal with the complexities of contemporary life and communication. The wheel has now turned full circle. While the return to idea-based design might have begun as a necessary attempt to purify design of self-indulgent noise that risked obscuring the message, the outcome today is a smooth and predictable set of visual procedures that pose few challenges to client or viewer.

These designers are naturally aware of the Netherlands' prodigious graphic tradition and, as if to reassure themselves and their design colleagues that they belong in its ranks, they sometimes invoke their forebears, even as they assure potential clients that everything will be simple and effective. Thonik follows its declaration about clear concepts and minimum means by stating that it "also has an anarchistic side and we regard each project as a chance to experiment." De Designpolitie's online profile informs visitors that "its members were brought up in the Dutch design culture and rich tradition of Dutch art, design and tolerance." Their ruthlessly stripped-down designs, they claim, are both critical *and* communicative. The inherent tension of trying to have it both ways and relate to the great Dutch tradition of graphic design, while moderating the visual freedom that gave it life, can be sensed in a comment that Hans Wolbers of Lava left on Dorresteijn's Visual Branding website in 2007. "I must tell you honestly that I am not very keen on theories," writes Wolbers. "One sees regularly all kinds of 'brand' gurus selling an incredible amount of bullshit. Personally I place more and more belief in talented creatives that touch the right chord."

This is another version of Studio Dumbar's "free spirit" plea: stop trying to micro-manage the design process with an endless stream of self-justifying concepts, precepts and admonitions. Trust talented and committed designers to come up with truly fresh and surprising visual ideas, and then trust visually aware viewers to respond to them. Accept the subjectivity of the creative process, the element of chance, the things you shouldn't even try to control. Eventually, the wheel might even turn again.

Perhaps it sounds as though I have fallen out of sympathy with Dutch graphic design. The disappointment, as I have tried to show, comes from the strength of admiration that preceded it. Dutch graphic design's astonishing, inspiring achievements showed what could sometimes be possible in visual communication. Its innovations provided unusually exacting benchmarks that could be used to assess graphic design anywhere. I can only suggest that it would be dishonest now – and self-deceiving on the part of Dutch designers – not to apply these benchmarks to the contemporary graphic design scene.

One of the most encouraging and energising developments in Dutch graphic design has come, since the end of the 1990s, from a perhaps unexpected direction. In *Word of Image: Metaphorical Thinking in Dutch Graphic Design* (2004), Jan Middendorp reprises the frequently heard view that Dutch designers are "no great theorists", preferring instead to concentrate on the practicalities of making things work. Wolbers voices his own reservations about the perils of theorising in the statement above. But the idea that theory-averse pragmatism is particular to the Dutch has always

Psyop: An Anthology edited by Karen Archey and Metahaven, Stedelijk Museum, Amsterdam, 2018. Design: Metahaven.

seemed questionable: first, because only a minority of graphic designers anywhere are ever much given to theorising; second, because some Dutch designers – Crouwel and Van Toorn to name but two – have always been prepared to reflect trenchantly on the ideas that support their design methods.

In the last decade, two design groups, Experimental Jetset and Metahaven, have taken this commitment to intellectual reflection to a higher plane. Although it hasn't been widely remarked, which may serve to underline the continuing paucity of close critical attention given to graphic design, both teams consistently offer some of the most cogent thinking about the discipline's present condition and future possibilities. In each case, independent critical reflection becomes an inseparable component of everyday practice. Nor are these the usual tiresome, spirit-crushing bromides about branding and marketing. Metahaven has recently published a book, *Uncorporate Identity* (2010), and both studios – they are emphatically studios – are interviewed in *The Reader: Iaspis Forum on Design and Critical Practice* (2010). Since space is limited, I will concentrate here on Experimental Jetset, the longer established team.

In Experimental Jetset's uncompromising statement of their position, we hear the authentic historical voice of Dutch graphic design, a reminder of how the country attained its elevated position on the global design stage. The three members, Erwin Brinkers, Danny van den Dungen and Marieke Stolk, explain that "the reason we exist as a studio is because we have a singular aesthetic/conceptual vision, a very specific language we speak." (See the book *Studio Culture*, 2009.) They are only interested, they say, in working with clients who understand this vision and who expect them to bring "a specific viewpoint, an aesthetic/conceptual language, an ideological approach" to the table. Clearly, this is a radically different style of self-presentation from one that promises a chameleonic ability to adapt the design output to fulfil a client's expectations.

Experimental Jetset have a self-conscious relationship with the Dutch design tradition, most clearly seen in their frequent tributes to Wim Crouwel, the elder statesman most revered today by young designers outside the Netherlands. As a viewer, I have sometimes struggled with the Crouwel-esque modernism of Experimental Jetset's visual palette. This doesn't excite me greatly in 2010, even though I appreciate the source and understand the thinking – their desire to stress the materiality of design and create objects rather than images – that led them to these stark visual conclusions. It is characteristic of their clarity as commentators, though, that they freely admit the drawbacks of their hero's former empire. "Total Design signalled in many ways the beginning of the sort of studios that we very much dislike: large communication conglomerates, where the actual practice of graphic design is overshadowed by branding strategies, marketing theories, advertising models, etc." In their view, the over-complication of the commissioning and design process has been caused by layers of marketing and communication people who create unnecessary work to keep themselves employed.

"We feel we are now at a point in history where we actually have to go in the opposite direction," they say. The solution to the bloating of the design business is not for design "agencies" to grow even bigger, but for marketing to shrink. Resolutely, Experimental Jetset remains a three-person studio that only takes on what it can handle. Here again, we encounter a variation of the "free spirit" argument, only this time from a studio that has found a way to make freedom of manoeuvre a central plank in its self-determined charter. If we care about graphic design – Dutch graphic design – as a still potentially limitless means of visual communication, then this modest proposal from one of the most thoughtful studios now at work in the design field must be correct. The future of graphic design, if it is to have one, can only lie in focusing on graphic design. Dutch designers who refuse to give up the ideal of studio practice are keeping the flame alight.

Counter Points

Objectivity or subjectivity in design?

In the perennially careful world of graphic design, where most people avoid potentially embarrassing slugfests with colleagues at any cost, a good argument is rare to find. Yet a public clash of views and even a bit of righteous anger from time to time can be useful, because it helps to establish the allegiances, priorities and values of both combatants and bystanders, and reminds everyone why they wanted to pursue a life in design in the first place. Graphic designers always say they want to be inspired, and who ever got inspired by a polite chat?

One of the most outspoken conflicts between two designers holding diametrically opposed views occurred in the Netherlands in the 1970s, and it lasted for at least a decade. That might sound too remote in time to matter any more, but both participants, Wim Crouwel and Jan van Toorn, remain in the public eye,* and the points they made with unswerving fidelity to their carefully defined positions prefigure some of the most significant themes running through design in the last three decades. Their ideas continue to mark out the possibilities, and limits, of practice.

Crouwel will be most familiar, perhaps, from his appearance in the *Helvetica* documentary (2007), though his inclusion represents just a small part of the admiration that his body of work attracts among younger

A Selection from the Collection of the Van Abbemuseum by Marinus Boezem, poster,
Van Abbemuseum, Eindhoven, 1971. Design: Jan van Toorn.

designers. "I'm a modernist, you know," he says in the film. "I was trained in the period. I lived in the period. I love modernism." When I first met Crouwel in 1987, he had recently been appointed director of the Museum Boijmans Van Beuningen in Rotterdam. The work that made his name in the 1960s, as co-founder of Total Design in Amsterdam, was long behind him, postmodernism was all the rage, and Crouwel was, to put it bluntly, out of fashion. But thanks to some well-placed British admirers, such as 8vo – who collaborated with him at the museum – Crouwel was back in the limelight by the end of the 1990s, the perfection of his modernist typography celebrated around the world, his work highly collectible.

Van Toorn's influence has been of a different kind. A notable educator, as well as a designer, he was an associate professor at Rhode Island School of Design in the US for 20 years and, in 2007, he was the subject of a retrospective exhibition at the Maryland Institute in Baltimore. Van Toorn has a reputation for being uncompromising in his design work, for being motivated by strong social and political convictions, and for his commitment to cultural theory, which has sometimes baffled more pragmatically minded Dutch colleagues. I have enjoyed a stimulating dialogue with Van Toorn over the years and I published a monograph about him in the Netherlands.**

By the late 1960s, the acute differences in Crouwel's and Van Toorn's views of the design task were clear. Where Crouwel's posters and catalogues for the Stedelijk Museum in Amsterdam are harmoniously resolved typographic constructions, generally using a single typeface – Helvetica – Van Toorn's posters and catalogues for the Van Abbemuseum in Eindhoven take a messier, more promiscuous approach to type. They find their form in the artists' imagery and each one looks different from the last. If Crouwel aspired to produce work that appeared timeless, as though the ultimate aim was the gallery wall, Van Toorn preferred designs that were informal, personal, provisional, and situated in their cultural and political moment.

In 1972, at a public debate in Amsterdam that has acquired an almost legendary status in the annals of Dutch design, the two locked horns for the first time. In *Helvetica*, Crouwel recalls how committed he was in those years to the idea of "neutrality" that Helvetica represented. The type shouldn't have a meaning in itself: the meaning resided in the content of the text. In Crouwel's view, the subjectivity of Van Toorn's approach was wrong because it meant that designers could only work on projects that they personally supported. "You must not try [...] to get the message across better than the one who is emitting the message," said Crouwel. Van Toorn agreed that the designer's task was to convey the content, but insisted that designers still had a crucial contribution of their own to make. "Crouwel's fear of subjective interference leads to uniformity, causing a distinct identity to disappear," he said.

As the 1970s progressed, Van Toorn's designs for catalogues, calendars and journals became increasingly confrontational in both content and form. The scattergun typography of one calendar provoked Crouwel so much that he designed and printed his own version, with an open letter to his misguided colleague, showing him how it should be done – using Helvetica, naturally. In 1978, a pamphlet about design for museums by Van Toorn and his friend Jean Leering produced the same inflammatory effect. Van Toorn's persistent questioning of the museum's authority as custodian and arbiter of art, and his desire to involve the museum-going public in a dialogue, were once again at fault. "What we're talking about here," writes Crouwel, "is information that should be as objective as possible, for the benefit of all people interested, without any other aim than to inform." He complains about viewers being forced to make sense of the "meaningless and fashionable compilations of images" offered by Van Toorn.

Just three years later, Crouwel felt the need yet again to publish a detailed rebuttal of something Van Toorn had written. After their initial debate, the pattern was always the same, with Van Toorn carrying on regardless, and Crouwel, as self-appointed guardian of the true path, taking it on himself to indicate the error of his ways. If Van Toorn had once resented these attacks – and who wouldn't? – he showed no sign of it in any of our conversations.

Today, the two appear to be on good terms as colleagues, and when Van Toorn published a book of essays in 2006, Crouwel was there for the launch. Crouwel still has a problem with designers using too many typefaces, but he seems to have mellowed. Twenty years ago, when I first met him, he told me that he had always been more present in his designs than he realised at the time, and this is clearly true. Neutrality was always a myth. More recently, in a book about the Alliance Graphique Internationale, he acknowledges that his work for the Stedelijk Museum, far from being timeless, "can be dated quite accurately".

Crouwel is absolutely right about that. Here, I have to declare my colours because while I think he is a fine designer, the fetishisation of his way of designing by a new generation of followers is as revealing as it is troubling. Crouwel was always much more interested in typography than images. His work appeals because it can be imbibed unproblematically as pure form, and the designers who most admire it often specialise in the same kind of modernist – or, more accurately now, neo-modernist – typographic craft. Today, much of this work is merely trendy; it couldn't be further from the modernists' utopian social dream. Its over-processed surfaces and sterile perfectionism reflect the sheen of the marketplace, without commenting on this commercial reality or questioning it in any way.

As a model for the role that the graphic designer might occupy as a critical public communicator, Van Toorn's work was always much richer than Crouwel's, and it is an enduring refutation of Crouwel's unnecessarily circumscribed definition of design. While its confrontational content and abrasive, even ugly, texture might alarm some designers, it has a lot to offer anyone who thinks that the most significant visual communication concerns itself with the task of articulating and complicating meaning through form. Smooth, disengaged and aesthetically enraptured design is much too easy now. We need a few more awkward, socially motivated designers with the nerve to irritate, provoke, challenge and involve viewers. We need a new generation of Van Toorns.

* Wim Crouwel died in 2019; Jan van Toorn in 2020.
** *Jan van Toorn: Critical Practice*, 010 Publishers, Rotterdam, 2008. For more on Crouwel and Van Toorn's discussion, see *The Debate: The Legendary Contest of Two Giants of Graphic Design*, Monacelli Press, New York, 2015.

The Death of Form

The denigration of aesthetics

I have witnessed in recent years a curious thing happen to graphic design. While I can sympathise with the development up to the point, it still perplexes me. It flies in the face of everything we valued about graphic design since the beginning of its life as a professional practice in the early 20th century, and turns its back on a key motivation that led so many to become designers in the first place.

I'm talking about what has become of the love of visual form, the desire to seize its possibilities and mould it into original, surprising and spectacularly expressive new shapes. Of course, graphic designers still carry out this task – sometimes, though less often now, with great panache – but they don't discuss visual concerns much, nor do they appear to value them greatly. At times it almost seems as though form is becoming a taboo, a dirty secret from the past that everyone is too embarrassed to mention, and which we are working hard to recover from and leave behind.

The response I received to an essay I wrote in 2010 about Dutch graphic design for the *Dutch Design Yearbook* drove this point home (see page 66). The Dutch used to be extraordinary inventors of graphic form, from 1920s modernists such as Piet Zwart to the extravagant creations of Studio Dumbar in the 1980s. Work like Dumbar's exerted great influence on postmodern

American graphic design and my argument in the essay, a polemic aimed primarily at Dutch readers, was that a decade later (and ever since) Dutch designers seem to have lost interest in graphic invention.

My criticism of contemporary Dutch design caused some local annoyance and I was invited to Amsterdam to take part in a panel discussion – fairly good-natured, as it turned out. What interested me, though, both there and when the piece was republished on *Design Observer*, is that, once again, no one responded to the specific issues I had raised about form by speaking up for its importance and value. Among these designers there was clearly little sense of concern about the diminished value assigned to form in contemporary graphic design. The general feeling was that designers had different concerns now. They had many more platforms to think about, more complex demands from clients to satisfy, and a supposedly greater sense of responsibility about fulfilling client needs than earlier generations of form-loving designers.

There isn't space to explore these assumptions except to say that none of them are reasons to neglect form, and form is the subject I want to concentrate on here. I find myself in the strange position of being a non-designer who seems to value form more – apparently a lot more – than many professional form-makers, and this has obliged me to think again about the underlying reasons for this attraction.

As a child, I had been impressed by comic book art, packaging, product logos and lettering, and I liked to draw. In my teens, I started to look consciously at art – first in books, and then in art galleries because I had to see the real thing. My principal concern at that stage was with painting. I had never been told how to analyse a picture, not even by art teachers, so I set out to learn how to do it myself. This required patient and sustained looking, as it does for each and every viewer.

I already understood the aesthetic pleasures of reading. It was a tremendous revelation to discover just how much pleasure there could also be in looking. The closer you looked at a picture, the deeper into the visual field you ventured, the more you considered the relationships between each element and how they combined to convey meaning, then the more satisfying the viewing experience became. Having made this discovery as a teenage art fan, it surprised me how few of the people I knew seemed aware that this sphere of aesthetic sensation existed as something to seek out and enjoy. What I did receive from one favourite art teacher was the complementary insight that the artist should look as attentively as possible at the world and notice details that many tended to overlook out of habit. The two activities, paying attention to the texture of reality and looking at art, were in a vital sense linked. It was all about learning how to see.

Painting rapidly led me to photography, and photography, in turn, to the artistic potential of film. While each medium has different capabilities, the visual aspects they have in common – composition, colour, use of light – were always central to my pleasure as a viewer, and I took it for granted, because experience repeatedly demonstrated it to be so, that in good work, form is inseparable from meaning.

Graphic design attracted my attention a few years later because it, too, was highly visual. I had always loved record sleeves, book covers and flamboyantly visual magazines. Now, with an eye trained by other media, I began to explore the wider possibilities and achievements of graphic communication – writing about it all came a few years later. The great designers, I found, had been shaped by many of the same visual influences that determined my own reactions to graphic design. It made complete sense to me that the discipline's history was closely intertwined at key moments with that of art. During the period when my interest developed and became a passion, from the early 1980s to the mid-1990s, graphic design was going through one of the most visually inventive phases in its history.

In deciding what has been valuable about graphic design, I cannot avoid starting with my own experience, which tells me that an aesthetically abundant environment has deep value to the individual and to society. Graphic design has been central to the visual culture of modernity. We see it everywhere we turn. It expresses in the most immediate and compelling form – note, *form* – our hopes, desires, convictions, values and dreams. A densely imaginative, formally inventive visual culture tells us something about who we are as a people and how we aspire to live. Conversely, a lacklustre visual culture would be a sign that we no longer feel the same sense of hope, freedom and possibility, and that's how I read the failure of aesthetic nerve and retreat from the manifold pleasures of form in some areas of graphic design: as evidence of something crucial gone missing.

Some designers and design educators seem convinced that earlier designers committed to the visual were unacceptably self-indulgent. I understand the need to purge that many felt in the late 1990s after the beanfeast, but abstinence has become a self-defeating habit and it's time to move on. For sure, there was plenty of self-indulgence during that decade of technological experiment; at any given moment there is always bad work. This doesn't invalidate the continuing mission to use an inherently visual medium as expressively as we can. No one complains that the enormous aesthetic pleasure provided by every kind of music is exhausted, old-fashioned, indulgent, excessive, simple-minded, or compromised by being merely aural, as in Marcel Duchamp's famous but inaccurate complaint that pre-conceptual art was "merely retinal". The eye craves to be treated with tender regard just as much as the ear. If graphic designers neglect the challenge of form, others will step in and do the job.

The Takeaway Effect

Why less is less in visual imagery

In 2012, a London publisher relaunched its backlist of books by the Japanese cult author Haruki Murakami with a striking new set of covers. Now, I have always thought that previous British interpretations of Murakami fell a long way short of the luscious Surrealism and fantasy of John Gall's American paperback covers, particularly for *The Wind-Up Bird Chronicle* and *South of the Border, West of the Sun*, two Murakami books I very much admire.

But the new covers, with images by Noma Bar, a highly regarded designer-illustrator, I found deeply irritating. Bar specialises in extremely simplified vector art that can often be read in two ways depending on whether you concentrate on the positive or negative spaces. To achieve this effect, he reduces colour to a minimum – the Murakami covers are red, white and black – and eliminates every kind of surface detail and texture, to produce a flattened design. Most of the covers are based on circular motifs. The *Wind-Up Bird Chronicle* image can be seen either as a flying bird in a circle or an old-fashioned clockwork key. On *The Elephant Vanishes*, the white negative space forms a spiral that terminates in the outline of a trunk, as though an elephant were vanishing into the cover's surface.

Vintage UK's selection of Bar to undertake this major 15-book series is a sign of just how fashionable both his work and this form of uncompromising graphic reduction

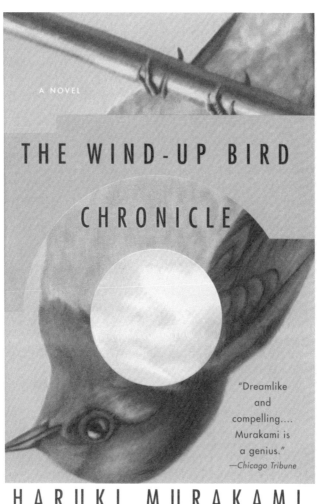

A NOVEL

THE WIND-UP BIRD CHRONICLE

"Dreamlike
and
compelling....
Murakami is
a genius."
—*Chicago Tribune*

HARUKI MURAKAMI

The Wind-Up Bird Chronicle by Haruki Murakami, Vintage, 2002.
Design and cover art: John Gall.

have become. When the covers were shown on the *Creative Review* blog, they drew a chorus of approving comments: "lovely series", "consistently clever, impressive work", "sublime!" and so on. Bar is undeniably good at this kind of graphic compression. He seems to represent an ideal for some designers, though I'm not aware at this stage of a school of Bar-like work. Yet the general effect, the pictorial simplification and flatness, the so-called minimalism, has become a popular, if not yet dominant, style of the moment in contemporary illustration. You can see it in the stylised, linear magazine illustrations of Malika Favre and Olimpia Zagnoli, or in Vahram Muratyan's *Paris versus New York* blog, which spawned an entire book of ultra-simplified visual comparisons of the two cities.

For Bar and his admirers, the "idea" is the most important consideration. This has become so much a mantra in contemporary graphic design that I'm inclined to treat it with suspicion now whenever I hear it, since I don't believe that in visual work there can be any useful separation of idea and execution. The idea is embodied, realised and made convincing in visual form. In forms as sparse as Bar's, the idea is particularly exposed. Representing a book titled *The Wind-Up Bird Chronicle* with a bird-and-key illustration could hardly be more literal or less interesting as an idea. The mental image of the strange bird was already present in the mysterious title; a good Murakami cover needs to compound the mystery with an image that matches, without duplication, the title's oddity. This is what Gall does with his upside-down bird pierced by a hole through which we can see the sky. Atmosphere is also a kind of idea and here it's expressed through visual treatment, texture and complexity of composition.

Bar says that he is trying to achieve "the maximum communication with the minimum elements." This, too, is a recurrent aim in graphic design. A monograph about the poster designer Abram Games is subtitled "Maximum meaning, minimum means". But Games' example is instructive. Despite his avowed intention to simplify, the posters he made from the 1940s to the 1960s were rich with painterly texture and his images were never merely flat. Games leads the eye into deep pictorial space. The central forms might be sharply defined and rapidly graspable, but the pleasure and effectiveness of the image and its persuasiveness as visual rhetoric come from accumulations of detail that can be felt subliminally or lingered over and enjoyed.

Nevertheless, the idea persists that one can "say the most with the least" – as another contemporary designer, Anthony Burrill, puts it. As an axiom, this doesn't stand up to a moment's consideration. If it were true that less is always more, we wouldn't have any further use for the ceiling of the Sistine Chapel, or *War and Peace*, or "The Waste Land". We welcome complexity in art and communication because we have the mental equipment to derive meaning from it, and because the aesthetic dimension of this complexity can provide a great deal of satisfaction.

Is graphic design perhaps a special case, a form of communication that manages, almost uniquely, to impart more with less? Does the reduction of elements magically increase the amount that is said? Certainly, a simple idea may best lend itself to being communicated simply – no argument there. But a work of fiction, particularly fiction as expansive and idiosyncratic as Murakami's, is another matter. Cover designers and illustrators face an enormous challenge in trying to express the special qualities of a fictional universe in the restricted format of a book cover. It's perverse to imagine that additional self-imposed restrictions will somehow improve the odds of successful communication. How many admirers of the covers are also close readers of the books? It doesn't matter how niftily Bar forms a face from a cat's profile against the red disc that contains both figures on *Kafka on the Shore*. It's still just a rudimentary cat and a face, and not much to look at. The basic problem with simplification is always that it risks becoming deadly dull.

Still, there is no denying that contemporary taste appears to embrace this kind of wrinkle-free graphic reduction. These days, even protest posters, once so rough and ready, often come with cleanly defined outlines and flat, bright, unnuanced forms. It's a style of illustration that vector art facilitates, though reductionist illustrators still tend to work out their ideas on paper before moving to the screen. "My process is to draw everything, then take away bit by bit," Malika Favre told *Wallpaper.* "And I love it that way; it's very soothing. I take away until I can't take away any more, until that last necessary line." For Favre, who created the cover of the Penguin Classics Deluxe Edition of *The Kama Sutra*, suggestion allows viewers more room to exercise the imagination; consequently, it's more erotic.

For that commission, which needed to strike a balance between explicitness and good taste, she might be right. But it's also true that every style of illustration sets out to encourage the viewer to enter the image, and to conjecture and dream. Many illustrations are tantalising fragments of something much larger that cannot be shown in full. The image-maker's perennial task is to develop visual tools that will be the most effective prompts to imagine that unseen world. Only in the work of a mediocre illustrator will this visual information add up to nothing more than pointless decoration. "Ultimately, when the idea is there I feel like I'm just wasting my time on decorations," Bar told *Computer Arts.* Again, we come back to that false dichotomy. In reality, fully achieved style is a vital embodiment of meaning.

The limitation of illustrative reduction is that its tools are much too basic. Where else do we routinely expect to encounter severe simplification of form and a preference for strong outlines, unruffled flatness and cheerful colours? Young children respond to this style of illustration in children's books because their perceptions, imaginations and understanding are still developing. Experienced viewers are capable of processing far more complex material. Pictorial minimalism isn't necessarily childish, but it still offers a needlessly curtailed form of visual experience. For both illustrator and viewer, it's like choosing to use only a few hundred words when you could employ a vocabulary of thousands.

Thinking Outside Ourselves

What is an ethical designer?

In 2003, D&AD, the British design organisation, put on a panel discussion in London about ethics in design and advertising. One of the speakers was Ken Garland, who wrote the original 1964 *First Things First* manifesto updated by *Adbusters* magazine in 1999. The organisers probably assumed that Garland would position himself as a supporter of ethical design. But Garland – always a charming contrarian – would have none of this. He had no wish to be seen as an "ethical designer". The idea seemed almost distasteful to him.

Garland shows every sign of being a deeply ethical person, but I can see why he did this. He didn't want to seem sanctimonious and preachy, or to appear to be setting himself up as a moral paragon, someone who claims to have the right answers about all these issues. He sensed that this would irritate and perhaps alienate his mostly young audience. In any case, it's no good talking about how ethical you are. What counts is whether your convictions translate into actions.

Yet Garland's response that evening was also a sign of how difficult it is to deal with these issues today. He and a design educator* were there to debate ethics with a couple of admen; these guys smelled blood in the water and went in for the kill. Garland's hedging may have reflected the reality of a complex situation, but the ad boys viewed things in much starker terms. They saw nothing to apologise for. It was the old Gordon Gekko "greed is good" rhetorical tactic. Come right out and admit what you are doing. Exult in your own self-interest. Dare people not to be impressed.

Today, putting yourself first is seen as entirely reasonable. The media hammers this home, day after day, with stories about super-successful celebrities, living the greed-is-good lifestyle to the limit. Except there is no limit. People who do this are the new idols of our culture. They flaunt their furs, their fleets of cars, their private jets parked outside the front door, their three nannies for one child, their unbelievable cribs, their outrageous demands, their bling.

Ethical positions, on other hand, require you to think beyond your own self-interest. It may be necessary to deny yourself what you want in order to live in an ethical way. In a have-it-all society, this is not something we find easy to do.

In design, the issue of ethics is certainly on the table. The topic comes up in student projects and at academic conferences. Books have appeared with ringing titles such as *Citizen Designer* (2003) and *Conscientious Objectives: Designing for an Ethical Message* (2004). But there are still not many designers prepared to speak out about the subject. At the American Institute of Graphic Arts' "Voice" conference, in 2002, Milton Glaser pointed out that while the AIGA's "Business and Ethical Expectations for Professional Designers" document has quite a lot to say about designers' responsibilities to the profession, to their clients, and to other designers, it doesn't mention designers' relationship to the public. "In daily life," Glaser notes, "we expect a butcher to sell us eatable meat and not to misrepresent his wares [...] once a butcher betrays our trust by knowingly selling us spoiled meat we go elsewhere. As a designer, do we have less responsibility to our public than a butcher?"

This is surely a key point, but it poses a profound challenge. The AIGA's ethical guidelines concern themselves with internal matters. For instance, "A designer shall acquaint himself or herself with a client's business and design standards and shall act in the client's best interest within the limits of professional responsibility."

A stated responsibility to the public could interfere with this. The public's best interest might conflict with the client's best interest. What then? Putting the public first could mean losing the commission. Of course, on a personal level, designers face these dilemmas all the time, and they may sometimes resolve them by challenging the client and even abandoning the job (or not taking the work in the first place). But you can see why the AIGA, as an organisation trying to find common ground for 18,000 members, with a multitude of professional interests, prefers to duck the issue and leave it to the conscience of the individual designer. Introducing the idea of responsibility to the public leads down a path where a great deal of what designers do might need to be called into question.

If we really want ethical design, though, the issue is unavoidable. In 2004, finding that the AIGA's code of ethics remained unchanged, Paul Nini, associate professor at Ohio State University, proposed six additional statements about designers' relationship with the public. (It does the AIGA credit that his article appeared on its website, as did Glaser's criticism.)

In the proposal with perhaps the most significance, Nini states, "The designer's main concern must be to create communications that are helpful to audiences and users and that meet their needs with dignity and respect. Any communication created by a designer that intentionally misleads or confuses must be viewed as a negative reflection on the profession as a whole." Other proposals deal with the need to include users in the process of developing communications and to refrain from using information gained through such consultations unethically. It is also important, Nini notes, to pay due regard to the needs of all potential users, to contribute to public wellbeing, and to foster the free flow of essential information.

Even this brief summary should indicate that such sentiments would be open to a variety of interpretations.

What does "helpful to audiences" actually mean? The dumbest ads for the least essential products could still be said to be helpful – they help viewers decide what to buy. Would "needs" be defined as anything a person wants ("I need an SUV") or should they be measured by some stricter yardstick? Whose conception of dignity and respect would we apply?

This brings us back to our starting point – the deep contemporary resistance to ethical priorities. This is not specifically a design problem. It's a social problem. In his brilliantly lucid book *How Are We to Live?* (revised 1997), philosopher Peter Singer, professor of bioethics at Princeton University, offers a way forward. People with a higher ethical consciousness, he says, are able to adopt "the point of view of the universe". Instead of staying inside themselves and seeing everything in terms of their own needs and desires, they are able to step outside. "From this perspective," he writes, "we can see that our own sufferings and pleasures are very like the sufferings and pleasures of others; and that there is no reason to give less consideration to the sufferings of others, just because they are 'other'."

Along with this comes a development away from what Singer calls "arbitrary subjectivism" – regarding ourselves as the centre of everything – to a rational mode of thinking that allows us to see that our individual subjective perspective is no more privileged than anyone else's. Singer points out that the major ethical traditions all have a version of the golden rule that encourages equal consideration of everyone's interests – as in Christ's "Love your neighbour as yourself." It is from this larger perspective, he argues, that we gain the objectivity needed to find a worthwhile cause in a way that is independent of our own desires.

"We have to take the first step," Singer concludes. "We must reinstate the idea of living an ethical life as a realistic and viable alternative to the present dominance of materialist self-interest." There will always be a tension between self-interest and ethics. There will always be people who don't care about anything but themselves. Design presents its own dilemmas. Perhaps much of design really is part of the problem, as its critics often say. There is no reason, though, why a less self-centred, more rational perspective – from the point of view of the universe – could not be the basis of a fulfilling life in design. Any improvement in a situation, however small it might seem, is a step in the right direction.

*This was the late Ian Noble, an influential design teacher. Ken Garland died in 2021.

Power by Design

The virtues of soft power

The issue of power goes to the very heart of the graphic designer's self-image. Graphic designers never feel as though they have enough power. They believe that their multidisciplinary skills equip them to make a wider range of decisions than they are ever actually called on to make. They think that things would run better if they occupied a more elevated position. Yet the world never seems to see it that way (no one is handing out power) and designers' authority relative to other groups doesn't increase; it might even be lower today than it has been at favourable moments in the past. Even within the pecking order of design, where architecture is immovably ensconced at the top, graphic design falls below other disciplines.

Of course, the powerless resent their own impotence, and envy those in positions of strength. The ultimate kind of power is the ability to control organisations, environments and the lives of others; to determine questions of policy; to decide what will be made and what will get done. This is the power possessed by politicians and civic leaders, business supremos and plutocrats, as well as crime bosses. Power is one of the fundamental problems of life. For better or worse, someone always ends up wielding it. We are rightly suspicious of the powerful, since even at their most idealistic they are primarily out for themselves. But if we stand by (as most of us do) and let others seize

Niccolò Machiavelli by Santi di Tito, oil on panel, late 16th century.

power without contesting it, we cannot be surprised when they use it for their own ends.

If you're strongly motivated to seek this kind of worldly power – let's call it hard power – then graphic design is a curious line of work to pick. Most graphic designers are not driven to grasp the reins of power. Their first motive is to design and they are highly focused on the craft of the work. Historically, they have often been solo operators or happiest working in small teams focused on a common goal. They might be perfectly sociable (though many are insular), but they are unlikely to be compulsive mixers, social networkers and glad-handers, constantly manoeuvering to extend their influence into fresh territory. Most designers are far removed from the labyrinthine intrigues of politics and policy-making. They don't often count people in high places among their friends and acquaintances and most show little desire to involve themselves in design organisations, let alone other kinds of groups where worldly power and influence reside. (This is why design associations have such a vital part to play: there can be no wider public influence for graphic designers without them.)

Perhaps this seems a little harsh or dismissive. Naturally, there are always exceptions and possibly you are one of them – a born Machiavelli who had no trouble scheming your way into a position of influence working alongside politicians, CEOs, media owners and other entrepreneurs. For readers who have never given the question of getting power much thought, I would recommend *The Concise 48 Laws of Power* by Robert Greene (2002). If attaining power is your goal, here is your handbook. If it isn't, treat this fascinating guide as a warning bell alerting you to all the ploys those determined to gain influence will use to try to manipulate you. And if you discover that you already practise a lot of Greene's ruthlessly self-serving precepts ("Court attention at all costs"; "Preach the need for change, but never reform too much at once", and so on) without having been fully conscious that you were doing so, then you are probably a natural power-seeker, somewhat miscast as a graphic designer. Embrace your true nature and go for it!

While designers lack – and, as a profession, will probably always lack – hard power, what they possess instead as public communicators is a great deal of soft power. By this I mean the ability, through their work, to influence, mould opinion, persuade, change behaviour, initiate and spread visual trends, shape the aesthetic environment, and help to inform the public. Truck drivers, mail carriers, nurses, construction workers, hotel receptionists and accountants, to name only a few ordinary workers, have no such influence on the public sphere. Graphic designers are in the highly privileged position of using their creative talents to devise messages viewed and read by thousands or even millions of people around the world. This puts them in the company of other public communicators such as journalists, writers, broadcasters, filmmakers, photographers, web designers, and those in advertising and PR, though the association with this last group also underlines some of the problems inherent in design's soft power.

The extent to which graphic designers perceive themselves as having power is likely to depend on how their skills are routinely used. Designers who see graphic design mainly as a commercial service undertaken for clients do still exercise power. Their power isn't personal, however, but derives from a client that has power in the world – this client might be, for instance, a big brand. Those who argue that design is "just a job", to be done with the same impersonal "professionalism" as driving a truck or delivering the mail, ask designers to suspend personal judgment and voluntarily set aside their soft power. But these forms of work are fundamentally different. The postman has no control over the messages he carries and there is no creative agency involved in performing his task. If the postman has concerns about the nature of the invisible content he is required to deliver, then his only recourse is to stop being a postman. In practice, this isn't a dilemma that anyone expects postal workers to ponder.

Designers, on the other hand, can examine the nature of each project in personal, contextual and ethical terms and choose what kinds of message they want to create. Even if they take a purely pragmatic, business-led view in their choice of clients, they are still responsible for the messages they bring into the world at their clients' behest. The message travels outward, seeking to persuade those who receive it and perhaps encourage them to act. Collectively, these messages constitute the profoundly influential visual culture and mental environment in which we spend our lives. Once graphic designers fully accept their responsibility to the public realm – the same responsibility held by journalists and broadcasters – then there is every reason to embrace their soft power with full consciousness (and a clean conscience).

Instead of using their abilities in a disempowered way – purely at the service of their clients – designers can apply their talents and skills to projects they believe in. This is how many designers prefer to work, even in a tough economic climate. My intention here is not to restate a possibility that has always existed but rather to set this possibility in a less familiar frame, as a privileged form of soft power to be actively engaged. Some kinds of hard power will remain inaccessible to designers, as they are to most citizens within the social and political structures that exist today. But the special nature of designers' work means they have access to a type of public influence available to only a few other professional groups. This can become the basis of a rewarding practice. A degree of networking and alliance-building with those who possess hard power remains essential, but shrewd graphic designers have always accepted this. The key thing is to recognise the reality of soft power and make good social use of it.

2. Tools

Singular Sensations

The limitations of anonymity

There is one complaint made by designers about other designers that baffles me. It's a gripe that surfaces regularly and I have been hearing it for as long as I have been writing about design. It isn't helpful, it's counterproductive and it flies in the face of everything that is going on in our culture today. This means that the complaint is unlikely to have any conceivable effect, which is perhaps the basis of its appeal: at a stroke, the malcontent establishes him or herself as someone who stands apart from the crowd.

The complaint I'm talking about is the idea that in our considerations of design – in magazines, books, lectures and, I daresay, even in our everyday chat at the water cooler or at the bar – there is too much emphasis on individual designers. Years ago, I published one of these jeremiads in *Eye* magazine. Getting into the spirit of things, we called it "No More Heroes". The magazine was young and it was the first time anyone had expressed this bracing view in our pages. More recently, also in *Eye*, the assumed over-emphasis on individuals has been roundly condemned as the "myth of genius". Roland Barthes, Michel Foucault (author of "What is an author?") and a platoon of art historians are usually brought in at this point to demonstrate how deeply oppressive it is to know the names of the people who designed the artefacts we use.

Speaking as someone who writes about individual designers without losing too much sleep over it, I have never been a subscriber to the myth of genius. "Genius" is a lazy, meaningless journalistic term that has no place in serious discussions of design. Nor do I count designers as heroes, unless they happen to have rescued a baby from a burning building. I am interested in work and ideas, not personalities, except where a consideration of someone's personality helps to illuminate the work.

The problem with this complaint is often one of context. In its more penetrating form, it is usually made by academics (this was the case with both *Eye* articles), but the venue in which it is delivered is usually journalistic. Art historians were first to recognise the profound limitations of a view of history that confined itself to presenting the lives of individual "great artists" organised into a smooth linear sequence. Design historians followed their cue. As John A. Walker notes in *Design History and the History of Design* (1989), "Texts recounting the story of design in terms of chronologically arranged summaries of the careers of individual designers [...] offer a single line of development akin to the progress of the Olympic torch from runner to runner which cannot cope with the multiple, parallel (and cross-linking) strands taking place in reality." Walker then explores the rich variety of approaches that design historians might bring to these complexities instead: the study of materials and techniques, the comparative method, content analysis, the typological approach, national histories of design, and the anthropological, social, structuralist and semiotic approaches.

This is all fine. More power to you, graphic design historians. I look forward to reading your books. But journalism has different priorities and strengths. It concerns itself with people and their activities, with events unfolding here and now. It is absurd to posit design journalism that doesn't focus on individuals, as well as organisations, companies and institutions, which are also composed of people. Imagine the "myth of genius" embargo applied to the field of politics. It would be impossible to report on or analyse politics as a daily activity without referring to the sayings and doings of politicians. You could discuss matters of policy, but policies are made by people subject to drives, ambitions, pressures and the requirement to compromise, and they have an impact on actual people's lives. Or you could discuss political theory, though this takes us, once again, into the realm of the academy. Extract the people from *Print* or a similar design publication and the dry husk left behind would no longer be a magazine as we understand the term.

The question is not whether we should pay so much attention to individual designers. Rather, it's how do we improve this coverage? I take issue with the "myth of genius" argument not because I think it lacks a certain validity, but because it often seems to be applied willy-nilly, without making any attempt to distinguish between intelligent appraisal and thoughtless puffery. Four out of five magazine profiles may indeed be vacuous celebrity worship, or just not very insightful. If we give up on the possibility that such an article – or a whole book – might be done well, then we increase the likelihood that all such coverage will become vacuous. Without support and encouragement, good things wither.

There is another side to this, which is in many ways more troubling. Here, envious objections to the emphasis on individuals come not from design academics, but from working designers. This surfaced in connection with an item I posted about Bruce Mau for *Design Observer*. I was interested in the way Mau has acquired or cultivated what I described as an aura of power. It might have been possible to discuss the question of power in relation to graphic design in the abstract, but it seemed more revealing to use a strong example as a starting point. It quickly became clear, though, that some of those who commented on my post resented Mau. His "fame" was nothing, it was suggested, when compared with truly famous people in the other fields: hardly anyone outside design had heard of him. The feeling seemed to be that design just doesn't merit this kind of acclaim. On occasions like this, it's hard not to conclude that one thing holding back design is designers.

Of course, when you use global fame as a yardstick, even graphic design's best-known figures – Paul Rand, Milton Glaser, Neville Brody, Paula Scher, David Carson – are a long way from being household names in the Britney Spears sense. But so what? Designers of this stature are known, admired and discussed by some outside the design world, and that is an achievement for which designers at every level should give thanks. Does it really need saying that graphic design can only benefit from high-profile figures able to talk engagingly about the subject to the public? We need more people of this kind, not fewer, and the publicity process, with all its flaws, is the main conduit for their emergence.

What the objections to focusing on individuals have in common, whether they emanate from academics or non-academics, is that they fail to embrace the real state of things. "There is no doubt that individuals do make unique contributions to design, but the magnitude of this element is generally exaggerated out of all proportion as a result of the ideology of individualism which has been so powerful in the West since the Renaissance," writes Walker. Apart from the element of exaggeration in the part of the sentence about exaggeration, this statement is unarguable, but it is written with great detachment by someone taking the long view of history and thinking in the broadest terms, not by someone grappling, as an individual, with the daily struggle to produce design in the world as it is. Sometimes the best way to achieve an understanding of that process is to climb down from the security of your vantage point and move in a little closer to the subject.

Loaded Choices

The usefulness of the canon

In just about any area of cultural endeavour you care to mention, the idea of a canon – a body of work that represents the highest achievement in a field – has been challenged in recent years. Time was when it was commonplace to come across guides to the 100 literary classics that any well-educated person should have read. Unfortunately, most of these works tended to be written by those dreaded Dead White European Males (exciting thought: I'm going to be one myself one day!) so it was reasonable for cultural critics to point out that quite a lot of excellent work from other cultures was being excluded. Was it really so inferior, so undeserving of attention and study? Or was this a clear case of one group reinforcing its cultural power over everyone else?

As so often with persuasive arguments, there were unforeseen consequences. I am willing to bet Tolstoy's complete works that, if we were to pluck 100 people off the street and ask them to name 100 essential literary masterpieces from distant lands, very few would be able to name these previously neglected volumes, let alone be spending their evenings devouring them. In other words, an expanded literary canon familiar to non-specialists has not emerged. Of course, you might still say that the attempted demolition of the old canon was a good thing (I say "attempted" because much of it is still in place.) Better a free-for-all in which there are few fixed points of reference than a cultural system based on assumed superiority and institutionalised exclusion.

About ten years ago, in a fascinating article (reprinted in Steven Heller and Marie Finamore's *Design Culture*), design academic Martha Scotford posed the question, "Is there a canon of graphic design history?" Scotford took five general historical surveys produced in the previous 20 years and subjected them to close analysis – the books included Philip Meggs' *A History of Graphic Design* (1983) and Steven Heller and Seymour Chwast's *Graphic Style* (1988). She made a careful count of the reproductions in these volumes to discover which designers' work was most frequently reproduced, how large it was shown and whether colour was used. From an intermediary list of 63 designers, she arrived at a final canon of eight: Herbert Bayer, A.M. Cassandre, El Lissitzky, Herbert Matter, László Moholy-Nagy, Josef Müller-Brockmann, Henri de Toulouse-Lautrec, and Piet Zwart. Scotford, as a feminist, was quick to note the lack of women in this group born before 1920, though she acknowledged the only real surprise was Toulouse-Lautrec, important to poster history, but probably not a highly significant figure for most graphic designers.

Scotford was ambivalent about the whole idea of a canon. "I want to make it very clear at the outset that in suggesting a canon here, I do not wish to perpetuate one," she writes. She concludes, though, that a design canon exists and is being created and that this will continue at an increasing pace. This being so, she urges readers to evaluate and control this process to make the canon "intentional, conscious, responsible, and truly meaningful for all." Clearly, this is much easier said than done.

Without further research of the kind undertaken by Scotford, it is impossible to know how the canon has developed in the past decade. There is, in any case, a difference between the type of objective measure she sought to apply – even though decisions about picture placement are often subject to random factors – and designers' actual perceptions. The canon may be tenderly midwifed by critics, historians, curators and collectors, but it is the audience that sustains its life. And this, surely, is an objection one might make to canons: that they help to determine and thereby limit our sense of what a field has been, or could be. For instance, women's absence from the canon might lead us to believe there have been no significant women designers, but is that the case? Scotford's book about Cipe Pineles, published in 1999, posed a noteworthy challenge to this assumption, though only time will tell whether Pineles will achieve a place in an expanded future design canon.

As a journalist, editor and writer of books, I have always been conscious of the extent to which these processes are the first stages of a possible canon. By selecting something for publication, you endow it – and often the person who created it – with importance. Yet it's striking how arbitrary, how irresponsible, as Scotford might say, this process has become as design publishing grows. Book after book comes out offering collections of contemporary design. Most of these titles lack any critical or historical perspective. It's not clear why their compilers deem this material significant, or what they are trying to say about it, if anything at all. It's just "new work" tossed hopefully in the direction of an audience presumed to have an insatiable hunger. Often these volumes full of pieces by designers one has never heard of are assembled by people with no track record who have written nothing substantial on the subject and have no reputation as observers of design. Yet publishers, who also often seem to know little about the subject, sign them up to deliver the books nonetheless.

Perhaps this sounds like protectionist talk. In fairness, you have to start somewhere and, in any field, good people come out of nowhere and prove themselves all the time. Even so, contemplating the amorphous sludge of published material that will confront future researchers, you wonder what form the canon for our own time will take, or whether it will be possible to discern one at all. You wouldn't find this kind of thing happening in art publishing where, even now, the significance filters are more finely graded. Critics of the design canon would say this is the point: singling out "masters" and "masterpieces" for special reverence is a misrepresentation of the reality of everyday design that blocks alternative, less designer-centred ways of reading the material. In many respects, the vast, semi-differentiated flux of ephemera served up by the plethora of contemporary design books is truer to the public's daily experience of a medium that is more often than not destined for the trash can.

My own view is that the canon is nonetheless an extremely useful, indeed vital, tool. It is much better to have a flawed canon, as any conceivable canon will be, than to have no canon at all. The canon provides a common body of knowledge, a shared basis for judgement and a starting point for discussion. It exposes us to essential material we might otherwise overlook and helps to set the agenda. A living canon will be fairly stable at the centre, but constantly shifting at its edges, as earlier assessments are revised in the light of fresh discoveries and new thinking. If, as a designer, you believe there are degrees of talent, expertise and achievement in your field, then it is reasonable to suppose that professional observers – journalists, critics, historians, curators – can also acquire this understanding and knowledge. If you believe that the history of your profession has a value, then it makes sense to entrust it to competent hands, and to discriminate between publishing ventures that have value and those that do not.

One of the notable things about Scotford's canon is that it is concerned with individuals, not with pieces of work. In 2002, the film magazine *Sight and Sound* published the results of an international poll it organises every ten years to find out critics' and directors' top ten films. As ever, many eminent film people took part, and the number one film from both groups, based on individual lists, was *Citizen Kane* – for the fifth decade running.

Some saw this as evidence of ossification, though there was plenty of movement elsewhere in the two lists.* It was a valuable, popular reminder of the canon of great films and a prompt to seek out unseen titles and fill some personal gaps. Is it possible to imagine a similar top ten or top 100 for design? Which are the masterworks and why? If we were to conduct a similar poll about graphic artefacts, among hundreds of critics or designers, would there be any consensus at all?

*In the 2012 *Sight and Sound* poll, *Citizen Kane* was finally dethroned by Alfred Hitchcock's *Vertigo* (on the critics' list) and Yasujirō Ozu's *Tokyo Story* (on the directors' list). In 2022, an unexpected result provoked wide discussion. The Belgian director Chantal Akerman's *Jeanne Dielman, 23, quai du Commerce, 1080 Bruxelles* (1975), a feminist masterwork influenced by avant-garde film-making techniques, topped the international critics' poll and rose to fourth equal in the directors' poll. It was a sign that when the time is right, canons may be subject to far-reaching revision.

Absolutely the "Worst"

How the graphic canon is formed

Canonical designers are easy enough to identify. The situation with canonical designs is more complicated. Graphic designers create millions of new designs every year. How does a tiny percentage of these pieces, which most viewers will never hold in their hands, come to be regarded as crucial works, designs of influence that deserve a lasting place in the narrative of graphic design?

Reproduction alone is not enough. Much of the work that appears in magazines and annuals for a brief moment in the limelight soon falls by the wayside, even if it remains in the published record, notionally available for future consultation. Online archiving will increase its chances. Projects that have not been published in any form are unlikely to be remembered for long, but if someone – usually the designer – takes the trouble to preserve good copies, there remains a slender hope of discovery someday.

The crucial requirement is repetition. The more often the work appears in the right places, the more its future appearance is assured. These "right places" are simply the venues that critics, historians and curators are likely to consult when trying to gauge the most significant examples of a particular type of work to show in their projects. Once a graphic work becomes part of a major museum collection, its longevity is guaranteed, though this alone will not be enough to make it canonical. It needs to be seen regularly.

A good example of the process in action is the American designer Allen Hori's "Typography As Discourse" poster, produced in 1989 at Cranbrook Academy of Art, while Hori, then 29, was an MFA student. This first surfaced in 1990 in the book *Cranbrook Design: The New Discourse* (edited by Katherine and Michael McCoy). To some eyes, it looked untutored, chaotic and alien.

Rudy VanderLans describes sitting in on one of Wolfgang Weingart's design classes at the Kunstgewerbeschule in Basel. Weingart, a regular visitor to Cranbrook, pulled out a copy of the poster. "This, he proclaimed, was the absolute worst of what was currently happening in graphic design," recalls VanderLans. "I knew then that the Typography As Discourse poster was a very special piece of graphic design."

The poster's subject is a lecture given at Cranbrook by Katherine McCoy, co-chair of the design department – an expanded version of her article with the same title published in *I.D.* magazine (March/April 1988). The outsized parenthesis and bracket recall similar devices in the magazine's layout by another Cranbrook designer, David Frej. Hori constructed the poster as a mechanical artwork, with manual letterspacing, Rubylith masking film, tracing paper and acetate overlays, and an elaborate mark-up. He sent intricate type compositions from the Macintosh to an output service and collected the hard copy the next day.

A communications theory diagram referred to by McCoy and the students provides the poster's underlying conceptual framework. It encapsulates the idea that text can be perceived as a visual image as well as read, while images can be read as well as seen. If visual communication is intuitive, holistic and simultaneous, then verbal communication is traditionally regarded as rational, linear and sequential – all keywords that appear in the poster. The scattered nodes of information, linked by meandering typographic pathways, challenge the usual seeing/reading distinction by encouraging exploration, which can begin anywhere and proceed in any direction.

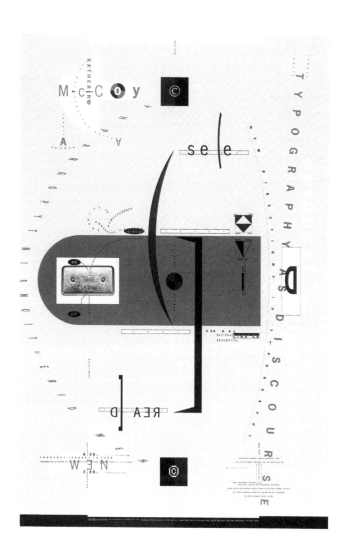

Typography As Discourse, lecture poster. Cranbrook Academy of Art, Bloomfield Hills, Michigan, 1989. Design: Allen Hori.

Hori refined the design over several nights and he recalls how McCoy would leave Post-it notes for him in the morning with questions and comments. There was also discussion in the studio about the way his design interpreted the familiar diagram.

In spring 1991, *Eye* no. 3 published an article about "deconstructed" design at Cranbrook by Ellen Lupton featuring the poster. I could hardly fail to include such an extraordinary and emblematic piece of new typography in the survey *Typography Now: The Next Wave*, published later that year. Around the same time, VanderLans reproduced the poster in *Emigre* no. 20, along with other work by Hori and an interview.

Nevertheless, it might have stopped there. Plenty of work from that time is now forgotten. Lupton, one of the most perceptive critics of Cranbrook design, helped to prolong the poster's iconic afterlife by publishing it twice in 1996. It features in her collection with Abbott Miller, *Design Writing Research*, in the essay "Deconstruction and Graphic Design", where they describe it as "a manifesto for a design practice informed by literary theory." Lupton also included the poster in her book *Mixing Messages*, which accompanied a major exhibition of contemporary American graphic design that she curated at the Cooper-Hewitt National Design Museum in New York. The poster is in the collections of the Cooper-Hewitt, the AIGA Design Archives and Cranbrook Art Museum. Only a few other copies survive.

Even if I hadn't known the poster already, all of this would have been enough to ensure its place in my own *No More Rules* (2003), a study of graphic design and postmodernism. The ultimate sign that the poster has entered the graphic design canon and is likely to stay there is its appearance in chapters on postmodernism in Stephen J. Eskilson's *Graphic Design: A New History* (2007) and Johanna Drucker and Emily McVarish's *Graphic Design History: A Critical Guide* (2008). Drucker and McVarish describe it as "a classic of postmodern design", noting its "clean and rather distilled aesthetic".

This is an astute observation. Although detractors professed to see only disorder and confusion in Cranbrook's output, Hori's poster is an entirely self-aware, delicately controlled visual essay, which makes its case with great precision. Current typographic taste doesn't much care for the complexities of this kind of work. It is a measure of the poster's originality, and the way it still radiates the heat of its moment, that it lives on regardless.

The Death of the Critic

What is design criticism for?

Does design criticism matter anymore? It's certainly not a term you hear bandied about by designers. Busy professionals have clients to meet, projects to plan, studios to run. If designers pause to think about design criticism at all, they probably imagine that it is still going on somewhere – and good luck to it.

But if we aren't actively looking for design criticism, how do we know whether it's flourishing or not? There is plenty of design journalism, but criticism and journalism are different activities. While it's certainly possible for journalism to have a critical intention, most design journalism simply reports on the latest news. There is nothing wrong with that, but it isn't criticism and it tells us nothing about criticism's state of health. We will call design criticism in for a fitness check and take its pulse in due course, but first it might be useful to look at what criticism in general – whether in the fields of art, architecture, literature or film – is for.

Perhaps the most basic service provided by criticism has been to champion the new. The idea here is that without the intervention of the critic, the public would fail to understand or appreciate artistic innovations. People might ignore or even attack them. The critic is presumed to have special insight into the motivations and meaning of the work that comes from a deep personal engagement. It may be necessary to challenge earlier ways of thinking to explain why these creations are timely and significant. The critic may become strongly identified with particular individuals, movements or causes, a fellow traveller with the innovators he or she champions, influencing their artistic development and ideas.

If we consider this model in terms of contemporary design, some problems emerge. Most obviously, there is no public resistance to design today and there is no provocative design avant-garde requiring the critic to step in as intermediary and advocate. Twenty-five years ago, Memphis might have needed this kind of critical support. The movement was controversial with modernist designers, and writers trotted out various theories to explain it. Where are the contemporary equivalents? Postmodern design caused a ruckus for a while, but this passed and nothing as turbulent has occurred since then. Meanwhile, adventurous design has become something that any modern consumer appreciates. People need updates about the latest sofas, mobile phones, bars, restaurants and hip hotels, but they don't need anyone to argue the case for these things or to explain their relevance. Journalism handles the publicity – from the glossy interior mags to reports in the daily press.

The same reservation applies to criticism's more general function of promoting a discipline's cause. Fifty years ago, design needed all the support it could get. "The role of the serious critic is that of an educator," wrote advertising designer Ashley Havinden in 1952. "By searching out the many examples of good design and appraising them constructively, he may convince the manufacturer or the printer of the merits of good design associated with his product [...] Such constructive criticism in the press would teach the public, not only to appreciate, but to demand good design in the products they buy." Today, in Britain, we have plenty of organisations and initiatives to beat the drum for design: the Design Council, the British Council, D&AD, the London Design Festival. It's debatable whether writing produced for this well-worn purpose can be regarded as criticism.

The third possible function of criticism goes considerably further than mere promotion. This kind of writing takes design's presence for granted as something that no longer needs to be argued for, and it arises from a commitment to design's cultural possibilities. The emphasis here falls on the depth, subtlety, sophistication and complexity of the critic's response. The writing is more discursive and playful; it weaves around its subject; it offers pleasures of its own. Making assessments of quality might once have been a key task for this type of criticism, but this has become unfashionable in other art forms, particularly in visual art, and today it is less likely to be attempted in design writing, where there is an inherent tension between subjective aesthetic reactions and more objective assessments of whether or not a design fulfils its functional purpose. The problem with the more rarefied forms of criticism is that they can too easily seem arcane and elitist, and in the age of public access this is unacceptable to many. Even art people seem to find much of what is written about art unreadable.

The final category of criticism takes a more questioning and sometimes even hostile view of the subject. This is the cultural studies approach. It treats cultural production as a form of evidence, taking these phenomena apart to discover what they reveal about society, and viewing the subject matter through particular lenses: feminism, racism, consumerism, sustainability. Design, as a primarily commercial endeavour, makes a particularly good subject for this type of analysis and unmasking. The problem, from a designer's point of view, is that this form of design commentary can be deeply sceptical about many things that a working professional takes for granted. Designers who read it are often confronted with two bald alternatives: feel bad about what you are doing or change your ways. Combative, campaigning criticism – Naomi Klein's *No Logo* is an example – is more likely to come from outside the design world.

This summary suggests some of the difficulties facing design criticism today. There are other factors that need to be taken into account. It has been publishing wisdom for years that the reader's appetite for ploughing through long articles has dwindled. We are busier than ever, the thinking runs, and other forms of media compete for the browser's attention. Magazines respond with an easy-to-swallow diet of captions, sidebars and pictures. If criticism needs space to flex its muscles, then today's design magazines are not always eager to supply it. You can see this at work in the industry bible *Design Week*, never the most critical of organs. Since the magazine's redesign, which increased the page size, articles appear to be shorter, with smaller type that only adds to the feeling that the words take up space that might be better allotted to more colour pictures. The "Private View" opinion column was hardly an unduly taxing read at 800 words; it has been slashed to just 500.

The notion of criticism has been undermined in other ways. The critic, as traditionally understood, was a person of superior knowledge and insight. Critics presumed to know best about their areas of expertise. They made judgements on behalf of other people and their authoritative pronouncements about books, films or art used to count for something. New York theatre critics could famously close plays with a damning review. People are much less prepared now to regard critics as sources of authoritative opinion. A consumer guide with handy star ratings may be all you need to decide which CD to buy this week or which movie to see.

It's often said that everyone is a critic today and the internet, with its challenge to all forms of printed authority, has taken this democracy of opinion to a new level. A growing army of bloggers offers commentary that editors would never dream of publishing in print on every aspect of cultural life. When everyone can broadcast their views so easily, the position of the critic looks much less distinctive and necessary. Still, the torrent of words unleashed by blogging and the popularity of some sites seem to contradict the idea that people are less prepared to read than they were.

When it comes to design, it's sometimes suggested that blogs might offer a new forum for design criticism and, as a design writer, this certainly attracted me. In 2003, I co-founded a site called *Design Observer* with three American designers and for a couple of years I wrote short essays for it as often as I could. What I soon realised was that as a medium for writing (as opposed to more diary-like uses), blogging software is a kind of Trojan horse. The open-to-all-comers comment box at the end of each entry can generate a vast trail of digression that overpowers the original article, no matter how carefully it is written. One 1,000-word *Design Observer* essay by a colleague produced more than 60,000 words of comment – the size of a book – and much of it utterly pointless. Internet publishing might, in time, provide a way forward for criticism, but I am not convinced that blogs will. Attempts to define a distinctive position disappear beneath the hubbub.

Whether design criticism has a future or not, we should at least be clear about what it can do. Here, I want to turn to an example that shows what critical thinking used to mean in the design field, and that suggests why we still need it today.

In June 1955, *The Architectural Review* published a special issue, written by the brilliant architecture critic Ian Nairn, then just 25, which it titled *Outrage*. The issue documents the spread of what the AR calls Subtopia – a compound of suburb and utopia – across Britain. "Subtopia," Nairn writes, "is the annihilation of the difference by attempting to make one type of scenery standard for town, suburb, countryside and wild." The AR documents this with great thoroughness. Everything about the issue – the use of drawings and different coloured papers, the typography – glows with visual intelligence. Nairn shows scores of photographs of street lamps, arterial roads, overhead wires, street advertising and bungled attempts at "municipal rustic". He undertakes a 400-mile car journey from Southampton to Carlisle, producing a written commentary supported

Outrage by Ian Nairn, book cover, Architectural Press, 1955.
Drawing: Gordon Cullen. Reprinted from *The Architectural Review*, June 1955.

anti-urbanism, part 2, cont.

rural third-degree If anti-urbanism as applied to an industrial town is a crime, what can one say about the third-degree practised in some rural districts? These examples of the halves of our inevitable equation (decay of the good, replacement by bad) come from the Ploughley RDC, around Bicester, where in ten years one authority has gone a long way towards eradicating what centuries of local building has bestowed and—the worst crime—replacing it by estates that might as well be in Outer Birmingham. The slum drive which is being pursued with the same height-and-sanitation rules, applied blindly, whether the environment is a Salford slum or an Oxon village, will intensify this destruction, as local authorities seem unable to see that they save money if they convert instead of demolishing. England's heritage, going down for the last time, gentlemen: won't someone see sense, even if it's only for the tourists' dollars?

key: Old: 1, Charlton on Otmoor. 2, Bucknell. 3, Godington. 6, Finmere. New: 5, Souldern. 4, Oddington. 7, Kirtlington. 8, Bletchingdon.

The village c___ subjection to ___ is shown oppos___ happened to deve___ that have beco___ sprawl: what ___ the same tech___ applied to village___ countryside—they h___

Outrage by Ian Nairn, Architectural Press, 1955.
Drawings: Gordon Cullen. Photographs: Ian Nairn.
Reprinted from *The Architectural Review*, June 1955.

by pictures of everything he sees, then switches his attention to the Scottish Highlands, where he looks at housing, roads, tourism, hydro-electricity. The issue ends with a manifesto about what needs to be done aimed at the person in the street, which sets out some precepts ("The site's the thing, not a set of rules, and your eye's the thing, not the textbook") and offers a comprehensive list of malpractices to watch out for ("Has the town lost its centre to the car park? Or the open square to a wired-in public garden?").

What is remarkable about *Outrage* is its controlled anger and passion. The purpose of criticism here is to force open people's eyes, to change opinion and make a difference. The writer has a view of Subtopia grounded in a philosophical awareness of what it signifies for the person who lives inside it: "Insensible to the meaning of civilization on the one side and, on the other, ignorant of the well-spring of his own being, he is removing the sharp edge from his own life, exchanging individual feeling for mass experience in a voluntary enslavement far more restrictive and permanent than the feudal system." The issue became a book, and it's clear from the many reviews quoted on the cover that it received a level of attention in the papers that a design magazine initiative would never be granted today. "Sameness can become a most virulent form of ugliness," writes *The Observer*. "If we are not shocked into recognising it in time, we shall ourselves become subtopians, sub-humans, no longer individuals but for ever members of a herd."

To produce a scorching critique like this you need profound idealism and a shared sense of what matters, and we have lost this now. Much of what Nairn and the AR feared came to pass in spite of their protests. In their terms, the visual environment of Britain was carelessly ruined. Subtopia – sprawl, if you prefer – continues to throw a dull blanket of sameness over everything in its path. Design and its offshoot, branding, were instrumental in stamping this uniformity onto British high streets to a degree that Nairn, who died in 1983, can scarcely have imagined. Many people find it harder to feel such a keen sense of outrage today because they have ceased to believe that it's likely to have much effect. What counts is to find ways of accommodating things as they are and of making whatever practical interventions you can lever, though these aren't expected to bring about fundamental change. In architectural circles, the term "post-critical" has gained currency as a way of describing some younger architects' acceptance of the prevailing social, economic and cultural reality. In a recent issue of *Harvard Design Magazine*, Reinhold Martin notes that this form of architecture is committed to "an affect-driven, nonoppositional, nonresistant, nondissenting and therefore nonutopian form of architectural production".

Reinhold wonders, with some justification, whether post-critical polemic might just be part of the general political swing to the right, an authoritarian manoeuvre intended to kill off once and for all any lingering traces in architectural thinking of the radical politics of the 1960s. If the post-critical position purports to be "realistic", then Reinhold proposes "utopian realism" as a riposte. "Utopian realism is critical," he writes. "It is real. It is enchantingly secular. It thinks differently. It is a style with no form [...] It is utopian not because it dreams impossible dreams, but because it recognizes 'reality' itself as – precisely – an all-too-real dream enforced by those who prefer to accept a destructive and oppressive status quo." We are back to the idea that criticism's purpose is to strip away the layers and try to expose what is going on underneath. This task has nothing to do with professional and institutional needs to build careers and promote the design business.

So where does that leave the possibility of design criticism today? Britain has plenty of outlets for design journalism, but design criticism is much harder to find. The quickest way to assess its state of health is to try naming some design critics, writers who are well known for consistent preoccupations and points of view, who are prepared to speak out and take a stand, and whose writing has a distinctive style and voice. If we use, say, the great writer and critic Reyner Banham as a yardstick, is there anyone who measures up? Recently, I took part in two panel discussions about design criticism organised in London by *I.D.* magazine and Rhode Island School of Design. Part of the way through the second event, I pointed out that no one on either panel had mentioned any design critics. I challenged my fellow panellist, *Icon*'s editor Marcus Fairs, to name some – he proposed himself and his team. I threw in the name of Sam Jacob, whose writing about design and popular culture in *Icon* and *Modern Painters* seems to me to display an individual voice. And that was it.

I would say we have a problem. We desperately need criticism. It's a vital part of the development of any creative discipline. It helps to shape the way practitioners think about their work and it plays a crucial role in fostering critical reflection among design students. Conducted convincingly, design criticism might even establish design in the public's consciousness – at last – as an activity that has a little more to it than dreaming up cool things to buy in the shops.

It comes back to our publications. The standard of design criticism is in the hands of the editors who commission most design writing. New writers cannot possibly emerge without places to publish and sympathetic support. The greatest gift an editor can give a writer is the space and freedom to explore a subject in a personal way; this was the opportunity that AR gave Nairn. Nurturing writers is a basic editorial task, but it's not clear that editors see it that way anymore. Most magazine writing is publisher-led: this is what we need, this is our style, 1,200 words, go away and do it. What we see in the best blogs is a desire, in both writers and readers, for writing that shatters the chains imposed by narrow journalistic formats and agendas. If design magazines learn one lesson from blogs, it should be to put the emphasis back on good writing. Let's be utopian realists and ignore the old saw about designers not wanting to read. It isn't true. Publish commentary that is so timely, lively, perceptive, provocative, informative, irreverent and entertaining that people can't afford to miss it.

There is no reason why criticism has to follow set paths. Analysis of the designed world can, and should, take visual forms. The AR knew it 50 years ago. Yet it's surprising how rarely design magazines use the resources at their disposal – photographs, diagrams, illustrations – in partnership with words to deliver an incisive commentary on the visual realm. Why is the prevailing visual mode always celebratory? That might be appropriate for the glossy, weekend-break, luxury-lifestyle end of publishing, but not for magazines professing a commitment to design thinking. And why isn't humour used more often to puncture pretension and cut the over-mighty down to size? Music magazines have been doing this for years. While criticism needs space to stretch out, it can also be delivered in sharp, concentrated bursts. It should be as unpredictable and inventive as the best design.

Designers Need Critics

Has criticism's moment passed?

It is curious that in the 21st century the idea of design criticism remains such an issue. Design has been a matter for serious discussion in Europe since the Second World War. Bruno Munari's wonderfully fresh critical reflections on design, now back in print, were written in the 1960s. Reyner Banham, one of the greatest design writers and still a model for aspiring design critics, also made his mark in that decade of accelerating change. For the last 30 years design has been a hot and increasingly public topic. During the "design boom" of the 1980s, when I landed a writing job on *Blueprint* in London, I couldn't believe my good fortune. Many of the best design and architecture critics of the day – Deyan Sudjic (*Blueprint*'s editor), Stephen Bayley, Peter York, Martin Pawley, James Woudhuysen, Janet Abrams, Jonathan Glancey, Rowan Moore – wrote for the magazine. Nobody ever needed to say that writing was important, that it should be sharp, textured, closely observed and critical, that it was a reason for buying *Blueprint*, or that it deserved plenty of space. That was all self-evident.

Yet today a huge question mark hangs over design criticism. Is it needed? What does it have to offer? How many readers even want it? Designers sometimes complain that design magazines aren't sufficiently critical. Then, if they happen to find their own work on the receiving end of even the mildest criticism, they yelp with dismay at the perceived injustice. I have seen this myself. A couple of outspoken design superstars I had the temerity to criticise in the 1990s refused to speak to me for many years. Such easily bruised egos, such astonishingly thin skins. Editors and publishers must defend their ethical and intellectual right to publish reasoned and fair critical comment on a field that can only benefit from the careful examination of new ideas, trends, received wisdoms and fads. What is meaningful and valuable now, and what isn't? If critical inquiry was continuous and normal, the design profession would gain immeasurably in critical self-awareness, sense of social purpose and public understanding.

Some believe it is already too late. There is a persistent claim that if criticism hasn't given up the ghost already, then it is drawing its last breath. A recent collection of writings by the late Martin Pawley, a titan among architecture critics, serves notice in its title, *The Strange Death of Architectural Criticism*. Joe Clark, a Canadian blogger, has a category devoted to "The death of graphic-design criticism", where he tolls the bell for this allegedly moribund practice with gleeful relish. An earlier essay I wrote about design writing for *Icon* magazine went out with the title "The Death of the Critic" – not quite my intention (see page 118). And design criticism isn't alone in hastening the last rites. Critics of literature, film and art agonise over whether their much longer established and more publicly accessible trades are coming to an end.

It is too easy to say that this is all down to the way that the online environment has changed our information-gathering and reading habits. In the 1990s, before the internet was even an issue, there was already a widespread assumption in magazine publishing that "readers" had less patience or inclination to read and that magazines needed to become more visual, with more pictures and more intricate page design. *Blueprint*, then in the hands of a different editorial team, began to reduce the length of its articles. This self-defeating move was a troubling sign for anyone who understood that ambitious critical writing needs space, but it rapidly became the new wisdom among magazine-makers convinced their audiences were more likely to scan and graze than to engage in attentive reading. Looking at almost any kind of magazine from the 1960s today is a shock: there are so many towering columns of words to take in.

There can be no doubt, though, that the internet has had a profound impact on design magazines with inevitable consequences for the way they handle critical writing – if it matters to them at all. As readers abandon print or just never acquire the habit, many advertisers are no longer convinced that this is the way to reach them. The economic downtown intensified the pain. The most alarming events have been the closure in December 2009 of *I.D.* magazine after 55 years as the leading American design title, followed in 2011 by the sudden demise of the British magazine *Grafik*, which until then had appeared to be thriving. Other titles, such as *Metropolis* in New York, look worryingly malnourished. Advertising has dried up, the page count has fallen and the long critical reviews it once published have been dropped. *Icon*'s earlier commitment to 3,000-word critical essays is another casualty of leaner, recessionary times.*

These magazines still show plenty of pictures, of course, but as a long-term survival strategy this seems inadequate since the internet will win every time when it comes to delivering instantly available new images. Even the superior quality of print won't in the end be enough. The same goes for industry news and topical comment, which blogs are better positioned to provide. Design magazines' online presence, on the other hand, often looks half-hearted – *I.D.* was left standing by web competitors such as *Core77*, *Designboom* and *Dezeen*. Magazine sites and blogs exist in an uneasy relationship with the parent publication and brand they are supposed to support and promote, diverting resources that were previously focused entirely on producing the printed page. They look like transitional ventures, place holders waiting for the moment when the burdensome weight of the paper magazine can finally be cut away and abandoned because the online world has found a way of properly monetising internet-based publishing.

Core77 publishes well-written essays and reviews, as does *Design Observer*, but the online world has not seen the outbreak of compelling new critical voices in design one might have expected – writing equal to the insight and panache of Pawley, Sudjic or Bayley in their prime. Dare one suggest, then, that probing critical commentary and analysis by knowledgeable writers is one area where magazines still have the potential to supply something valuable that's not easily found elsewhere. The more pictures come to dominate a design magazine's pages, the less it will look like a writer's – or a reader's – medium. To stand any chance of commanding attention, the text needs a strong graphic presence of its own (1980s *Blueprint* managed this awkward image/text balancing act with aplomb). It is also worth noting that the dependence of design magazines on pictures supplied or authorised by a project's clients and designers has frequently limited their writers' power to comment freely on what the pictures show.

For the sake of argument, let's say we did have a fully mature design criticism in the design press. What would it look like and what would it be doing? First of all, it would need to find a way of staying close to its subject while maintaining a sceptical distance. This is not easy to pull off. Journalism is a good starting point because a journalist has access. Only by meeting the key figures, going behind closed doors and seeing things from the inside is it possible to gain a real sense of the milieu. (Designers who turn to writing have an initial advantage – they already inhabit this world – but naturally then find it difficult, if not impossible, to achieve detachment; they worry too much about their design colleagues' reactions to what they write.)

One would expect writers in any field to be passionately engaged with their subject and to keep surprising us with their knowledge. We take this for granted in political writing in the press where commentators show a detailed command of recent political history: what happened when, who said what, and how it relates to what's happening now. When I started, the best design writers brought wide experience and hard-won insight to their writing, making it denser, richer and more convincing. This kind of knowledge is rarer now in design. Forever frothing with excitement about the latest thing, too much design writing exists only in the fast-evaporating moment; it lacks a cultural memory and shows no sign of realising what it doesn't know. Without a close understanding of context and the ability this brings to make comparisons and arrive at carefully weighed judgements, a subtle, sophisticated criticism is simply not possible.

Another crucial point about criticism is that it needs to be genuinely critical. This is taken for granted in other kinds of cultural reviewing and criticism: films, novels, plays, art exhibitions and music are all subject to continuous evaluation (though these consumer-orientated assessments also have their flaws). The reader's awareness that adverse criticism is not only possible but merciless when necessary gives favourable judgements more reliability and weight. By contrast, design receives a consistently easy ride in the specialist press, which often seems to aspire to be nothing more than a glamorous PR platform and support service, while general media, with no other model of design discussion to go on, treat design as a lightweight consumer subject in the style and lifestyle pages. Not for the first time we need to remind ourselves that there can be no serious, well-informed, mainstream design criticism if design publishing has not already set a high standard of critical inquiry to show how it should be done. Design is a fusion of commerce and culture. For design criticism to develop, we need to place a great deal more emphasis on investigating the cultural implications of that union.

If design criticism remains an ideal more talked about than engaged in, there have still been some notable educational initiatives of late. In 2008, new master's degree courses in design writing and criticism started at the London College of Communication and at the School of Visual Arts in New York. The Konstfack design school in Stockholm also runs an MA in critical writing and curatorial practice. In October, another design and art criticism MA opens its doors at the Royal College of Art in London.** For anyone who believes that criticism could have an important role to play, courses exploring its methods and applications can only be a positive development. The obvious question to ask next is where do these graduates expect to find work in a shrinking field? And assuming they do find viable places to write, what do they and their teachers, for that matter, understand the purpose of design criticism to be?

Alice Twemlow, founder of SVA's D-Crit course, provides one possible answer to the question of purpose in a post for *Design Observer* titled "Howling at the Moon: The Poetics of Amateur Product Reviews". Designers of all kinds are finding new ways to involve design's end-users, ordinary people, in the design process and Twemlow approaches design criticism from the same angle. Analysing the often hilarious user reviews on Amazon.com of a self-flushing cat toilet and a T-shirt with a howling wolf motif, she proposes that this kind of imaginative user feedback is "not a deviation from the true path of design criticism but, rather, a logical extension of a democratizing impulse that has always been at its core." She goes on to argue that Reyner Banham anticipated these developments in his accessible critical writing about everyday subjects and "empowered the casual and independent observer to comment on their own designed environment." This, Twemlow believes, is a key task for the 21st-century design critic: to educate and encourage design's users by generous example. "Criticism is only really productive," she concludes, "if it reaches its intended audience in a way that surprises, goads or otherwise convinces them to act."

I wouldn't put it as baldly as this. Who is to say, after all, what is "productive" and what isn't? Why is it so important to act? And what constitutes an act, anyway? In the context of a product review, does acting mean buying something? Deciding not to buy something on the basis of a bad review would be a non-act, though still a positive, active decision. Is criticism only fully productive if it inspires readers to compose reviews of their own? Why isn't simply thinking and reflecting enough? Twemlow's efficiency-driven argument looks like a bid for certainty, a desire for an objective, measurable outcome, where certainty is neither achievable nor necessary.

The truth, I would suggest, is that excellent criticism will always find readers and those readers will use it in whatever ways they need. All the committed critic has to worry about – no easy task – is trying to do the best possible job. As for the reader, the most trenchant response, never more so than now, is to encourage criticism's continuing existence by supporting the platforms that provide it. Good critical writing is vital to the design field, to any cultural field, in a looser, less easy to quantify sense that can be best apprehended through our own histories and experiences as readers. Criticism prises open doors, reveals unforeseen possibilities, enhances our awareness, refines our values, hones our taste and exerts a myriad of influences on the judgements, decisions and actions we will take in the future. Whether we are fully conscious of this web of inspiration or not, criticism helps to shape our mentality.

---

*In 2019, *Print* – where most of the essays in this book first appeared – also ceased publishing. It was later born again online.
**It proved to be a false dawn. The London College of Communication's Design Writing Criticism course closed in 2011 and the Konstfack course also closed. The RCA's Critical Writing in Art and Design course flourished for several years before becoming a more general "writing" course. D-Crit, the ambitious SVA course in design criticism, shrank from two years to one, although it retains a focus on design.

Standing Still

What is true visual literacy?

Our speaker's subject was convergence. In the future, the young designer informed us, music and image-making would no longer be separate creative activities. Produced on a common platform, the endlessly adaptable computer, they would fuse into a single, dynamic new medium. If the painter Titian were alive today, the speaker continued, warming to his theme, he would be Steven Spielberg. This was such a misguided notion that a colleague sitting in front of me turned around and shot me a look that could only be interpreted as "Huh?!"*

My sentiments exactly. There had to be a better comparison than that between one of the greatest painters of mythological and religious scenes, and the stylistically gifted but artistically shallow box-office hit maker. Still, the speaker's meaning was clear. Titian crafted antiquated, immobile images using quaintly outdated equipment, while Spielberg draws on all the wonders of digital technology to deliver a flowing stream of hallucinogenically intense *motion pictures*. Given the choice, who wouldn't want to make and, for that matter, look at movies?

Graphic designers have suffered from moving-image envy for decades. Once in a while someone succeeds in making both static and animated forms of communication, usually by designing film titles (Saul Bass, Robert Brownjohn), and a particularly intrepid ship-jumper will occasionally manage to direct an entire feature film (Kyle Cooper, Mike Mills). Of course, it's different now because the availability of low-cost digital tools means that almost anyone can become a temporarily famous supplier of YouTube clips. Meanwhile, digital video has made professional filmmaking much cheaper and more flexible and even a celluloid-loving auteur of David Lynch's stature is happy to give it a try. Today, the easy availability of the means only serves to underline the primacy of the moving image.

Even so, it's wrong to assume that moving images are inherently superior to the still image, and it's tempting to say that anyone who thinks so probably doesn't know how to look at pictures. One of the great untested claims of our time is that people are far more visually literate than they were in the past. This is an assumption based on the proliferation of visual images in advertising, design, media and computer games, the ever-increasing sophistication of these images at a technological level, and the apparent ability of audiences to decipher, assimilate and enjoy these products. But is it really the case?

When you spend time in art galleries, it's striking to see how few people pause to look – really look – at the paintings they pass. Even the greatest masterpieces are dispatched within seconds. Viewers take in the image as a whole, as a kind of mental snapshot, but the only way to appreciate and understand a painting of any complexity is to give it time, allow your eyes to wander over its entire surface, and permit it to act on you. Paint is a medium of expression and a carrier of meaning, and these meanings are only available to viewers prepared to make a modest effort to scrutinise colour, the stylistic effects of brushwork and the use of light. The composition may be crucial to what the painter is trying to say about the subject matter and it needs to be studied carefully, as well as savoured as a source of aesthetic pleasure. Questions will probably arise about the painter's relation to the subject and about the painting's relation to other artworks. It isn't excessive to spend ten minutes, or considerably longer, looking at a good picture, but it's unusual to see a viewer devote this much attention to a single image – though everyone sits happily in a cinema for two hours staring at a screen. It's also revealing to observe what happens when galleries show films: the viewing rooms fill up with spectators.

The critical element when looking at a complex static image is time. The image might not move, but the viewer's relation to the image is far from static. Still images withhold what comes before and after, freezing a single defining moment for contemplation, and this challenges the viewer to engage imaginatively with the image and interpret it: why show this scene in this way? A still image of an occurrence or event will always be more iconic than a filmed version of the same episode.

Moving images, by contrast, oblige the viewer to move and react at the speed of projection. Momentum exerts its own irresistible seduction, regardless of what is shown. Watching a film, we can be absorbed by narrative and performance without paying conscious attention to the construction of the images as imagery. Using a DVD player, it's always possible to "stop time", allowing us to study a frame at leisure, but this is an artificial extension of our ability to reflect on what would otherwise be transient, a violation of the essential nature of the motion picture as a viewing experience, where one image follows another and the editing and flow within a sequence of images becomes a source of meaning.

Some might argue that the depth and complexity of painting is irrelevant in a media environment where speed of communication is vital. But the study of art from all epochs provides the best possible form of visual education, a grounding that underpins every kind of applied art. If gallery-goers are unable to appreciate fully the works of art they nevertheless feel compelled to file past as tourists in major museums, then it's hard to see how the same viewers could have developed the skills of visual interpretation needed to engage critically with advertising and design. For the highly developed visual literacy the public is said to possess to mean anything at all, it must entail an ability to read visual images – to apprehend their full range of meanings and understand how they contrive to influence the viewer. Merely being familiar with the conventions of image-making doesn't in itself constitute genuine visual literacy.

The remarkable thing, looking back now, is how narrow the gap between fine art and commercial art used to be. Old advertising images frequently match the paintings of their period for visual quality, transcending their commercial origins. If I owned a copy of Niklaus Stoecklin's 1941 poster for Binaca toothpaste, I would happily hang it on my wall because I doubt I would ever tire of looking at that heroic, oversized tube and toothbrush rendered with hyper-real, lithographic precision. While the image anticipates Pop Art's compellingly ordinary iconography of the everyday by a good 20 years, it also conveys a profound sense of mystery produced by placing the tube, brush and glass against a background as black and ineffable as the voids of deep space. These ordinary objects seem to be about much more than mere dental hygiene.

A similar depth of sentiment and realisation can be found in Milton Glaser's *Typewriter with Dog* poster from 1968, an advertisement for Olivetti's classic Valentine. Glaser based his drawing on a section of a picture by Piero di Cosimo (circa 1495) of a satyr mourning over a nymph. All that can be seen of the nymph in Glaser's tribute is her sandaled feet next to the little red typewriter. A melancholy brown hound, modelled with tender, immensely assured, criss-crossing strokes of the pen, stands watch over the fallen girl.

Neither of these posters can be accused of failing to deliver the client's message, though Glaser's is an audaciously understated piece of product placement by any standards. His image subordinates the once fashionable Italian typewriter to more mortal concerns

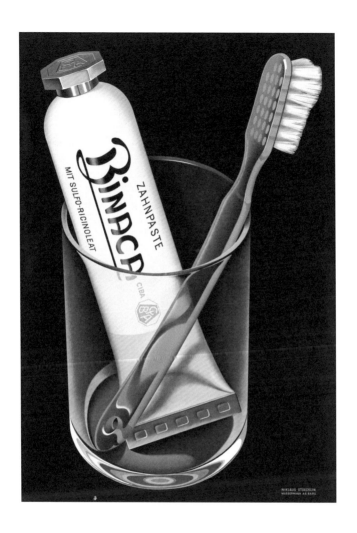

Binaca by Niklaus Stoecklin, lithographic poster, 1941.

and elevates it to become a symbol of rumination, a writing device for musing on some of life's most pressing and personal questions, a presence as natural as water and plants. Both Stoecklin and Glaser took it for granted that their picture was to be looked at, and as with any work of art, the more time and effort you put in, the more you will get back. A culture of making and viewing that routinely turns first to the moving image, forgetting the contemplative value of stillness in pictures suffused with the passage of time, is choosing, in a real sense, not to see.

*The colleague was the late designer Ken Garland.

Sexy Nextness

Chasing the new to no purpose

There was a time when I was obsessed with the new. The most obvious reason for this is that all journalists are obsessed with what's new(s). That's our job. It doesn't matter how great today's story is; tomorrow there must be a new one, and another, and another. None of this would be necessary were it not for the reader. Whether the new is earthshakingly momentous or a passing trifle, readers want to know about it, and if you aren't there to bring it to their attention, what are you there for? Newspapers, magazines, online publications and blogs are giving their audiences what they want. Not for nothing was "new" long ago understood to be one of the main hot words in any communication.

It was exciting to engage in the battle – first as a writer and then as an editor – to hunt down and deliver the new. The aim was to find it first, then to tell it and show it better than your rivals. It was also to try to distinguish between developments that were genuinely new (because they contributed something we hadn't seen before) and those that were merely novel (superficially different, but familiar at the core). If you could do that, your publication would have an edge. Readers would understand that this was the real new, not just the old new dressed up to give it new life.

As subject matter, graphic design provided a never-ending river of newness. Or so it seemed in the late

1980s to mid-1990s – the years when I was most actively chasing the new and was most impatient with anything that didn't meet the brief – because this was a phase when graphic design was constantly coming up with remarkable new things. The field was in turmoil and the nature of this newness, the challenge it posed to old ways of thinking and working, the dismay, disapproval and fierce commitment it generated, made for the most compelling kind of news. Designers wanted to know where we were going and what it all meant.

Yet there comes a point when endlessly chasing the new can start to seem like a hollow pursuit. One thing you might then begin to wonder is whether all the effort that goes into this search might be better directed into trying to gain a deeper insight into what you have already discovered. With its urgent demands for our attention, the latest piece of shiny, unmissable newness tends to push aside the last new thing we were persuaded to care about by the news cycle's relentless churn. More information doesn't necessarily add up to greater understanding. Sometimes it just gets in the way.

Some of these thoughts were running through my mind as I turned the pages of *Contemporary Graphic Design*, put together by those indefatigable survey compilers Charlotte and Peter Fiell. Four years ago, the Fiells produced a similar volume for Taschen – that one was called *Graphic Design for the 21st Century*. Has so much changed in graphic design since then to make necessary another huge book of pictures, organised alphabetically by designer, with only the most cursory and unprobing of introductions to set the scene? *Contemporary Graphic Design* is "new" in the sense that we probably won't have seen a lot of these images before, but is it actually new? Does it reveal and explain something that we didn't know already? The question seems to have given Carlos Segura a moment of doubt when he was asked, like all the contributors, to provide a few words to introduce his way of designing. "I don't have a *new* approach ... still the same old one," he notes apologetically.

Even though I don't really believe in the new anymore, and I don't have high expectations of finding it in a volume so obviously put together for commercial reasons, I still felt a sense of anticipation. Perhaps there would be work by someone I had never heard of that takes design in an unexpected new direction. In 1996, in an essay for *Emigre* titled "The Next Big Thing", Rudy VanderLans reflected on the prolific visual experimentation of the previous few years. "Picturing what has passed before us," he wrote, "I cannot for the life of me think of what it could be that hasn't already been done." The sense that graphic design had reached some kind of postmodern terminus of style beyond which it wouldn't be possible to travel has persisted for more than a decade now.

While graphic designers remain conflicted about the whole issue of style, worrying that it is trivial if not actually immoral to be preoccupied with surfaces, the expressive manipulation of form has always been central to what graphic designers do. Take that away – as some of the more disenchanted or fastidious designers tried to do in the past decade – and you are left with a dry, threadbare "conceptual" design. "My objective is to go beyond the surface, presenting dematerialised concepts and ideas within the context of art and graphic design," British designer Daniel Eatock tells the Fiells. Eatock's rigorous purification of "superfluous elements" is witty and has genuine human warmth. But while it works for him, as a way forward in any larger sense it is surely a dead end, although it does at least avoid the snare of being merely trendy.

A great deal of contemporary graphic design – if we are to take the book's title and survey purpose at face value – seems to aim no higher. The work juggles fluently enough with the codes that signal "now" and "fashionable" to the digitally oriented young consumers at which it's aimed (dolls, doodles, cartoons, stylised foliage, retro type, friendly monsters, whimsical ornaments), but the combinatory aesthetic has been around since the era of Victorian collage and is easily achieved on screen. Young American design seems especially prone to this tendency. The book does contain work by a number of well-established older designers: Pierre di Sciullo, Philippe Apeloig, Peter Saville, Jonathan Barnbrook, Rick Valicenti, Stefan Sagmeister, Ralph Schraivogel, Irma Boom, Karel Martens, and Jan van Toorn. Aside from pieces by M/M – the dullest projects by the arty Parisian duo I have seen anywhere – much of the work is exemplary, but we didn't need this book to tell us about it. These bodies of work are already familiar contributions to the story of the last two decades of graphic design.

There are, however, examples from a few lesser-known figures who extend graphic form in original directions, though even this work I had seen elsewhere: Dutch designers Maureen Mooren and Daniel van der Velden's covers for *Archis* magazine and posters for the Holland Festival; Swiss designer Martin Woodtli's posters for the Museum für Gestaltung in Zurich (in the late 1990s, Woodtli worked in New York with Sagmeister and David Carson); and pieces by the French designer Toffe (Christopher Jacquet). Can it be a coincidence that all four designers provide subtle and interesting rationales that display a degree of self-awareness as noteworthy as the work that arises from their ideas? Many of the statements supplied by other designers are, to put it politely, less than original.

Toffe's work is particularly intriguing. He is in his early 50s, and his work possesses a kind of meticulous anarchy. He unites diagrammatic computer-drawn elements with simple patterns and textures, and his use of type is equally precise and playful. "My graphic production is political and utopian," he says, as only a French person could.

When you encounter work such as Toffe's, which has the benefit of not having been reproduced to death already, it becomes clear that new elaborations of graphic form in the service of worthwhile ideas are possible even now. To uncover them, what we need is not the include-anything-and-everything approach taken by *Contemporary Graphic Design* and similar publishing efforts, but a more refined, exacting and curatorial sifting of graphic output. The problem that graphic design presents is the ceaseless, overwhelming flood of fresh things. That is the nature of communication. We need to weave finer critical nets to capture and isolate what is truly unfamiliar. If there was less to see because we took the trouble to exclude the endless, unrevealing duplication, there would be more to talk about.

Stars in Our Eyes

Design celebrity in the digital era

I have a pretty good idea of who the best-known graphic designers are, seen from an American perspective, and you probably do as well. But these days, thanks to the miracle of search engines, we can take a more scientific approach. Just type in "Who are the most famous graphic designers?" and Google will respond with a horizontal strip of thumbnail pictures under the title, "Graphic designers frequently mentioned on the web." Results varied a little whenever I tried this, but the last time there were 51 designers featured.*

The first four were all names one would expect to be high on any list of notables: Paul Rand, David Carson, Milton Glaser and Saul Bass. Next came Paula Scher, Stefan Sagmeister, Alan Fletcher and Neville Brody, followed by Michael Bierut and Herb Lubalin.

There is no question that these are all household names among designers. It hardly needs saying, though, that being famous within the design community is no guarantee that anyone else knows your name. Bass is the most widely famous in this group because of his parallel career as a filmmaker. Rand and Glaser are so stellar within the field that their names are also known outside it. Carson and Brody made an impact beyond design through their connection with popular culture, and Peter Saville, a little further along Google's strip, is in the same category, at least in Britain.

I said that Google was more scientific because it counts the numbers, but the list had some oddities. Some designers who are not singled out have thousands more mentions than some on the list, and these anomalies suggest that Google must be using some other forms of computation than numbers alone. We might wonder, anyway, whether uncategorised mentions could ever be a reliable guide to the true standing in which someone is held. Lester Beall, also in Google's top 51, has a comparatively modest number of mentions – 24,300 – and yet he is one of the most considerable figures in American graphic design history, a trailblazer, as a book about him was subtitled, that every properly educated graphic design student should know.

This has traditionally been the meaning of fame. The condition of being famous arrives because a person has done or achieved something out of the ordinary and this attracts attention. Famous designers of the past became famous by producing designs that stood out and enlarged the sense of what design could be. No one in the first ten is under 50, and three have died, but during the years spanned by their careers the terms of "fame" were mutating. Anyone who was famous could in theory be dubbed a celebrity – in the dictionary sense of "one who is celebrated" – but celebrity (as both noun and adjective) has evolved into a special kind of relentless public visibility that feeds off itself. The phenomenon, as we know it now, is an invention of the media age, and its vital currency is the photographic image, whether still or moving. Celebrities need to look good, to be personalities and to possess a voracious desire to bask in the limelight. No great talent, apart from an aptitude for publicity, is required to ascend the foothills of contemporary mass audience celebrity – you can be "famous for being famous".

It's unlikely that a graphic designer who is unduly modest or shy about self-promotion will ever become truly famous, even among fellow designers. The most renowned designers, such as those in Google's first ten, tend to be (or were) highly comfortable talking about their work in interviews and lectures. They enter and win design awards and invariably publish monographs – Bierut's *How to* (2015) is the latest – and sometimes other books expressing their philosophies, as did Rand and Fletcher.

In the 1990s, though, a new kind of graphic design star began to emerge. The leading lights were Saville in London and Sagmeister in New York. From his early days as a sleeve designer for Factory Records, style was always everything for Saville. Louche and glamorous, clad in black turtleneck sweaters and white jeans, fashionably unshaven with long disheveled hair, he posed for photos with effortless cool. Saville possessed a magnetic media appeal and a stream of admiring profiles appeared not only in the design press, but also in men's magazines and national papers. The life, career history and personality of the man himself, more than anything he now produced for his clients, had become the focus of interest for both Saville and his fans. As a raconteur, he endlessly burnished his own myth.

With the image-consciousness of a fashion designer or a rock star, Sagmeister also used his own iconicity as a way of gaining attention. The images of his body – the nude studio announcement (with sock), the carved torso, the designer "on a binge" and another we'll come to shortly – are indelibly etched in the profession's memory. Sagmeister reinforced his regular appearances as an unforgettable image with a programme of entertaining lecture engagements around the world that continues to this day. He developed a catchy personal theme, the pursuit of happiness, and produced an exhibition and a film about it. His design work is good, without a doubt, but would it have been sufficient on its own to put him in the same league of international design fame as Rand, Glaser and Bass?

The question arises again, even more pressingly, in the case of the most startling figure in Google's "frequently mentioned" list. Nestled among design textbook stalwarts such as El Lissitzky, Josef Müller-Brockmann and Muriel Cooper, we find the name of Sagmeister's professional partner, Jessica Walsh. Like many observers, my first sighting of Walsh came in 2012 when she appeared naked alongside Sagmeister (unclad as usual) in a photographic announcement that they were joining forces – it was all over the web. This was before I knew a single thing about her work, or had any reason to take an interest in it. That manoeuvre alone was enough to launch Walsh as an instant design celebrity. "It did exactly what we set out for it to do," she told *Print*'s editor in a profile. "Even more so than we could have ever expected. So no, I don't regret it."

After the jaw-dropping photo, anything Walsh did was likely to gain traction, and in 2013 she scored another viral hit with the *40 Days of Dating* website, now a book, with designer Timothy Goodman. This, too, I heard about from a distance despite it being of no intrinsic interest to me – it turned up everywhere from *Time* magazine to the BBC news website. Whatever the quality of Walsh's design work might be, her celebrity has come about by other means than simply being a good designer, and she could hardly have found a better mentor in the publicity process than Sagmeister.**

Will Walsh's rapid rise prove to be a marker in graphic design's evolution? The days of pure visual innovation appear to be over and there isn't much left to say about basic design principles that hasn't been repeated many times before. In the last decade, few graphic designers have shot to fame, as Carson or Irma Boom did in the 1990s, because of the invention and originality of their design work – in Google's list, Marian Bantjes is a rare post-2000 example of this kind of luminary. In the same period, the possibilities for attracting attention through astute use of social media have multiplied enormously for everyone. It was only a matter of time before designers who possess the natural advantage of expertise in communication, plus the qualities it takes to become a celebrity (looks, ego, an exhibitionist streak), put everything together to fashion a compelling media presence. Having pulled this off, Walsh has built a platform to do anything she wants. Other young designers will watch her progress and learn.

*Google no longer generates this strip of images when asked the question.
**Sagmeister and Walsh ended their seven-year design partnership in 2019.

Between the Lines

Designers and writers must be allies

For a writer, "text" is almost a sacred word. Text is the object we produce, a material made of strings of words, which have to be eked out, crafted and, sometimes, when the words aren't working, torn up and replaced. Do designers feel the same intense ownership of the words that pass through their hands?

As communicators, designers, writers and editors ought to be natural allies and sometimes they are. Every designer works with text and for editorial designers there is always a massive quantity of words to process. But unless the designer is also the author of the text, a degree of distance is built into the relationship. Some designers see the text they work with as a pretext for the design ideas and visual approaches that preoccupy them. The page becomes a formal shape rather than something to be read. For writers, text only exists when readers feel motivated to read it.

In the mid-1980s, when I started to write for magazines, the future of writing seemed assured. But the feeling of connection to a history of writing for print that could be expected to go on forever turned out to be short-lived. The arrival of the World Wide Web changed everything. In 1993, in a column for *Blueprint*, I voiced doubts about the rhetoric coming from some designers about the future of text: "Nobody reads anything anymore" (this was magazine supremo Roger Black) and

Illuminated letters for a Latin text in a Gospel Lectionary, Paris, late 13th century.

"the book is dead" (almost a credo for some). The growing feeling within graphic design that, when it came to how we process text, *everything must change*, was crystallised in 1995 by David Carson's monograph, *The End of Print*. Print turned out to be stubbornly popular, but the title had the ring of a catchphrase, and as we gravitated online, it undeniably caught the mood of the digital times.

In those early internet years, working as a journalist, I was torn about these changes: part supporter and part sceptic. I was fascinated by the experiments taking place in digital graphic design and typography, I found the theories about communication and reading intriguing, and the provocative look of the work appealed to me. Many of the most interesting and experimentally inclined people I met on the design scene, often Americans, were preoccupied with the question of how typography and textual design should evolve in a digital world.

But there were also forcible arguments that the reader's essential needs hadn't changed, expressed most incisively by the British writer Robin Kinross (in his 1994 pamphlet *Fellow Readers*) and his colleague Paul Stiff. I knew them both and their seriousness of purpose was persuasive, even if their designs (Kinross was a publisher) conformed to established and, at that point, unfashionable ideas about what makes a printed text accessible and useful to ordinary readers. In an essay Stiff later retitled* "Look at Me! Look at Me! (What Designers Want)" he disputed the claim that the postmodern graphic designer's task was to cajole and prod people into reading by turning the experience into a convoluted visual puzzle. In an article in *Eye*, Kinross observed that "multiplication of text is a social act" and that line stuck with me as a maxim. All those printed copies that designers labour over create vital links between writers and the community of readers.

In the years since then, uncertainties about the status of text have multiplied. As with CD-ROMs in the 1990s (the failure of which should give us pause), each technological innovation – mobile phone, e-reader, tablet, social media – appears, at least at first, to herald a change in how we read, what we are prepared to read and the viability of old media. The widespread assumption that many people have neither the time nor the inclination to engage in deep reading is seemingly unshakable now, even if we still do it ourselves and know plenty of people who are similarly inclined, whatever platform they happen to prefer. The growing use of the term "long read" by online magazines and newspapers, as well as the site longreads.com, implies that lengthy articles requiring sustained concentration are not the norm and need to be labeled as a specialty item for the unusual folk still prepared to fritter away precious time on longer bouts of unbroken reading.

For someone attempting to write during these years of change, all of this led, unavoidably, to a feeling of being embattled, as though one had invested, with potentially diminishing returns, in an activity whose days were numbered, at least as a professional pursuit. This isn't the place to dwell on the economics of writing, but writers need to put bread on the table just as often as everyone else does. Economic feasibility will be the final decider of what kinds of writing are allowed to thrive in the reading (or non-reading) future.

My early experiences had sensitised me to the relationship between writing and design. Way back in the 1980s, when the main distraction was still television, graphic designers had a reputation for not reading – and therefore not understanding – what they were designing (at least in Britain, where I was based). They were said not to read much at all. I could hardly be unaware of these potentially discouraging assumptions, but preferred to proceed as though this wasn't the case as I worked first as a writer, and then as an editor of a magazine for graphic designers. To do anything less seemed to run the risk of patronising those designers who were dedicated readers of all kinds of writing.

I believed, as I still do, that people who are serious about a subject do want to read about it because this is by far the most effective way of deepening their historical knowledge and critical thinking. Those who choose not to read about their field remain stuck at a more superficial level, though naturally they can't know this because they don't read. Eventually, though, I had to face the fact that even design book publishers, citing sales figures as evidence, didn't believe that the majority of graphic designers were readers. What designers wanted were books consisting mainly of pictures, with only skimpy text. One publisher told me that a book I had written in clear English about the tricky subject of postmodernism and graphic design had probably "gone over readers' heads", while another informed me I was an "elitist" for believing that design books could be both accessible and make demands of the reader.

We are now at a critical moment. A generation has grown up digitally connected without the experience of deep reading instilled by books that older readers draw on to compare different sources of information, both printed and digital. As design educators report, this leaves their students unable to make assessments of quality and reliability in the sources they automatically consult online. Websites and apps presenting information in small, easily digestible chunks encourage an expectation that everything will be chopped up into little pieces, and breed an intolerance for anything less immediately manageable. Sustained experience of engaging with longer texts, whether printed or digital, is the only way to learn how to read with close critical attention and to develop the attention span this requires. This applies to designers just as much as anyone else. Well-read designers are invariably the best designers in my experience.

Earlier I said that designers should be the natural allies of writers and editors. The alliance is dependent on designers taking writing as seriously as writers and editors do because they, too, are committed readers. This is only likely to happen if an appreciation of language, and constant engagement with sophisticated texts, is central to the way that graphic design is taught.

Over the years, many farsighted designers and educators have understood this and argued for the primacy of writing. The point constantly needs remaking. While it's a fine thing when a page or a screen of text is beautifully designed, the ultimate measure of its success as a piece of communication is not how it strikes the detached aesthetic eye, but its vitality as a medium that calls out to be read.

* The original title was "Stop Sitting around and Start Reading", *Eye* no. 11, 1993. The essay was republished in Michael Bierut et al., *Looking Closer 2*, Allworth Press, New York, 1997.

A Delicate Relationship

Balancing words and images

Bookshop browsing has always been a ruthless activity. A book attracts your attention. You pick it up. You flip through it, perhaps only for a few seconds. And then, likely as not, comes that moment no author would want to see. You put it back down again. This one's not for you – no sale. Then it's on to the next.

That happened to me with a book I hadn't heard about before I saw it on display in a shop. I was familiar with the author, Stephen Bayley, one of Britain's best-known design writers, and the title was ambitiously sweeping: *Ugly: The Aesthetics of Everything* (2012).

Bayley is a stylish, erudite and highly opinionated commentator, so this promised to be a read that would be both informative and entertaining. But as I saw immediately when I began to turn the pages, the book wasn't what I had expected. There were pictures – countless pictures – punctuated by occasional patches of writing. No matter how enlightening the text, colour images dominated the book, making the words seem secondary. Since this was a work by Bayley, a writer who can sustain interest with no pictures at all, the effect was all wrong. After only a few moments, I replaced the book.

The longer I write about graphic design, the more preoccupied I am by the issue of how to balance text and images, particularly with longer texts in books. Writers of all kinds are naturally inclined to be a little suspicious of images. They want to be read with close attention, they believe their writing merits this engagement and they know instinctively, without needing to give it much thought, that other visual elements on the page will act as distractions, dividing the reader's attention.

As a writer, I'm conflicted because I love images as much as words and because the subject of my writing is visual culture. More than this, I want to work with images, and find, select and edit them in combination with other images, in a way that illuminates what I'm talking about in the text and gives me pleasure as a viewer. I see this activity as being a fundamental part of the design writer's task and I believe that any design writer who doesn't seize the opportunity to act as his or her own visual editor, and simply leaves it to the designer to sort out the visual side, is overlooking a meaningful and potentially satisfying aspect of the job. The same might be said of any other form of visual subject matter.

Yet I still face the dilemma that pictures can easily overwhelm a piece of writing so that the potential reader concludes instantly – almost subliminally – that the writing is not the primary reason for perusing these pages and can probably even be dispensed with.

Over the years, I have bought many visual books on this basis, mainly for their pictures. The writing may be excellent (that's the tragedy), but it hasn't been presented in a way that makes it likely that many readers will settle down, in shifting locations, to read it from cover to cover as one devours an ordinary pictureless paperback. Not only are the pictures the main event, but their preponderance has led to other unreaderly outcomes: big pages, tall, austere columns, unusually wide columns (sometimes made worse by over-small type) and a thickness and weight that make a book a pain to handle.

Another thing to mention, and I wish it wasn't so, is that graphic designers retain a reputation, as a group, for being reluctant readers. Since I know many who love to read, I prefer to view designers like any other readers, but book publishers take this supposed reluctance very seriously. It dictates the appearance of their books. They are convinced that dull grey text needs to be broken up as much as possible by pictures and by other even shorter texts to make it look attractive and digestible.

That's why design books have become so relentlessly magazine-like in page structure and appearance. This might help to sell them. It might mean that some parts of a book get read as a result of the "grazing" that a high degree of structural and visual fragmentation encourages. But it also affects and limits the kind of sustained writing – taken for granted elsewhere – that can be attempted when writing for graphic designers. If you doubt this, try to name just five long, continuous texts about graphic design with only a modest number of pictures. (I concede that a graphic design book with no pictures at all risks being a non-starter.)

I suspect the issue comes down to the relative amounts of surface area covered by pictures and text. For a book to look as though it's intended for continuous immersive reading rather than browsing and sampling, the text needs to occupy most of the space – an occasional full-page picture every few pages isn't going to change that emphasis.

As I have found when making books, there can also be advantages, when there aren't too many pictures to accommodate, in separating a picture from the spread where it's discussed. The description and analysis of an image often works better when it's absorbed before moving on to consider the image. Otherwise the experience of viewing something before reading about it can easily override the description – why describe what we can already see? The answer is that an observant description is also a form of interpretation. This will be missed if a noisy image makes the words appear superfluous.

Where there are numerous pictures to pack into a book, we need another solution. To that end, the work of the British graphic designer and design historian Richard Hollis deserves close attention. In *About Graphic Design* (2012), a collection of his articles published over the years, Hollis uses a method, founded on being both author and designer, that has come to be identified with him.

His 296-page book runs to 100,000 words of text, mostly in a single column, occasionally in two. It also contains more than 500 images, though it doesn't feel anything like that many.

As with his earlier *Graphic Design: A Concise History*, (1992) Hollis reduces most of the images to small, black-and-white reference pictures, which he places in the inside margin, running parallel to the text. The text block holds together as a strong, clear reading path to which the illustrations remain subordinate. The proximity of the image doesn't negate the discussion in the text because its size makes clear that it's there not as a substitute for reading but to support it. The serif text is relatively small but the characters are black, well-defined and highly readable; graphic unity expresses clarity of thought. Where an illustration such as a magazine spread needs to be shown a little bigger, Hollis permits it to break the column at the point where it's mentioned in the text. He doesn't allow the forking paths of a needlessly complicated layout to lead the eye away, as so often happens in visual books. Once the image has been looked at, the reader continues with the text, like diving into a pool and climbing out briskly on the opposite side.

For Hollis, this has been a career-long way of working as well as a point of principle. I suppose some prospective buyers might find his pages to be a little serious-looking, but I doubt a motivated reader would make that mistake. Reading is a consuming experience. When the subject is visual imagery, we need to view it without becoming distracted.

Many designers and publishers think the answer to the challenge of selling the printed book in a digital age is increasingly elaborate design. That doesn't remove the age-old challenge of crafting pages that demand to be read. If Stephen Bayley's inquiry into the aesthetics of everything had achieved the finely honed balance of writing against visual evidence seen in Hollis' books, I would have bought it without hesitation and read it with pleasure.

One Week in Pictures

Photographs without a purpose

If quantity alone is the decisive factor, we live in a great age of photography. It has never been easier to take a picture, and everyone is doing it. In the bygone days of film, a camera was still something to be brought out for special occasions. Processing pictures cost money, so cameras were used sparingly. Digital changed everything. With lightweight pocket cameras and camera phones, snapping pictures became a daily activity for many, particularly the young. The result is a peculiar new kind of photographic "literacy": more people taking more pictures than ever, yet a feeling that the individual picture, particularly the well-taken picture, counts for much less than it did. A "photo" is now just an easily deletable particle in an infinite stream of images that will probably never materialise as a print and be invested with meaning as an object.

The devaluation of photography can be seen most clearly in the places where the medium once thrived: in newspapers and magazines. These developments have been incremental, so it is easy to take the situation for granted without realising how much has changed. It is equally easy to assume that what we see in papers and magazines now is all that photography is capable of doing. The changes were already under way in the 1970s, as printed publications increasingly lost out to the visual immediacy of television, long before digital photography became the norm for professionals as well as amateurs. By the 1990s, photography as we had known it was struggling to hold its place. The past 15 years, if you care about photographic reportage, have been calamitous.

It is not just that the pictures are often mediocre and formulaic. The problem also lies in the way they are used. There is good reason now to doubt that many of the art directors who commission or select these pictures, and the designers who lay out the pages, have any deep understanding of, or commitment to, photography's possibilities as a documentary or narrative medium. But how can this be? Isn't the sensitive handling of photographs one of the fundamental tasks of a fully competent graphic designer? It certainly used to be regarded that way. "Of all the related visual disciplines, photography is probably the one of greatest importance to the graphic designer," wrote Allen Hurlburt in *Layout: The Design of the Printed Page* (1977). "Working with photographers is one of the most important aspects of the designer's work." Those observations hold even truer for anyone engaged in editorial design.

If you doubt the situation could be as bad as I say, do what I did. Go to the newsstands and buy a big pile of papers and magazines and spend some time sifting through them all. To narrow down a potentially vast task, I followed a couple of rules. I chose to look only at British examples and I concentrated on publications where you would expect to find – and would once be certain to have found – high standards of photographic practice. This meant quality newspapers and supplements, and magazines with general subject matter, whose reputations depend on high-quality journalism. By comparing what was available from a particular publishing culture in a particular week (at the end of June 2009), I hoped to produce a picture that amounted to more than a series of random impressions over time, and that could be fairly taken to represent the current condition of photography and its use.

So I ploughed through them all: *The Times, The Sunday Times, The Guardian, The Observer, The*

Telegraph, *The Sunday Telegraph*, *The Independent*,
The Independent on Sunday and the *Financial Times*,
with a particular focus on their proliferating supplements.
Magazines were a trickier task. I flipped through many
with photography so perfunctory that they weren't
worth obtaining for this survey. I found material worthy
of comment – whether to commend or criticise – in
New Statesman, *Intelligent Life* (published by *The
Economist*), *Wired* (UK), *GQ* (UK), *Esquire* (UK), *Grazia*
(UK) and, slightly to my surprise, *Jamie*, celebrity chef
Jamie Oliver's then new magazine about food.

I mostly avoided specialised publications (sport, music,
computing etc.), which show endless pictures of essentially
the same subject. A golf magazine art director could be
performing wonders but it makes no difference to the
more crucial standards of mainstream visual journalism.
I also left out the independent subculture documented so
effectively in *We Make Magazines* (2009) because, again,
my purpose was to find out what was happening at the
heart of British publishing culture in ordinary newsagents.
I broke my rule for *The Drawbridge* magazine: its ambitious
content makes it a natural in this company.

The simplest test I applied was the stun factor. I hoped
to find pictures that stopped me in my tracks because
the image was extraordinary, presenting something
unexpected in an unfamiliar way. This only happened twice
in all of these publications. The first, in *New Statesman*, was
a picture showing a People's Liberation Army ceremony in
Taiyuan, China in 2008. The seated recruits, stretching
away into the distance on both sides of the image, like a
huge green human wedge, contrast powerfully with the
hazy grey buildings behind them. This library photo from
Rex Features is good rather than brilliant, and much of its
impact comes from the confident way it fills the opening
spread, forming an open window on the story that follows.
The other photograph, in *The Drawbridge*, was a picture by
Jason Orton of a glove, a rug and some bones in Dartford
Marshes. This enormous image, centrepiece of an issue
titled "Horror", is extremely unsettling.

In publications of this calibre, with thousands of pictures, there should have been many more images with this kind of power. But so many of these colour photos are dispiritingly bland. In an era when the public is supposedly fixated on celebrity, everything is about personalities and the portrait has become the mainstay of contemporary visual journalism. Yet these portraits, whether they show someone famous or an ordinary person, lack strong character as images. The figure will usually be presented in the middle ground. The light tends to be even, flat, descriptive: it is given no role in defining form or suggesting the person's depths or drama. There often seems to be only a minimal attempt to compose the picture, and visual surprises – unusual viewpoints, angles, shapes and details – are avoided. The surrounding environment, the subject's work space or kitchen, is presented as "information" in the same neutral, faux anthropological manner. The picture cannot escape being some kind of interpretation, but what these images mainly offer is their timidity in the face of the subject, their reluctance to make an authorial statement by risking a point of view.

The same blandness and lack of clear journalistic purpose also afflicts more obviously newsworthy subjects. A feature in *The Telegraph Magazine* about students facing an uncertain future in Swindon opens with a shot (by Mark Power) of the town centre. The image is static and uninteresting in content and drab in colour, its inexpressive flatness recalling the detached, "objective" style of so much contemporary art photography. The picture certainly conveys a feeling of sterility, even hopelessness once you start to think about it, but it offers viewers no identification with the subject, no warmth. This unenticing visual hook is followed by three more shots of the town – one shows five luckless students posing in microscopic long shot on an outdoor staircase – accompanied by pull-quotes working hard to provide a context for pictures that do little on their own to involve readers in the students' plight, or to make them care.

This must, after all, be the reason for publishing such a story. As the French critic Christian Caujolle argues in *Things as They Are* (2005), a superb collection of photojournalism since 1955, it is only by creating a more incisive photojournalism that mass-market magazines will be able to offer a unique position that truly competes with TV and the internet. "If that is to happen," he writes, "greater attention and analysis must be devoted to every stage of the process that results in the production of meaning, including the choice of photographer, the selection of the images, the organisation of the sequence and its graphic development, always bearing in mind that typography, like layout, affects the way photographs are interpreted. It is absolutely essential that we continue to ask the fundamental questions: for whom am I publishing these images? What is the point of view I am seeking to express, to render intelligible?"

The essential principles that should guide any newspaper or magazine designer working with photographs are plainly stated in this quotation. The problem with many publications clearly starts from the failure to answer Caujolle's final questions in any way other than "celebrity worship", "fashion" or "stuff to buy". This can be seen in a lifestyle title such as *GQ*, which prides itself on being the home of intelligent writing for men without seeing the contradiction. *GQ*'s strongest visual statements in its July 2009 issue – the meaning it is really producing – are a set of pictures of the actress Megan Fox (its cover story) and a set of surfer swimwear pictures. Both come with the usual supplier and price lists for the models' clothes.

The issue contains nothing remotely comparable in social awareness to the abrasive, compelling "Gun Nation" photo-essay about American gun culture by photographer Zed Nelson, which *GQ* published in 1998 when Tony Chambers was art director. "It was genuinely fascinating, disturbing and thought-provoking," says Jeremy Leslie, who shows it in his book *magCulture* (2003).

"The obsession with celebrity is a major factor generally in the positioning of magazines," Leslie continues, "and photographically who needs an expensive and complex shoot when a cheap paparazzi shot is all that's required? The stories themselves are dictated by these images. A whole industry has built up around providing pap images for the celebrity weeklies and, increasingly, the monthlies use the same images, too."

Only in *The Guardian*, and in the Spectrum section at the back of *The Sunday Times Magazine*, once home to some of the finest photojournalism, are there occasional reminders of the intensively researched and costly to produce photographic essays that most British magazines long ago ceased to provide. The Spectrum section I looked at included six pictures by the photojournalist Patrick Barth, who spent three weeks flying with the US air-ambulance squad in Afghanistan. Barth's shots are a poignant example of the kind of report that could often be seen in news magazines in the 1960s and 1970s. Nevertheless, his pictures are second on the bill, after a tacky set of photos of burlesque artists posing at home, and they feel a little squeezed, their scaling against each other and placement on the page less certain than it could have been.

Elsewhere, though, my survey confirmed that papers that once knew how to identify a visual story, source excellent pictures and present them on the page in gripping visual narratives have completely forgotten how to do it. In the early 1990s, *The Independent Magazine*, where Colin Jacobson was picture editor, constructed superb photographic essays, usually in black-and-white, about subjects such as Nicolae Ceaușescu's legacy in Romania, a Russian women's prison, and an AIDS ward in Zimbabwe. The paper's once sure instincts are nowhere to be found in a story about the 20th anniversary of German reunification published in June 2009. The opening spread pairs a black-and-white picture from 1961, showing a defecting East German solider leaping the barbed wire, with a present-day shot of the same street, where tourists are visiting a Cold War memorial. The older picture, a remarkable news moment, is shown too

191

Editing for point of emphasis

On March 3, 1974 all 346 passengers and crew were killed when a Turkish Airlines DC10 fell 12,000 feet, out of a clear blue sky, into the Forest of Ermeonville, outside Paris. The jumbo jet cut a path through the trees about 500 yards long and up to 100 yards wide and in this terrible scene of annihilation the remnants of the victims were too tragic to photograph. Captain Jacques Lannier, who led the search, is haunted by one image of two hands clasping each other, a woman's and a man's hand which withstood disintegration. It would have been insensitive to give any other than a general view, and Aubrey Hart achieved this in a moving manner with his picture (above) of the swathe through the forest and a man—a bereaved husband—walking through it.

Should the picture be edited? The answer must lie in what one judges to be the emphasis of the story, and the

occasion of publication. The full frame (above) gives equal emphasis to the devastation and the man. Different cropping is suggested if the imagination is to be directed more to individual grief and less to the circumstances of the crash. The crops (right) bring the figure into the foreground with varying effects—he can be made to appear to be walking away—but these describe the scene less well. If the picture is to be accompanied by others showing waiting relatives there is a strong case for the full frame; if, on the other hand, another picture emphasises the devastation, a crop to focus more on the man might supply a missing element.

In later days, when the public has absorbed the idea of the crash, a smaller picture serves as a reminder; versions as limited as those on the far right can be considered. Of course it would be unthinkable to crop like that on first publication.

Pictures on a Page by Harold Evans, Heinemann, London, paperback edition, 1987 (first published 1978). Photographs show the crash site of a Turkish Airlines passenger plane.

small on the spread to transmit its full drama, while the over-scaled picture of a group of teenagers milling about has no more information, drama or interest than a casual snapshot. No meaningful relationship has been achieved between the two pictures.

While publishers and editors must take the blame for succumbing to the values and imperatives of an increasingly narrow and culturally damaging obsession with vacuous celebrity and consumer lifestyle, designers have also contributed to the decline in standards of photographic practice, if only through ignorance. Photography was pushed to the side, as an essential concern of the graphic designer, in the digital type revolution of the early 1990s, and as image-making, too, went digital, it has never recovered its place. Few designers now see their primary task in terms of the "production of meaning" by choice of photographer, selection of images and the organisation of sequence. Looking through contemporary manuals of graphic design, photography receives little attention. In *Graphic Design: The New Basics* (2008) by Ellen Lupton and Jennifer Cole Phillips, for instance, an otherwise thorough and popular guide, the authors allot the subject only a few brief entries. Pattern, on the other hand, a specifically graphic, largely decorative and mostly fashionable concern, has an entire chapter.

As software enables ever more intricate and rococo page designs, the graphic aspects of page construction increasingly preoccupy designers. "I think there is a perceived notion that good editorial design means lots of design," says Richard Turley, art director of *The Guardian*'s G2 supplement, "lots of intricate elements, lots of typefaces, and concept after concept. Often photography gets lost in that fiddle, with pictures getting a bit overwhelmed by it." *GQ*'s pages are cluttered with this kind of stylish but editorially redundant paraphernalia.

Turley dismisses his own design education, crediting Mark Porter, *The Guardian*'s creative director, with teaching him about the use of imagery, pacing a story and the importance of scale. He points to a tradition of editorial art direction ("we're still standing on their shoulders") that includes Willy Fleckhaus, Michael Rand, David King, Pearce Marchbank, Fred Woodward and Tibor Kalman – also a crucial figure for Porter, who worked with Kalman on *Colors* magazine. It comes as no great surprise that both Porter and Turley cite *Pictures on a Page: Photojournalism, Graphics and Picture Editing* (1978) by Harold Evans, editor of *The Sunday Times* for 14 years, as a key influence on their approach to working with photographs. Evans' book is a masterpiece, the best study of this subject ever written; it should be required reading for designers, yet, as Turley points out, it is a book that few designers seem to know about.

Porter encountered *Pictures on a Page* in the mid-1980s. "I think I had a vague instinct about this before, but reading Harry Evans taught me that the narrative is at the heart of every good picture decision," he says. "I still remember the examples he gave about how the meaning of a picture changes with the composition, use on the page and – especially – cropping, and I've been putting those lessons into practice for over 20 years. *Pictures on a Page* helped me understand that in the editorial environment the picture is not a finished artefact, but a raw material."

Cropping is a vital tool for refining images and constructing narratives, yet today it appears to be a declining art. Turley observes that the activity is "really overlooked now, considered to be a skill you just pick up, or maybe even not much of a skill at all". Evans devotes 50 pages and many pictures to the possibilities of picture editing and creative cropping, and to cropping problems that might arise. *Graphic Design: The New Basics* assigns a single page, three photos and just 120 words to the subject.

The reasons for this neglect are as much technological as cultural and they impose awkward restrictions, even on publications as sensitive to the possibilities of photography as *The Guardian*. "Some of the digital images we now work with," says Porter, "particularly in newspapers, barely have the resolution to fill the space we need them to, so we simply don't have the option of cropping them significantly, otherwise the resolution wouldn't be up to it. The fact that so many are compressed JPEGs makes it worse. So digital technology has taken away one of the picture editor's (or art director's) most powerful tools for working with pictures."

Magazine pages used to be constructed around photographs that were carefully selected, cropped and sized to tell the story. Too often now the pictures are relegated to a subordinate role. Images are dropped into predetermined boxes on InDesign templates and cropped to fit this frame (where cropping is possible) rather than cropped for narrative reasons.

"I believe that every element on a page – writing, imagery, design – has to combine to tell the story of the piece," says Leslie, "but, sadly, too many times on the newsstand the magazines use imagery to fill a predefined space. This is the same as pouring text into text boxes without reading it. It's just space-filling."

The "space-filling" problem is just as acute on the web. The finely judged placement of one picture against another, and the dynamic visual and semantic relationships potentially achievable within the fixed frame of the page, are the first casualties online. On screen, the multiple diagonal axes of the asymmetrical page are replaced by the unvarying vertical axis of the single column, seen most typically in blogs where all the pictures within the main column are sized to fit the column width. As you scroll down, the photos ascend into view one at a time. Each image has more or less the same visual weight and the narrative, where there is one at all, can be read in only two directions: down and up, forward and back. The photo galleries popular on newspaper websites are no better. Here, the images must conform to approximately the same size and position, irrespective of the nature of their content or degree of interest, and on this horizontal axis, which is closer to a constrained form of television than it is to the flexibility of the printed page, each new image wipes away the last.

I wish I could have found more in my survey of newsstand magazines to excite me. I hoped the exercise wouldn't confirm what I felt to be the case before I began. At a time when we are deluged with more photographic images than ever, we seem to have lost faith in the power of the photograph to express anything other than our personal reality. We don't take the production of meaning seriously and we use pictures with less fluency and purpose than earlier generations of editors, photographers, designers and readers. We don't know what we are trying to say and we don't know who we are saying it for. We would rather not pay for the photographer's expertise and commitment, we don't believe in the photographer's mission and we don't think it is likely to have any effect. Yet we take our pictures, regardless, and pour them into our boxes. Lacking a clearly defined purpose, rejecting the need to reveal and reform, our ocean of photos still tells us uncomfortable stories about who we are now.

Typographic Selfies

Why fonts are not enough

The title did exactly what it was intended to do: it stopped me in my tracks. I was killing time browsing in a bookshop – a surprisingly large one – in a big London train station, and there in a display surrounded by books covering every kind of subject was the title: *Why Fonts Matter*. Just those three words in heavy capital letters on a plain white background. No subtitle or qualifying text. Bold and unmissable, with no hint of apology for thumping the viewer with a proposition that would once have seemed thoroughly arcane, if not incomprehensible.

I remember those font-blind days well because my own discovery of graphic design involved a mini revelation about type several years before the arrival of personal computers put us on a path to where everyone knows what a font is, and it's possible to assert with confidence that fonts really matter. I had always liked letterforms, occasionally messing around with sheets of dry transfer type for high school art projects. Then, in the late 1970s, I took a temporary menial job at a company that carried out typesetting and book production. I started to become fascinated with typefaces, peering closely at the letters, finding out their names and reading introductions to typography. Before long, I was learning how to set type, using strings of code, on the little screen of one of the company's Compugraphic EditWriters, an early photosetting system.

Away from work I knew no one who took an interest in any of this. The word that people probably used if they ever paused to think about such matters was the catchall *printing*. The word *font*, now preferred in everyday speech for *typeface* – as on the book cover – was then obscure for ordinary viewers (no designer should need the difference between typeface and font explained).

Sarah Hyndman, author of *Why Fonts Matter* (2016), knows the difference, but no one can resist the tide of etymological change, so a shrewd publishing decision prevailed. *Why Typefaces Matter* wouldn't have made the same connection. Hyndman's book joins a small group of projects aimed at non-designers that celebrate the social and personal impact of typefaces, such as Gary Hustwit's *Helvetica* documentary (2007) and Simon Garfield's book *Just My Type* (2010). Think, too, of the fabulous letteriness of Netflix's "Abstract" episode about Paula Scher (2017).

I imagine plenty of designers have purchased Hyndman's book because designers always love it when the wider world takes notice of what they do, and Hyndman, too, is a graphic designer. But the project is astutely targeted to a general audience that knows nothing about the technicalities of type and has reached the point, by making selections onscreen in the font menu, of becoming aware of personal favourites and thinking more consciously about the barrage of typefaces that confronts us every day. A Hyndman introductory exercise for "type consumers" involves counting how many typefaces one encounters in the space of an hour; on a Saturday morning, she noticed 67.

But this is only the starting point. Hyndman bases the book on her experience running public events she calls "Type Tasting", which is also the name of her studio. She has devised a series of experiments and surveys – "tested on humans" – intended to reveal to participants how we respond emotionally to type. "I am interested in using these experiments as a fun way to start conversations and to dispel the preconception that typography is a 'dry' subject for academics and experts," she writes. The list of

"Type Tasting" graphic for an event at the Victoria & Albert Museum, London, 2017. Design: Sarah Hyndman.

surveys includes "Eat Me" (what do letterforms taste like as food?), "Font Fortunes" (how typeface choices reflect values and aesthetics), and the "Type Dating Game" (involving more than 5,000 participants at the time of publication). Here, people choose a typeface that will represent them at a speed-dating event and select the typefaces they would date, drop, or keep as a friend.

From this we learn that given a list of just nine typefaces, most men choose to be Futura Light or Caslon, while women choose to be Didot or Futura Light – what is it with Futura Light? Men say the face is "tasteful, modest, classic". Women deem it "sleek, crisp and to the point". The most dateable men, apparently, are those who proclaim themselves to be Franklin Gothic bold condensed ("You have an alpha personality") and for women, it's Didot ("You relish the opportunity to dress up in style"). But women who see themselves as Franklin Gothic, a real passion killer for men, are going to have a hard time getting dates. And men who favour Eclat and Cinema Gothic could also be out of luck, though men find Eclat women ("casual and laid-back") pretty appealing.

This is all very amusing and the considerable amount of detail in the book about people's reactions to type certainly makes the case – not that anyone with design knowledge has ever doubted it – that type choices are full of meaning, and also that viewers are increasingly sensitive to, and preoccupied with, how type works. Hyndman correctly points out that much of what designers think they know about type, based on their accumulated experience, is not verified in evidence from academic research, which has tended to focus on issues of legibility. She acknowledges that her surveys weren't conducted under anything remotely resembling scientific testing conditions, but hopes to highlight areas for possible future study in collaboration with more rigorous investigators.

How useful such evidence would be remains to be seen. Would it facilitate better (as in more precisely targeted) use of type in marketing strategies? We are quite good at that already. In any case, *Why Fonts Matter* seems much too reductive to me, as even its title reveals. By putting so much emphasis on the personality of individual typefaces, as though the answer to a design's meaning will reside solely in the emotional influence exerted by a single type style, the book neglects the larger issue of what happens when typefaces are put to use as part of an intricate design.

In a piece of design, there may be several typefaces. These combinations will produce subtle interactions and webs of association – how do we determine the meaning that arises dialectically from these counterpoints? Size changes and variations of font (original use intended here) will play their part in articulating possible meanings too. Colour has the potential to contribute a great deal, as will the placement of typographic elements within the space of the design. We also need to bear in mind what happens to meaning when these highly variable typographic units are part of a larger sequence of some kind.

There is another factor that leads to an even greater degree of complexity – the presence of imagery. Graphic design's full potential as a means of communication comes from the integration of type and image. It hardly needs saying, one might think, and yet it often seems today that the emphasis falls too much on type at the expense of the image. At the point where we might be better able than ever before to proselytise the purposes of graphic design, because public awareness of type and design in general in the 21st century helps to make this possible, instead we fixate on one component – the "font" – simplistically reducing public perception of visual communication to a matter of expressing our personalities by our type choices. According to Hyndman, "Fonts are like typographic selfies." Those are words to chill the blood of type masters from Caslon to Tschichold.

Designers collude in this narrowing of perception by preferring to focus on type concerns as an arena over which they can still exert a high measure of control. The global triumph of the image, once central to graphic designers' sense of what visual communication existed to do, has become too overwhelming. Many have turned away, opting for the craft satisfactions of typographic design.

Typefaces helped to ignite my interest in graphic design all those years ago. But for me, the central issue is not the letterform, but how the letters relate to everything else.

Revise, Reform, Rebuild

Does design history have a future?

In 2011, I was asked to take part in a conference in London about graphic design history. I'm committed to the subject, I write as a graphic design historian sometimes and I liked the people involved in organising the conference and wanted to support them. How could I say no? So I prepared my talk, which was about curating exhibitions of graphic design history, and spoke at the event, titled "Graphic Design: History in the Making", held at the St Bride Library.

I can't deny, though, that I did have some reservations. The subtitle, "History in the Making", had an optimistic ring, suggesting that there is not only work to be done in the field, as you would expect, but a new kind of history to be invented. Exactly how this history would be new wasn't entirely clear. The conference description said only that the event would "investigate the status of graphic design history today, with an emphasis on the making and using of it [and] review the state of affairs, looking at where we are, and questioning where we could go next." I expressed a degree of scepticism, for reasons I shall explain, but thought it better to keep my counsel. There is no pleasure in raining on someone's parade and perhaps the conference would reveal the presence of a new generation of design historians out to overhaul and advance the discipline.

My doubts came from having heard these hopes before. In 2005, also in London, we had the "New Views: Repositioning Graphic Design History" conference. Jumping back a decade, there were the three famous issues of the journal *Visible Language* titled "New Perspectives: Critical Histories of Graphic Design". The promise each time is that graphic design history, usually criticised for its profound limitations, will be rebuilt brick by brick until we at last have a critical-historical structure that is fully fit for its contemporary purpose. Yet somehow, despite the fervent good intentions, and the feeling that the will is there and the time is right for radical reform, the promised rebuilding never seems to happen. Time passes and another set of ambitious, bright-eyed reformers arrives on the scene with the conviction that graphic design history must be critiqued, demolished and built anew.

Between these moments of mild euphoria, I watch to see what happens. First, how much graphic design history gets published? The design journals are one index of serious scholarship in the field, though few journals publish any graphic design history. Even the *Journal of Design History* doesn't show much interest: just one major article out of 16 in the past year dealt with this subject. A rather more telling index, in my view, is book publishing. This is where we would expect to see significant activity if a new programme of committed graphic design history production were under way. Once in a while, a book dealing with some aspect of graphic design history will emerge from one of the art book publishers, though rarely from a university press. These few books won't be fundamentally different in kind from their (unreformed) predecessors, and their scholarship, measured against the academic standards routinely found in art history, is unlikely to be exceptional.

The other sign I watch out for is new writers, since there can hardly be a new graphic design history without new graphic design historians. Here, too, there are fewer new arrivals – far fewer – than one might hope to see.

Easily the most striking debut in the past year or two has been that of British author Patrick Cramsie, with *The Story of Graphic Design* (2010), published by the British Library. Cramsie is a graphic designer rather than an academic design historian and before the appearance of his book he wasn't a familiar name. Yet out of the blue, he delivered a hugely ambitious and largely well-received work of synthesis that rivals previous histories of graphic design by Philip Meggs, Richard Hollis, Stephen Eskilson, and Johanna Drucker and Emily McVarish. Even so, this is probably not the kind of history writing that proponents of a new graphic design history have in mind. (It should perhaps also be noted that the book's grasp of historical detail is not without its critics. Paul Shaw published a long list of complaints on his *Blue Pencil* blog, to which Cramsie responded at some length.)

Leaving aside exceptions such as *The Story of Graphic Design*, it's hard to believe that a sudden flowering of graphic design history (of any kind) is imminent. The problem is not simply "what is this history for?", but "whom is this history for?", and the two questions are related. The primary readers of graphic design books have always been graphic designers. If graphic designers don't buy books specially produced for them, then almost no one else will. Graphic design history books are some of the toughest to sell. The more specialised the area of research, the harder it will be to find an audience large enough to make publication economical. Even national histories of graphic design are unattractive to publishers because they know that outside the featured country, it will be a struggle to market the book. What publishers want, more than anything, are overviews that include work from many countries, making the books attractive overseas. Ideally, they will be able to sell co-editions translated into French, Spanish, German, Korean, and so on. US publishers, with an unusually large home market, need to worry about this less, but that still hasn't led to a profusion of books full of original, scholarly graphic design history research.

Over the years, graphic design educators have often complained that graphic design students know little about design history and care even less. Yet it would be perfectly legitimate to point out that the internet is awash with graphic design history, and that it is young designers who are consuming it. Here, we come back to the fundamental difference between history as scholarship and simply finding, displaying, sharing and enjoying historical images. I have a lot of sympathy for this kind of visual pleasure and it does develop aesthetic sophistication and promote a kind of limited understanding. But the blogs that circulate images in this fashion – *50 Watts* (formerly *A Journey Round My Skull*) is a good example – are not engaged in scholarly historical research and provide little information about the treasures they show.

Despite periodic calls for reform and renewal, for new voices and new approaches, the only committed and regular sources for historical writing about graphic design are graphic design magazines. *Print* has a long tradition of this kind of popular history writing produced with the professional designer in mind, with both Steven Heller and the late Philip Meggs playing key roles. In the UK, *Eye* and *Baseline* feature history pieces written by historians and designers (sometimes they are one and the same). In France, the occasional magazine *Back Cover* publishes similar pieces – in English as well as French – by Catherine de Smet, one of the organisers of the "History in the Making" conference, and other writers. The best we can say, in my estimation, is that we are in a holding pattern.

In an essay published on *Design Observer*, I argued that the development of graphic design history has stalled because, in design schools, the subject is too closely tied to the studio.* History is presented to reluctant design students as a course requirement in departments that continue to see it as secondary. To develop, graphic design history would need to become a fully-fledged academic discipline taught like any other humanity. After all, you can study art history without studying to be an artist. In my essay, I suggested that the academic discipline called visual studies, or visual culture, might provide an incubator where graphic design history could grow. The only problem is that visual studies academics have so far, inexplicably, shown barely any interest in the visual study of graphic design. By all means be a graphic design history reformer, but the main thing the subject needs right now is a lot more all-round support.

*Rick Poynor, "Out of the studio: graphic design history and visual studies", republished in Sara De Bondt and Catherine de Smet (eds.), *Graphic Design: History in the Writing*, Occasional Papers, London, 2012.

Future of the Past

The era of vintage everything

On the way to an opening, I stopped off at Habitat, one of London's most famous furniture shops, which I hadn't visited for quite a while. As I wandered around, some old posters mounted in fancy frames caught my eye. One of them showed a simplified globe with a teacher's mortarboard superimposed on it and the message, "For greater knowledge on more subjects use your library more often." The graphic style and typography suggested that the poster dated from the 1930s or 1040s, and according to a label, it was the work of Henrik Dybdahl, a designer or artist unfamiliar to me. "As a heritage adventurer," the label said, "he browses through hundreds of amazing collections at libraries, museums and archives around the world. When he finds 'visual gold' he often redraws the images, adjusting colours, contrasts and details to make them shine as they did back in the day."

So it seemed that Dybdahl wasn't the designer of this old image, after all, but rather an opportunistic 21st-century interpreter and re-publisher of a piece of "heritage" that he had found somewhere. Not only was the poster not an original, but it also wasn't necessarily a faithful reproduction of the original. This chunk of visual gold, along with the other Dybdahl posters on display, was a tweaked and "improved" version of something cool-looking from the past that was being presented to viewers and purchasers in 2014 without any indication of when it

City of New York Municipal Airports, silkscreen poster,
Works Progress Administration, c. 1937. Design: Harry Herzog.

was made, what it was for, who actually designed it, or the country it came from. So far as Habitat was concerned, Henrik Dybdahl created the poster.

Curious to know more, I visited Dybdahl's website. He is based in Denmark and offers a range of posters and greeting cards. According to a company statement, The Dybdahl Co. is "all about giving new life to old images. Through redrawing, remixing and mashing-up." The posters I had seen are part of a collection titled "WPA" and here, at last, comes acknowledgement of their provenance. From 1935 to 1943 – from the Great Depression to the Second World War – the Works Progress Administration, a "New Deal" initiative of the US government, printed two million posters from 35,000 designs. This was truly a golden age of the medium. In 1987, the Wheatley Press published a fine book about the posters and more than 900 of them can be viewed online in the Library of Congress collection, many in large file sizes. In all probability, this was Dybdahl's source. There appear to be no rights restrictions on the use of these marvellous historic designs.

Comparing one of the Habitat Dybdahls with the original, I could see more clearly what "giving new life to old images" involves. In a poster titled *City of New York Municipal Airports*, Dybdahl has adjusted the main colours, extended the sky above the top aircraft and the water at the bottom and, most troublingly, removed the distinctive WPA logo from the corner. In this case, the original designer's name is known – Harry Herzog – although it is admittedly missing on the Library of Congress site, which does credit some of his other posters. Needless to say, neither Dybdahl's site nor Habitat's label makes any mention of Herzog.

Pondering this cavalier treatment of graphic design history made me want to revisit an essay titled "Good History/Bad History" published by *Print* in March/April 1991. If the magazine were ever to produce an anthology of its most significant writing, this trenchant, multi-authored polemic by Tibor Kalman, J. Abbott Miller and

Karrie Jacobs – originally written for Kalman to present at one of Steven Heller's era-defining "Modernism and Eclecticism" conferences – demands to be in there. In its published form, the essay has a series of footnotes, presented in coloured boxes, offering additional perspectives on the main text.

The authors' central concern lies in the way that designers were, as they saw it, misusing history. There were too many projects where the easy solution was to borrow something seductive-looking from the graphic past, with barely any changes. "Designers abuse history when they use it as a shortcut, a way of giving instant legitimacy to their work and making it commercially successful," they argue. "In the '80s and even today, in the '90s, historical reference and down and outright copying have been cheap and dependable substitutes for a lack of ideas." They made the point visually by showing six contemporary designs next to their historical sources. These included a poster for Swatch by Paula Scher, a book cover by Carin Goldberg and (in a spirit of confession) a record sleeve by Kalman's company M&Co.

Scher's repurposing of a Herbert Matter travel poster to sell contemporary watches is probably the most emblematic example of this trend – I have written about it myself. If it's hard now to appreciate why the authors found these designs so unacceptable, that may be because more than 20 years later, despite their urgent warning, we have become thoroughly accustomed to treating the past as a heap of golden nuggets waiting to be ransacked and redeployed for our own gain. Today, a shrug of resignation rather than an outpouring of scorn is the more likely response.

"Good History/Bad History" expresses the authors' enduring faith in modernism, for its belief in the present, its awareness of the future and its desire to use design to change the world. They call the visual plundering they deplore "jive modernism", a form of revival that denies the true purpose of modernism by contributing nothing new, and they attempt to draw a distinction between jive modernism and postmodernism, though, for me, this doesn't hold up. References to historical sources were characteristic of postmodernism's historicism across the arts, as the cultural critic Fredric Jameson demonstrated convincingly in *Postmodernism, or, The Cultural Logic of Late Capitalism* (1991). But whatever term we prefer to use for these appropriations, it doesn't diminish the cogency of Kalman and co's argument. As they conclude, "Bad design history says, here, this is nice, use it. Good design history acts as a catalyst for our own ideas."

Today, there are many websites like The Dybdahl Co.'s, offering reproductions of old posters, including some of the same posters from WPA. It's clearly open season. Reprints are perfectly acceptable so long as they are properly credited, but remixes of earlier work for arbitrary decorative reasons, stripped of the original designers' names and any sense of context, do the history of graphic design a great disservice. Would it be reasonable to rewrite a Hemingway passage to suit alleged modern taste, or to repaint a Matisse to give it a brand new shine? As the "Good History/Bad History" authors write, "To look at artifacts without knowing what they were in their own time is to look into a vacuum." It's cold and empty in there.

Yet in the era of Vintage Everything that has flourished since the essay appeared, this is increasingly the trend. In 2015, Thames & Hudson published *Greetings from Retro Design: Vintage Graphics by Decade* by Tony Seddon. The book stretches from the early 20th century to postmodernism and the dawn of the digital era in the 1990s. (The 1990s! Vintage already? Feels like yesterday.) The blurb pays lip service to the idea of historical understanding, mentioning a timeline and profiles of influential designers, but the author is a designer, not a design historian, and historical illumination is patently not the volume's primary intention. This self-described "sourcebook" aimed at the graphic retronaut sets out to identify "the qualities, elements and quirks that defined the graphic identities of each decade" – a ludicrous oversimplification that ignores every lesson that good design history has tried to deliver since the 1980s. The book's ultimate purpose is made painfully clear by the inclusion of "step-by-step guides to recreating key looks and styles using modern software".

It seems we urgently need a "Good History/Bad History" for a new generation.

Show and Tell

Why illustrations need words

How seriously should we take illustration? I pose the question in this potentially offensive way because I often wonder how seriously illustration takes itself.

Let me say at once that I have always gained a lot of pleasure from illustration. After studying art history, examining the illustrated image was not a big leap, and my first writing about visual communication in the mid-1980s focused on illustration rather than design. The British illustrators I met at that time were well-read, highly educated, visually sensitive, historically aware individuals who were consciously attempting to challenge received wisdom about the practice and move it forward.* This permanently shaped my view of what illustration could be and gave me a set of critical expectations and standards that, allowing for changes in context, I have applied ever since.

One thing illustration has always lacked, compared to graphic design, is a strong critical framework by which to assess it. Design magazines have tended to treat it as an adjunct of design rather than a fully fledged discipline in its own right. Apart from Steven Heller, who patrols a wider territory than either illustration or design alone, one would be hard pressed to name a single highly active writer, an expert, primarily identified with illustration as a subject.

Graphic design criticism might be on the agenda these days. Illustration criticism isn't. Very few magazines have ever focused exclusively on the subject and there have been long stretches, particularly during the 1990s – illustration's years in the doldrums – when few books about illustration appeared. Monographs dedicated to contemporary illustrators were even less likely to show up. Leaving aside Heller and Seymour Chwast's *Illustration: A Visual History* (2008), which is mainly pictorial, no international history of illustration is now in print. This puts illustration at about where graphic design was circa 1982, before the arrival of Philip Meggs.

The crucial difference today is that there has been an illustration renaissance in the last decade. Books have appeared, but they are invariably how-to guides or visual surveys that merely aim to show what is going on. Nothing wrong with that, we might say, if such routine publishing fodder were bolstered by publications with the ambition to research and explain the field's key issues and developments. *For Love and Money* (2010), by Liz Farrelly and Olivia Triggs, collects some impressive new illustration, but it fails to display even a basic grasp of how to analyse images. After a cursory intro, the book settles into an alphabetical catalogue of image-makers. Each artist answers the same five banal questions about place of study, inspirations, what they collect, their favourite way of working, and where they work, play and travel. We aren't told the nationality or location of the illustrators unless they happen to mention it themselves.

Apart from the odd T-shirt or shopping bag, all of the images are shown out of context, a standard problem when reproducing illustrations. Without seeing an editorial image on the page where it was used, in relation to headlines, text and other images, we have no way of determining whether it was employed meaningfully or not. Showing the pictures in this disembodied manner turns them into art to be appreciated entirely on their own terms.

There might be a good case for doing this, but it can only be made by writing about the images as a form of art. No reputable art book publisher, art critic or art

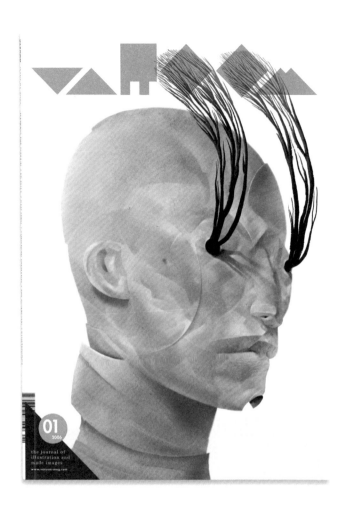

Varoom, Association of Illustrators, no. 1, 2006. Cover art: Sam Weber.
Art direction and design: Non-Format.

historian would patronise readers by presenting works of art in such an intellectually flimsy fashion and no one would take them seriously if they did. (The book's publisher adopts a very different approach to fine art.) The message coming from *For Love and Money* and other threadbare overviews is that illustration isn't a serious activity, so it doesn't require thoughtful consideration by writers with a close understanding of how the discipline has evolved, and that most illustrators aren't sophisticated enough to want this anyway.

The problems begin with the word "illustration". Illustration is no more a unitary activity than art is. There are many kinds of illustration for many kinds of contexts and many kinds of illustrators. Some focus on branding, packaging and advertising; some concentrate on children's books; some specialise in technical, medical or natural history illustration; some prefer editorial assignments. Others seek new kinds of surfaces to illustrate: clothing, curtains, objects, hotel walls, stage sets. Some have no problem seeing themselves as service providers. "As an illustrator, my job is to solve problems visually, and to inject a 'cool' factor into my client's product, service, or campaign," says Tavis Coburn in Taschen's 2006 compendium *Illustration Now!* Other illustrators strive to create individually coherent bodies of work – spanning client commissions and personal projects – that they regard as their art. Subdivision and classification of this wide field is necessary before anything perceptive can be said about a particular branch of illustration's purpose and potential, or what constitutes a significant level of accomplishment in that area. A randomly organised, directory-style list of names could never provide this framework.

A recent development adds other complications. After many years of being split asunder, graphic design and illustration have merged anew, their remarriage brokered by shared digital tools. On the evidence of *For Love and Money*, many of the most inventive image-makers have come from first degrees in graphic design, communication design, or digital media, rather than illustration courses. They describe themselves as self-taught illustrators. This reunion is a positive trend, though it raises further issues of classification. Designer-illustrators often have a strong feeling for decorative type. They also show a marked inclination for abstract or semi-abstract composition and a predilection for a picture plane where objects float and collide in non-naturalistic arrangements of shape and form.

At the same time, there are still many illustrators working in a straightforwardly pictorial manner. It would be graphic imperialism to overlook or marginalise this strand of work, which tends to be grounded in narrative rather than conceptual concerns, just because it remains less amenable to graphic manipulation. The kind of smoothly engineered illustrative design offered by Karlssonwilker in New York or Build in London provides an easy out for fastidious designers who never liked messy pictorial illustration much but know they need to move with the times and embrace the latest visual fashion. This trend hasn't supplanted more traditional methods and styles of image-making – nor should it.

The question, again, is how to disentangle these developments and find appropriate critical tools to study the aesthetic roots and recent growth patterns of these different species of illustration. A finely calibrated critical response will need to fall somewhere between design criticism and design history, with their focus on the marketplace and consumer, and art criticism and art history, with their focus on highly motivated individual agency. We are still some way from such a synthesis. Farrelly and Triggs recognise that "the history of image-making offers a canon of creative ancestors" available to the illustrators in their book, but show no inclination to unlock the putative "new illustration" with the keys provided by these forebears.

One ray of light in this poorly lit area comes from *Varoom*, a thrice-yearly magazine launched in 2006 by the Association of Illustrators in London. This was a brave and necessary venture, though the magazine's umbilical link to a professional organisation can make for conflicts of interest, and the AOI should probably rethink last year's curiously dated redesign. Nevertheless, *Varoom*'s content is often excellent, providing the illustration community with engaging, well-informed and timely commentary about contemporary departures and historical milestones. A long feature in the winter 2009 issue about the relationship between folk art and illustration had exactly the breadth of reference, command of cultural context and seriousness of purpose (while maintaining a delicate touch) that writing on illustration now badly needs if it is to bloom.**

*Figures such as Russell Mills, Robert Mason, Anne Howeson, Andrzej Klimowski and Dan Fern.
**In a retrograde step, *Varoom* ceased publication in 2021.

Illustrators Illuminated

The subject's study come of age

In 2010, I wrote about the state of research and writing dealing with the field of illustration, and lamented its missing critical history (see page 191). A survey of contemporary illustration had just been published, the latest in a long line of similar books, and it seemed to represent another missed opportunity to engage with the practice of illustration at a deeper level. I wasn't referring to how-to books aimed at the student or freelance illustrator – illustration has some good ones – but historical and critical studies of illustration that treat the subject as a potentially serious art form, which I have always believed it to be.

In the years since then, I haven't been paying illustration so much attention, though I remain a keen reader of *Varoom* magazine, published by the Association of Illustrators, which I cited as a positive sign. Then, in November 2015, I was invited to Rhode Island School of Design in the US to deliver a keynote at the sixth annual symposium convened by a group of academics and scholars who form the Illustration Research Network, based in the UK. The symposium's spectacularly ambitious and provocative title was "The Illustrator as Public Intellectual".

I was so intrigued I agreed to take part immediately. It was an eye-opening event, attracting more than 30 participants from Canada, the UK, Germany,

Australia, India, and Lebanon, as well as the US. In the manner of academic conferences, speakers presented papers organised by panels with sub-themes such as "Challenging Professional Identities and Roles", "Visual Satirist as Public Intellectual" and "Illustrators Usurping Writers". While a handful of well-known practitioners –Seymour Chwast, Nora Krug, Anita Kunz – took part in an informal roundtable discussion addressing cartooning and illustration as modes of authorship, most of the contributions were by educators who publish their research. These presentations were of a consistently high standard and the conference was one of the most stimulating and inspiring I have attended in a while. What it brought home to me forcefully is that, in the past few years, illustration has become a field in which there is a concerted international effort to establish benchmarks for the academic study of the subject, and to challenge perceptions elsewhere in academia that illustration is anything less than a fully-fledged discipline with its own history and theories of practice.

RISD went out on a limb to bring the symposium, usually held in the UK, to the US, and it deserved a bigger audience – the number of attendees probably didn't exceed the number of speakers. Any non-academic practitioner who stopped by would have been excited by the intellectual energy now pulsing through the field, but bridging the divide between academic symposia and professional conferences, and exposing illustrators to this kind of investigation and inquiry, is a challenge. American illustrators already have the big biannual ICON conference first staged in 1999. This offers a plethora of workshops, as well as talks by stars of illustration, and it focuses on the practical and professional needs of working illustrators. It's not the kind of event, on the face of it, where a presenter would have the temerity to unveil a paper titled, "Metapictures: Signposts to an Illustrated Public Space", as Stuart Medley from Edith Cowan University in Perth did at RISD. Yet the likes of ICON would be greatly enriched if it were possible.

In my "Show and Tell" article, I complained about the lack of a textbook attempting an integrated history of illustration, pointing to how the study of graphic design had benefited from the arrival, in 1983, of Philip Meggs' *A History of Graphic Design*, and from other general histories that eventually followed it. At the RISD conference, I learned that this shortage is being addressed with vigour. Since 2014, a mammoth research effort has been underway by a team of more than 40 writers, co-ordinated by main editor Susan Doyle, head of illustration at RISD, with the assistance of Jaleen Grove and Whitney Sherman.*

If the daunting task of interweaving so many contributions lives up to the editors' fighting talk on the project's website – "illustration has always been the most pervasive and popular of artforms in the world and is arguably the most influential" – then the book stands an excellent chance of decisively expanding our understanding of the field. My only hope is that the text and layouts aren't orientated in content and style so far towards the needs of teaching (a tagline describes the initiative as "an educational resource for students, teachers and practitioners") that the book neglects to propel its message outward to broader audiences in design, communication and the visual arts. If illustration really is as pervasive, popular and influential as they say, then everyone should know a lot more about it. But the signs of outreach are certainly encouraging. The editors took the trouble to introduce the project at ICON8 in Portland, Oregon, in 2014, and at ICON9 in Austin, Texas, in 2016.

Another welcome development was the launch of the *Journal of Illustration*, a twice-yearly, peer-reviewed publication, edited by Desdemona McCannon, a British illustrator and academic. Since 2014, three issues have appeared, and as I write, two more are scheduled to arrive at the same time. In the first issue, Doyle describes the "general lack of understanding [of illustration] by the academic community outside of illustration" and sets out the case for reform. "I have been asked repeatedly by colleagues as to what distinguishes illustration as a discipline," she notes, "or even more negatively, 'Is it a discipline?'" Illustrators in every branch of the profession would benefit from the elevation of the activity to the status of a fully accepted academic discipline, regarded as a branch of knowledge in its own right. But this growth can only occur through the processes and platforms of academic inquiry and discourse: research, writing, conferences, journals, textbooks, and plenty of them.

Catching up with these still new developments in the study of illustration – we are only talking about the last three or so years, after decades of existence as a professional practice – I could see what a milestone, and perhaps even a tipping point, the discipline has reached. For long-time watchers of graphic design, it's striking to observe the pressure drop that has occurred within what we might broadly call graphic design studies (history, criticism, discourse). Graphic design wanted the same historical credibility for itself that illustration now seeks. This drive started earlier, if we take Meggs' book as an indicator, and by the 1990s the discipline seemed to be getting what its more forward-looking members were convinced it needed. In 1994, the three "critical histories" issues of *Visible Language* indicated a field of studies on a roll, full of energy and hope for change. But two decades later the momentum hasn't been sustained, despite the numbers studying graphic design, and few believe today that graphic design history will someday achieve acceptance as a stand-alone academic discipline. How could it when graphic design, as it was historically construed, has become so unsure of what it is now, this uncertainty extending even to its often-contested name?

Illustration, on the other hand, has everything to play for. It's as ubiquitous as these researchers insist and it can be discussed in properly academic terms. In the span of ideas encompassed by "The Illustrator as Public Intellectual", and in the enthusiasm of its speakers, the symposium reminded me of graphic design events I attended 20 years ago. There is the same sense of deep commitment to the subject, a pleasure in belonging to a network of colleagues engaged in a shared mission, and an energy to carry out the work that remains to be done. It will be crucial, though, to get the message out and entice practicing illustrators, and also designers who use and enjoy illustration, into the public discussion.

* *History of Illustration*, edited by Susan Doyle, Jaleen Grove and Whitney Sherman, was published by Fairchild/Bloomsbury, London, in 2019.

3. Futures

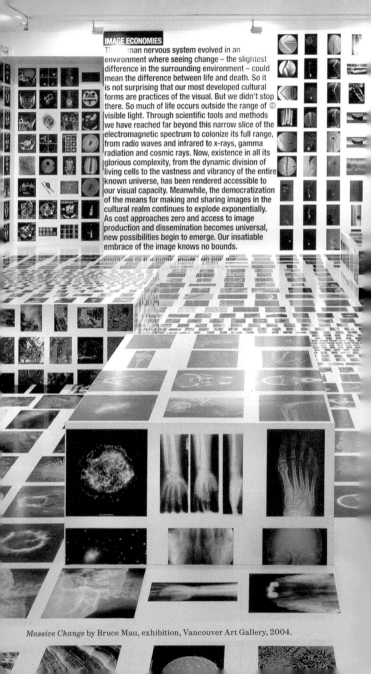

IMAGE ECONOMIES

The human nervous system evolved in an environment where seeing change – the slightest difference in the surrounding environment – could mean the difference between life and death. So it is not surprising that our most developed cultural forms are practices of the visual. But we didn't stop there. So much of life occurs outside the range of visible light. Through scientific tools and methods we have reached far beyond this narrow slice of the electromagnetic spectrum to colonize its full range, from radio waves and infrared to x-rays, gamma radiation and cosmic rays. Now, existence in all its glorious complexity, from the dynamic division of living cells to the vastness and vibrancy of the entire known universe, has been rendered accessible to our visual capacity. Meanwhile, the democratization of the means for making and sharing images in the cultural realm continues to explode exponentially. As cost approaches zero and access to image production and dissemination becomes universal, new possibilities begin to emerge. Our insatiable embrace of the image knows no bounds.

Massive Change by Bruce Mau, exhibition, Vancouver Art Gallery, 2004.

Questions of Authorship

The graphic designer as author

At the end of the 1980s, I had a conversation with Canadian designer Bruce Mau that led me to start thinking about design in a new way. What he wanted, he told me, was to achieve a sense of deep personal investment in his work. Mau wasn't, of course, the only designer to feel like this. But he was unusually clear when it came to defining his own position and he was already proving his point with some piercingly smart projects for the New York publisher, Zone Books. He mentioned a famous essay by the German writer Walter Benjamin, examining the "author as producer". The role he was aiming for, he said, neatly reversing the image, was the "producer as author".

In the last decade, the idea of the "graphic author" has gathered momentum. There have been essays, debates and exhibitions, especially in the US. Many other designers were also proclaiming – if not always achieving – authorial ambitions. In 1995, the appearance of Mau's name on the cover of the cult book *S,M,L,XL*, on equal terms with architect Rem Koolhaas, was a key moment. Recently, after a quiet spell, the authorship issue has flared up again, with the publication of Mau's 624-page *Life Style*, backed up by appearances in London, and British design team Fuel's *Fuel Three Thousand* (2000).

Much of this is admittedly fairly peripheral to everyday design and the term graphic authorship is still not widely used or understood. Even Fuel, authors in 1996 of *Pure Fuel*, claim not to have heard it until after that book came out. For others, the trend seems to offer only the opportunity to indulge in cheap sarcasm. "It is no longer good enough to be a plain vanilla designer," complained British designer Quentin Newark in *Design Week*. "There is an impulse among a handful of critics and designers to create a better class of designer: the designer as author." For Newark, graphic authorship's challenge apparently boils down to nothing more than a distasteful exercise in one-upmanship.

What is clearly needed at this point is a reappraisal of the possibilities and pitfalls of graphic authorship, starting with a definition of what it is. The first thing to note is that "doing" a design does not in itself make someone a graphic author. This needs stating because sometimes, particularly in some Japanese publications, "author" is used as a synonym for "person who made it".

Nor is graphic authorship merely a fancy way of saying "self-expression". All design work expresses the person who made it to some degree and all designs will involve an element of interpretation by the designer of material given by the client. Over the years, deciding exactly how much self-expression design should include has been the subject of endless debate and the profession has frequently acted to police itself. When a design becomes too personal and seems to leave its intended purpose behind, fellow designers are likely to pronounce that it is "art" not design.

Sometimes, too, the designer acts much like an editor, carrying out research, commissioning copywriters, shaping visual and textual contributions. However, this is most likely to happen in "soft" editorial areas such as brochures and annual reports. Such freedoms are much rarer in newspaper, magazine and book publishing. This is what made Mau's successful struggle for editorial recognition so notable.

Early discussion of graphic authorship often focused on graphic style as a vehicle for a coded extra layer of private communication superimposed on the client's basic message. Many designers developed highly visible signature styles, and some made no secret of their disenchantment with the messages they were asked to convey. But what, you might ask, made the designer's vague desire for self-expression more important than the client's content, banal or not? In retrospect, many of these experiments can be seen for what they were: signs of profound, underlying cultural and technological change, transitional pictures of the prevailing climate, but not the way forward. Few now argue that style alone, however inventive, can be the medium of authorial vision.

Graphic authorship recognises the self-expressive aspect of the design process, but pushes it to a much higher level of intention. Someone writing a letter or planting flowers in a garden expresses him or herself; that doesn't make the results literature or landscape architecture. Authorship is a more deliberate and self-conscious process. If they want to engage and enlighten others, graphic authors need – just like any other author – to have pressing, original or penetrating observations to make about their experiences of the world and the conviction to express them in public. Their work needs to be about something and this cannot simply be a superficial reaction to subject matter given by a client. No one prescribes the content of a novel, a sequence of poems, or a piece of installation art. The motivation comes from an inner urge to make some form of personal statement.

This is a point that hasn't been made strongly enough in discussions of graphic authorship. A designer may have the luck to find a long-term patron, who will offer conditions of unusual freedom and a continuous flow of projects on which to build a personal vision. Think of Reid Miles' relationship with the Blue Note jazz label in the 1960s, or Vaughan Oliver's with 4AD Records in the 1980s, or Mau's 15-year "intellectual adventure" – as he put it – with Zone Books. Then again, you can work for years and never encounter such a client.

If designers want full authorial control, the most effective way is to instigate their own projects. Design, as the designer's natural area of expertise, is most often the subject matter – from Jan Tschichold's *The New Typography* (1928) to Paul Rand's *A Designer's Art* (1985). More recent exponents are American husband-and-wife team Ellen Lupton and J. Abbott Miller, authors of the influential visual essay collection *Design Writing Research* (1996). Design historian Robin Kinross, having spent many years researching, writing and editing his study of Anthony Froshaug, then proceeded to typeset, design, proofread and publish the two volumes himself in autumn 2000.

These are impressive projects. Yet it seems to me that the real test of graphic authorship's viability and potential lies outside the self-referential domain of design. Could it be used to address the broad range of topics and audiences routinely handled by ordinary authorship? Might the techniques and devices of graphic design be borrowed to present ideas, impressions, arguments and analysis in brand new ways? Are there subjects that would benefit from breaking out of the traditional pattern, still firmly in place in mainstream publishing culture, that insists editors and writers define the agenda and says the visual person's role is to support and illustrate?

Here, examples are hard to find. One under-sung pioneer, based in London, is David King, former art editor of *The Sunday Times Magazine*. In the last 30 years, King has researched, edited, designed and sometimes written a remarkable series of politically engaged, photographic histories based on material in his world-class archive of Soviet photographs.* Without a demanding subject matter like this, would-be graphic authors tend to fall back on their own resources. It's obvious what King's documentary books are about, although they certainly don't lack depth, complexity or resonance. But what is *Process; a Tomato Project* (1996) about? Or *Fuel Three Thousand*? The constant danger with such projects is that designers mistake obscurity for profundity.

Fuel are painfully aware of the standard such work will need to attain to be convincing outside the design ghetto. They are similarly realistic in acknowledging there is a distinction between the work they make for clients and the work they make for themselves. This doesn't mean their commercial design lacks commitment or interpretative intelligence; it just means they have found they have greater freedom to express their own peculiar vision, without compromise, in their self-initiated magazines, films and books.

This is likely to be a sticking point for designers who would love to believe – like Mau – that graphic authorship might be achievable within the framework of a client's commission. In *Life Style*, Mau shows two diagrams comparing the typical trajectory of a book project, with design entering at the end after all the key decisions about content have been made, and his preferred model, with design involved from the start of the research process. *S,M,L,XL* appeared to vindicate the Mau method, but speaking at the time, one of his designer colleagues, Nigel Smith, was sceptical about his claims: "It's not about Mau, it's about Koolhaas. The author is the person who creates the text. You can't claim authorship because you made the page pink."

Listening to Mau promoting the book at the Institute of Contemporary Arts, London, those words of caution came to mind. "The content – what is being said – is the trigger for form," Mau writes in *Life Style*. "Our goal is to produce an environment of collaboration for the development and integration of form." Few designers would take issue with this. It's central, at least in theory, to almost all graphic design – but it isn't graphic authorship. At the ICA, Mau readily confessed he was both ambitious and "lazy" (his word) and happy to allow his employees to run with the ball. This makes perfect sense in a busy studio; everybody does it – but, again, it isn't graphic authorship. The term "designer as director", coined by American critic Michael Rock, is a more accurate description of this way of working.

Do these intricacies really matter? Yes, because there is a chance here, with self-awareness and rigorous thinking, to open stimulating new channels of communication. Some of the last decade's most adventurous graphic projects have come from people chipping away at limiting conventional definitions of graphic design. Graphic authorship makes a huge claim for itself and presents some tough critical challenges. It isn't a panacea. It can take many different forms. The only way to begin to decide whether it is truly present in a graphic project is by undertaking a critical reading of the work itself – the kind of reading more usually given to literature, art, music, or architecture. This sharpens our sense of the possible, introduces points of comparison, highlights problems and establishes vital benchmarks.

Beneath it all, though, lies a straightforward proposition. Why shouldn't someone with something urgent of their own to say, a subject to explore, a passionate point of view to transmit, choose to express these ideas by primarily graphic means? If you can see no reason why design shouldn't be used for this purpose at least some of the time, then you understand what graphic authorship is about.

*David King died in 2016. For more information, see my book *David King: Designer, Activist, Visual Historian*, Yale University Press, London, 2020.

Art's Little Brother

The art-design relationship

Designers have always had an inferiority complex when it comes to their relationship with artists and art. It isn't usually talked about in quite such bald terms – no one wants to admit to weakness – but that's what it is. It doesn't matter that design is playing a bigger role in culture than ever or that some argue that it has become the more significant activity. Old ways of thinking persist and the balance of power seems to stay much the same.

Designers rarely achieve the level of recognition and financial reward attained by the most successful artists. Media coverage of art and design constantly reinforces art's privileged position. While every paper has an art critic knocking out weekly reviews of new exhibitions for the arts and culture pages, design is still not seen as a subject fit for serious discussion. It's treated as a lifestyle issue and skimpy, superficial write-ups concentrate on showcasing enviable domestic interiors and things you can buy for the home. Design books and exhibitions tend to be ignored. If you ask editors why, they say it's because "historically, we haven't reviewed design" – as though it was written in stone.

Yet questions about design and art's relationship, their similarities and differences, and the ways they might now be converging, refuse to go away. People on both sides of the divide have a stake in the matter. Some artists are fascinated by design's role in contemporary society and commerce; they make art about it and create designs of their own. Some designers are increasingly inclined to use their creations as a vehicle for the kinds of personal expression and commentary that are usually seen as art's preserve. "As we move forward through the twenty-first century," notes Barbara Bloemink, curatorial director at the Cooper-Hewitt, National Design Museum in New York, "distinctions between design and art are likely to become increasingly difficult to define."

Ironic, then, that Bloemink's 2004 exhibition, "Design ≠ Art", unwittingly reinforced the old imbalance. It's perfectly true, as she notes in the catalogue, that "the current ascendance of design gives renewed relevance to questions concerning the validity of art's conventionally privileged position." So what was the museum trying to say with the mysterious mathematical symbol in the title, which means "not equal to, but not greater than and not less than"? The Cooper-Hewitt is a design museum, yet only works by artists acting as designers featured in the exhibition: figures such as Donald Judd, Scott Burton, James Turrell and Jorge Pardo. Visitors had no opportunity to compare artists' designs with designers' treatments of similar objects and no examples of designers producing more art-like forms of design were shown.

A study of the phenomenon of "design art" from Tate Publishing by art critic Alex Coles is similarly one-sided. *DesignArt* (2005) examines the way that artists such as Henri Matisse, Sonia Delaunay, Judd and Pardo have dealt with pattern, furniture, interiors and architecture. "A key issue to keep in mind while thinking through designart is that all art is designed even if it endeavours to appear otherwise," writes Coles. He hopes to encourage "a more flexible approach towards design" and who could argue with that? But the way he goes about it, whatever the benefits might be for artists, only ends up confirming that art remains the dominant term in the relationship. Coles' exclusion of designers producing anything resembling art could not be more pointed; artists are permitted to undertake forays into design to refresh and extend art, but it appears to be a one-way street since no one is travelling in the other direction. The established positions of art and design in the cultural hierarchy go unchallenged.

It's worth remembering at this point how designers have tended to view the question of what distinguishes design from art. One of the best accounts is a chapter called "Is a Designer an Artist?" in Norman Potter's classic *What is a Designer* (revised edition 1989). The answer for Potter is clearly: no. A designer, unlike an artist, "works through and for other people, and is concerned primarily with their problems rather than his own". A painter's first responsibility, on the other hand, "is to the truth of his own vision". This is the contrast usually made between the roles of designer and artist: the designer must deal with matters of practicality and function while artists are free to do what they like in pursuit of their self-chosen goals.

A key idea for Potter is that the essence of a designer's work, as a planner, problem solver and supervisor, is to supply clear instructions so that others can complete the production of the design. By contrast, a painter or sculptor is more dependent on feedback from hand and eye and develops the work through direct experience of the materials. Potter suggests that the designer will need to be capable of more detachment than may be necessary to a fine artist.

But it's rarely as straightforward as this makes it sound. There are more passionate, less detached designers just as there are highly cerebral artists. Like designers, many artists make work with photography, video and computers. Artists are often dependent on specialist manufacturing techniques to fabricate their pieces and installations and they need to give those who assist them accurate instructions. Meanwhile, the computer has transferred specialised tasks and crafts once carried out by others to the designer's desktop and control, eliminating the need to prepare detailed instructions. This is particularly the case in graphic design and typography. Using digital tools, all kinds of design work can proceed in a more exploratory and open-ended way and this might be compared to the intuitive shaping by hand of old-fashioned art materials.

So we come back to the essential split between function and vision. Donald Judd insisted on the difference between his art and his design work, which he kept hidden from public view for many years. In 1993, he explained why: "The configuration and the scale of art cannot be transposed into furniture and architecture. The intent of art is different from that of the latter, which must be functional. If a chair or a building is not functional, if it appears to be only art, it is ridiculous. The art of a chair is not its resemblance to art, but is partly its reasonableness, usefulness and scale as a chair [...] A work of art exists as itself; a chair exists as a chair itself. And the idea of a chair isn't a chair."

Judd had good reason to preserve the distinction. The worst accusation that could be levelled at abstract art was that it was "decorative". In 1967, art critic Clement Greenberg attacked the new minimalist art, saying that it was "closer to furniture than art" and comparing it, with an audible sneer, to "good design" executed by someone else rather than made by the artist's own hand. The obvious danger, if Judd's furniture started to gain attention, was that his art would be demoted to the same level.

But Judd hadn't so much resolved the issue as dodged it. Coles jokes that his "stack sculptures would make sublime shelving units and the floor sculptures comfortable stools". Others claim that Judd's furniture fails as furniture and must be art, after all, because it isn't comfortable to sit on and flunks the design equals function test. The art or design question comes up again in art critic Matthew Collings' long interview with Ron Arad in Arad's latest monograph (2004). Judd owned a Rietveld chair, displayed at his home in Marfa, Texas among his own pieces. What would happen, Collings and

Arad wonder, if you were to take a Rietveld chair and a Judd chair to Covent Garden and show them to a passer-by? "If you tell them which is art and which is design," says Arad, "they'll think you're having them on – they'll think, why the distinction?"

Why indeed? There are few better examples of the way in which ideas about design have been enlarged in the last two decades than the work of Arad, an obvious candidate for inclusion in any exhibition or book about "design art". In 1987, Arad participated in Documenta 8, devoted to art and design, in Kassel, Germany – the hoped-for inter-disciplinary meeting of minds failed to happen – and, the same year, he was one of the first designers in London to venture into art's territory with an exhibition at the Edward Totah Gallery. He created chairs – as well as concrete hi-fis and telescopic aerial lights – that were functional in their way, but also concerned with what Judd called the "idea of the chair". At the time, design critic Deyan Sudjic went so far as to propose that Arad be viewed as an artist whose subject matter was design. His work dealt not only with the qualities of a chair that are to do with sitting, but with its symbolic, allusive and literary dimension.

Arad was one of many designers who, in the 1980s, tried to endow his designs with an extra layer of meaning, but with such little discussion of design as a cultural activity, wider critical awareness of design's enhanced potential has been slow to develop. In his conversation with Arad, Collings says he feels that he knows when something is more a piece of design than art, but that he is "completely naïve" about what design is and about its history. He is embarrassed, he admits, by his ignorance. Offering his own version of the familiar riff, Collings suggests that the essential difference between design and art is that design has function while art has mystery, yet he acknowledges that "the art world's mystery often isn't all that mysterious any more." He is absolutely right there. Art's routines are often obvious, repetitious and stale.

The point about Arad, though, was that his work did possess a sense of mystery. His One Off display space in Shelton Street, London was a cave of billowing steel sheets that couldn't have looked less like a sleek furniture showroom. There are many examples of designs that exceed their functional role and take on some of the qualities associated with art: Charles and Ray Eames' LaChaise lounger; Shiro Kuramata's How High the Moon metal-mesh armchair; Daniel Weil's deconstructed radios in plastic bags; Anthony Dunne and Fiona Raby's Globally Positioned Table, which responds to the influence of electromagnetic radiation. The mystery comes from the way that our expectations of form's conventional possibilities and limits are overturned. The sensory, intellectual and emotional satisfactions they offer as pieces to look at, think about and react to – as well as to use – are akin to the experience of sculpture.

Hella Jongerius is another designer who regularly blurs the distinction between design and art. "If, as a designer, you don't grab the theme by the throat and probe it to its farthest consequences, you're inevitably going to get stuck at the outer surface," she says in a 2003 monograph. "In the long run it's a dead end. I believe we make a mistake if we restrict ourselves to pragmatic aspects." An interviewer suggests that she might be in the wrong profession and that designers should perhaps leave the other side of the story to art. "Usable objects have their story too," insists Jongerius. "Still, does it really matter all that much? Who cares if it's art or if it's design?"

There is a tendency, when design ventures too close to art, to say that it has ceased to be design and become art instead. Designers have often been the first to criticise colleagues deemed to have crossed the line. Some show a deep distaste for what they see as gratuitous self-expression and they make these complaints even when a design has satisfied functional requirements. What these criticisms reveal is often no more than a preference for a particular design aesthetic in which traces of the designer's hand are kept to a minimum. The unapologetic embrace of decorative motifs in Tord Boontje's work is a deliberate rejection of the cold, machine-like, modernist-derived design language of many industrial products and objects. Far from being something to be shunned, uninhibited decoration is now seen by some designers as a way of re-humanising design.

Stephen Bayley has always insisted that industrial design is the real visual art of the 20th century. This was good showmanship, but reversing art and design's position so decisively is not plausible at this point even if you suspect that history might one day share his opinion. The aim is not to pull art down. Nor is it to crown design as the new art. But it is certainly to elevate design. Art and design exist in a continuum of possibilities, and rigid definitions that might make sense on paper are not tenable in practice when both activities can take so many forms. The most interesting work often happens in the gaps where there is room for manoeuvre and scope for debate.

Dunne and Raby are a good example of why we need to approach the relationship of art and design more flexibly. They are emphatic that they don't wish to be seen as artists. They recognise that it is in the context of design, perceived as designers, that their speculative research could have most impact. If their self-initiated projects were to be classified as art and shown only in art galleries, their work would be seen as a kind of artistic fantasy and would be ignored by the companies, institutions and policy-makers they would most like to influence. All kinds of opportunities will open up if only we can enlarge our notion of what design practice might be to embrace new kinds of design thinking and research.

If design really is in the ascendant, it is perhaps for the most fundamental of reasons. Since the 1960s, art has become increasingly suspicious of forms of expression that are merely visual. Artists saw beauty as simple-minded. They regarded design and decoration, which still cared about aesthetics, as superficial and vacuous. The artist's role was to go deeper, to be a visual thinker, to deal in ideas. Marcel Duchamp's legacy, conceptual art, has become a catch-all and art based on the sketchiest of thoughts is routinely described today in these terms. A visit to the new galleries of the Museum of Modern Art, New York, reveals what art has lost in the process. The early 20th-century floor, showing masterpieces of Post-Impressionism, Cubism, Fauvism, Expressionism, Suprematism and Surrealism, is an inexhaustible banquet of visual stimulation and pleasure. MoMA's work from after the Second World War is a lot bigger, but it is also thinner. Its overblown gestures can often be absorbed in moments. There is much less to savour and study and consequently, in both aesthetic and intellectual senses, rather less reward.

Design has no such hang-ups about the beauty of visual form. It exults in it. Artists may resist beauty because it is too easy, too compliant or insufficiently critical, but this does not change the fact that people hunger for it. We seek retinal pleasure, things to run our eyes over, colours, lines, textures and shapes to explore and inhabit, and design has no hesitation in supplying these experiences. Design is becoming more elaborately layered, more spectacular, more pervasive in our lives. Design, rather than art, is foremost now in embodying the visual spirit of the age. Millions get by without going anywhere near an art gallery, but everyone is touched in some way by design. Perhaps what we are seeing in the inexorable rise of design is the gradual reunification of art, in the pre-modernist, "decorative" sense, and everyday life. If art is so important to our social, mental and spiritual well-being, why should we keep them apart?

In their books, both Bloemink and Coles quote Matisse's famous statement: "What I dream of is an art of balance, of purity and serenity, devoid of troubling or depressing subject matter, an art that could be for every mental worker, for the businessman as well as the man of letters, for example, a soothing, calming influence on the mind, something like a good armchair that provides relaxation from fatigue."

Matisse's sentiment, recorded almost a century ago, could not be more contemporary, though the stresses of modern living that he wants to heal with art "like a good armchair" are more intense than he could have guessed. He describes his hopes for painting, but he could just as well be talking about design's comforting sensorial embrace. "Design art" is an awkward compound term and it may not catch on, but at least it suggests the continuity between design and art. Neither word on its own seems fully adequate any longer to explain how our visual culture is evolving. To move forward, we need a wider public understanding that design is a means of personal and cultural expression with the potential to equal and even exceed art's reach. It's high time the media stopped treating design as a nothing more than a pleasant diversion and woke up to this. If *The Guardian*, for instance, can devote an entire issue of its daily review to a 17-page article about the painter Caravaggio, it can certainly find space to think more seriously about design.*

*"The Complete Caravaggio" by Jonathan Jones, *The Guardian G2*, 17 February 2005.

Kissing Cousins

Art's romance with design

Anyone who follows the art scene will know that in recent years artists have become increasingly preoccupied with design. They long ago turned to many of the same techniques and media used by graphic designers – photography, typography, video – giving their work numerous similarities to commercial visual communication. Many artists also design things, though this is not always an aspect of their work that they seek to publicise. Donald Judd designed furniture. Lawrence Weiner created posters for his own exhibitions. Japanese artist Takashi Murakami collaborates on fabrics.

This has been going on for decades. "High & Low", the landmark 1991 exhibition at the Museum of Modern Art, showed how, from Cubism's use of collage to Jeff Koons' porcelain Pink Panther sculptures, modern art engaged in a continuous relationship and sometimes a dialogue with popular culture. How could it be otherwise? If art's subject was the modern world, then it could hardly avoid the mass-produced images that shaped the visual environment of the street and home. There might be a place for still lifes of fruit or abstracts with no content, but if art stopped there, it would cease to tell us much about the nature of contemporary experience.

What has changed is that art's focus on our designed reality has become increasingly overt. *George Hanson Critical Forum* (2004), a new book from the Royal

We Want to Make Dreams a Reality by Mark Titchner, archival print on aluminium panel, 2005.

College of Art, London, refers to the tendency as "art's romance with design" and this description is apt. Design is seductive for everyone, including artists, who read the shelter magazines, dine in fancily designed restaurants and shop at the same designer stores as the rest of us. The more successful they become, the more they can participate in the comforts and pleasures of the designer lifestyle. The society in which art is produced has evolved and so have art's concerns and visual methods.

Not everyone is happy with these developments. A review of the Carnegie International exhibition at the Carnegie Museum of Art in Pittsburgh, published in *The New York Times* in 2004, criticised the survey for being dominated by "designer art". "The problem with designer art," writes critic Ken Johnson, "is that it can be difficult to distinguish from everyday commercial art." He gives many examples of artists whose work fails to satisfy him, often making a comparison with some aspect of commercial design. Philip-Lorca diCorcia's photographs of pole dancers "might have been commissioned by a slick magazine", while a project by filmmaker Yang Fudong would work as a clothing commercial.

Johnson acknowledges that designer art can be "bracingly provocative", but he finds a lot of it joyless and overcalculated, with a tendency for design to overwhelm the content. Even the best pieces are often more interesting to think about than to experience. "Designer art is ironic and strategic," he concludes. "It is not the product of a searching soul but of a critically articulate mind."

This is not a very probing explanation of what is going on in this kind of art, but it does throw up a couple of significant ideas. Johnson thinks that fine art should look different from commercial art and that it should be more concerned with soulfulness than cerebration. The problem for the artist, though, is that the media and communications landscape in which design plays a part is a much more powerful producer of imagery than art has been for years. Commercial communication has thoroughly absorbed visual strategies invented by pioneering modernist artists. At their most creative, pop videos, film titles and TV ads can be as oblique, abstracted and loaded with obscure symbolism as any avant-garde film from the 1920s. Graphic design of the last 30 years exhibits an astonishing range of styles and tactics to engage audiences assumed to be highly sophisticated.

There is a good case for suggesting that graphic design has exhibited rather more visual inventiveness than art during this period. It's no wonder that artists find themselves gravitating towards design techniques and devices of proven power since these, rather than oil paint and brushes, represent the visual language of the day. What art critics never seem to acknowledge is that, on a purely visual level, the commercial arts tend to handle these things much better. Take artists' typography. It isn't usually very accomplished and, to the trained eye, this failure of visual rhetoric is enough to render an entire work of art creaky and suspect. Do they expect us to make allowances?

This leads to the second point about soulfulness versus cerebration. At a time when art's power to produce new kinds of imagery has been eclipsed by pop culture's, it makes sense for the artist to place more emphasis on a critical exploration of the subject. Hence, the "conceptual" nature of so much art produced since the 1970s. Given that design is so central to our culture, it's logical for design to be one of those subjects.

Here, the artist enjoys a real advantage over the designer, who sometimes moves towards a similar position on the art/design interface, but from the opposite direction. Discussions in the last decade about the autonomy of the designer, or the designer as author, always run into the problem of the client. Clearly, the only way to gain complete autonomy as a designer is to initiate your own work, but this seems to deny the essential client-serving role of design. If art people have tended to disregard the critical potential of design, it's because, from their perspective, the client's control rules out the possibility of any substantial agency on the designer's part.

"What artists bring to design is an interface with art that goes beyond the literal production of design and instead looks at design scenarios," writes British art critic Alex Coles in *George Hanson Critical Forum*. "Few designers have the flexibility within the briefs they are set to do this with any real commitment."

And commitment is undoubtedly what it needs. Graphic designers have made little headway in convincing culture's power brokers that their activity deserves critical attention, let alone that it can be an autonomous form of practice. Even designers are inclined to doubt it and being a pro tends to win the day.

Shouldn't designers' work and thinking be central to such a discussion? While design has certainly moved closer to art, it has done this without much thought. If there was an overriding idea among young designers, it was that they had some kind of right to their own measure of self-expression. Looking at endless books of "designer art" published by designers in recent years, it's obvious that, while they possess exceptional technical skills, few have much to say about the role of design in society, or about anything else. This kind of designer art will not be taken seriously until it can show more evidence that it's the product of a critical mind. Even mediocre artists are educated to understand that without a set of carefully articulated personal concerns, they have no purpose making art. They need a high degree of motivation to pursue such a project and this gives them the confidence to establish the terms on which they will collaborate in any partnership.

What might be possible if only we could marry the artist's sense of individual purpose to the designer's understanding of media processes and image-making techniques? It all comes down to the way that designers are educated and to the kinds of expectation and speculation they are then able to weave around design.

Where is Art Now?

The question of quality in the visual arts

Does it matter whether art exists? I don't mean art in the ordinary sense of "visual forms of expression". This kind of visual output clearly exists in abundance. There is more of it coming at us, from every direction, than ever before in history. But what about "art" in the more particular sense of something that conveys deep meaning and is consequently judged to possess a special value – both cultural and monetary? Do we need that kind of art? And how do we decide what it is?

The situation has been confused for decades and it becomes more tangled with each passing year. To demonstrate the difficulty, try to come up with a brief and clear explanation of this higher kind of art that would be convincing to anyone, from any walk of life, who heard it. The task is all but impossible. Yet we proceed as though general social agreement exists about what constitutes "serious" art. We still have artists who believe themselves to be in a different category from other visual creators. There are still curators, critics, dealers and collectors. There is still art education and an art market, even if it's doing less well than a few years ago.

The art world is largely responsible for this confusion about definitions, too. They told us that anything could be art, so long as an artist said it was. Almost anyone who goes through a gallery door is likely to have heard about Marcel Duchamp and his urinal. The art world is less

Saint Francis Borgia by Juan Martínez Montañés,
polychromed wood, c. 1624. Photograph: José Morón Borrego.

good at explaining how certain people get to be artists and decide what art is for the rest of us. This process of selection might not make aesthetic or philosophical sense, but it works anyway. It's about power: whoever holds it gets to officiate and decide. The "art world" is a way of conserving, controlling and assigning this precious resource. Once a year, *Art Review* publishes a list of the 100 people on the international art scene who wield the most clout. So there we have it. Even the insiders admit what's going on.

I'm not part of the art world, but I studied art and I share some of its assumptions. I do believe the higher kind of art exists. It grips and fascinates me. There are few things I enjoy more than looking at art in museums and galleries. So all the time, like any committed gallery-goer, I'm confronted by the question: why is this object I'm gazing at art? And, conversely, why is something quite similar not art? Having reached that point, it's impossible to avoid even trickier questions. Am I being shown things by the art world that might not be art after all? Can a piece of work be serious art even though it isn't any good, while some other excellent piece of work fails to qualify as high art? One thing I feel confident about saying after years of looking at art is that I'm not automatically prepared to take the art world's word for it, even if I conclude they are right about an artist or an artwork. But how do I think I know? I'll come back to that later.

In an interview with *Variant* magazine, in 1993, Brian Eno came up with another way of looking at the "what is art?" question. First, he suggested that all the distinctions between high and low art boil down to commercial interests. If a work of art is going to command a high price, it has to claim a position in the centre of culture that other work doesn't have. Agreed. But Eno went much further: "The problem with the whole art object theory, the idea that art somehow resides inside objects because artists have put it there or discovered it, [is that it] creates a picture of an independent entity, a substance in the world called Art. And then the job of art historians is to decide which ones have it and which ones have more or less of it."

Eno went on to argue that art – in the sense of some special attribute or value, objectively present in the work – doesn't actually exist. So the question "what is art?" is a redundant enquiry; it cannot be answered. Instead, Eno switched the emphasis from the artist to the viewer. While art might not reside in the object, spectators can still feel that they are experiencing something that qualifies as art, at least for them. The artist should be redefined, Eno suggested, as "someone who creates the occasion for an art experience." This experience could be generated by anything at all and it will be different for every viewer. Art, like beauty, also turns out to be in the eye of the beholder.

At first sight this is quite persuasive. It appears to solve the problem at a stroke. We have simply been thinking about art in the wrong way. Eno's redefinition offers a relativistic view of art completely in keeping with all the other relativistic ideas and opinions we hold about morality, society and the meaning of life. His proposal also reflects what many people already tend to think about art, high or low. They know what they like; it's an entirely subjective matter; the official view about what is real art and what isn't is irrelevant to their private enjoyment and no one is going to persuade them otherwise.

The trouble with Eno's focus on the viewer's art experience is that it doesn't reveal anything about the aspects of an artwork that might cause the viewer to have that experience. It doesn't recognise that we might be able to analyse those qualities, aesthetic or conceptual, and learn how they affect us from studying many art experiences. Nor does it acknowledge that artists try to create art experiences by manipulating their materials, using an understanding gained as both viewer and practitioner, in order to affect other viewers in particular ways. It further suggests that there's no possibility of communicating with other viewers about our art experiences to see how our perceptions of a given art-experience generator (or artwork) might compare.

One issue we should be able to agree on, though, is that art requires intention and action. Reality has to be manipulated or rearranged in some way. A landscape isn't art. But a view of a landscape in the form of a painting is certainly art, according to both our linguistic and cultural uses of the term. Can it also be art in some higher sense?

The answer to this question isn't culturally convenient – that's why we struggle with it now – but we know how it goes already. High art has existed for centuries. It's still with us, though it coexists now with many other possibilities on a continuum that extends all the way from high to low, and it's much easier to identify in the past than in the present. High art is Dante, Shakespeare, Flaubert and Kafka. It's Titian, Goya, Monet, Picasso, and many others. Their creations survive as part of a canon of great works that educated people have felt they should know about. This isn't just some unscrupulous con trick practised by the ruling classes. Nothing stays in the canon over time unless enough people find it of lasting worth. This is not to say that the canon shouldn't be continually reassessed, edited and expanded, but it remains a collective judgement on what high quality means in the history of a cultural field.

This is a difficult idea for us because we are less inclined to believe in greatness now. Several decades ago, all the dead white European males who populate our cultural history started to look oppressive to radical thinkers. This distaste has led us down the blind alley of relativism and we need to rethink. If we set aside the impossible wish to re-play history and correct all its regrettable imbalances, what distinguishes great works of art from other works judged to be of lesser cultural value is that they represent a higher order of creative intention and achievement. In form, content and technique, they show an exceptional degree of accomplishment. They handle themes common to other art of their time (and later) with a degree of intelligence, depth, fluency, expression, sensitivity and drama sufficient to impress itself even on readers and viewers with only limited experience of these art forms.

Compared to these flaming suns, other works are pale discs without heat. The unusually rich "art experiences" reported by generations of ordinary spectators and critics are a response to identifiable properties in the works themselves. The more experienced the viewer, the more alert he or she will be to these effects, and the better able to measure them against similar kinds of art.

In 2009, the National Gallery in London mounted one of the most remarkable exhibitions I have seen in years. The 17th-century Spanish painted wooden sculptures in "The Sacred Made Real", staged and illuminated with a brilliant sense of theatre, were a revelation. It wasn't necessary to be religious to find these dark melancholy saints and martyred Christ figures profoundly emotive, or an art expert to appreciate that these were peerless masterpieces of the craft. The fierce blade of their humanity lanced out across time. And it wasn't only me. I can rarely recall *The Guardian*'s art critic, Adrian Searle, who mainly covers recent art, sounding as excited and overwhelmed – "I left devastated and deeply moved" – as he did writing about "The Sacred Made Real". It seems like bad etiquette to say it, and even a kind of modern heresy, but how often does a contemporary art exhibition poleaxe anyone like that?

Serious art criticism, like other kinds of criticism, might have given up on the idea of evaluation. But that doesn't lessen the viewer's desire to experience work that seems worthwhile or "good", and this perception of quality in relation to a work's properties and effects must originate somewhere. While it might be felt as intensely personal, the experience is not exclusively our own. One thing the internet has revealed more clearly than ever before is the presence of communities of taste – the discovery that other people often like the same cluster of things as us for strikingly similar reasons. Quality enriches our lives. Few things feel like a bigger waste of time than bad art.

At the same time, as 21st-century network democrats, we fervently wish to believe that everyone deserves access, that we are all creative and perhaps even artists, that elitism (being better at something and knowing it too) is totally unacceptable from other people because it affronts our ego and sense of self-worth. Miraculous tools allow us to dabble in visual pursuits we would once have left alone for lack of talent, opportunity, or both. Even the most modestly skilled image-makers can digitally bootstrap themselves to a high technical standard now. The disappearance of the old career filters and disincentives, the daily deluge of new imagery, and the intoxicatingly instant self-promotion to be had from blogs and social media seems to mock the very idea of striving against the odds, on your own, perhaps for years, to produce exceptional work. Everyone floats around happily in the same online sea of mediocrity.

Somehow, if we are committed to the idea of quality, if this remains a culturally meaningful goal – does it? – then we need to strike a balance between the social aim of greater participation and a continuing faith in the critical ideal that great things are still possible for those with the drive, dedication, talent and vision to achieve them. Quality will be defined by the same criteria that informed viewers have always used as benchmarks: strength of conception, depth of content, integrity of viewpoint, originality (there's no getting around it) and mastery of technique. It's an enduring conceit peculiar to the conceptual art of the last 40 years that the most important thing about an artwork is its "idea" and that the visual dimension really isn't the issue. This is like poets holding the view that crafting well-turned lines is of marginal interest for literature, or jazz musicians claiming that being able to play their instruments is a red herring and then informing audiences that they are simple-minded to see it any other way.

So we need to put more emphasis again on the visual in art, and it's clear that many young artists with visual talent have decided to ignore the art world's weary, self-serving conceptualist strictures and just go ahead and make the art they feel like making. They want to create optical art experiences of their own. By paying too much attention to the extremes of high or low we run the risk of undervaluing what's happening in the densely populated middle – graphic novels, graphic design, illustration, low-cost film-making – where the expressive possibilities of the visual are still embraced with conviction. This, rather than art scene-mediated art, is the real centre of visual culture in our time. Are we overlooking great work only because we have been instructed for so long to assume that anything presented outside the art world's walls must be inferior?

Non-official art of this kind is a contemporary *Salon des refusés* for anyone who resists the by-invitation-only policy of the now thoroughly professionalised and institutionalised artist/dealer/curator nexus. It remains to be seen whether this zone of wild, unregulated and largely unmonitored creativity is where the masterpieces of the future will come from, but with the gates wide open, there is every reason to hope.

Rigorous Anarchy

Earthquakes and aftershocks at CalArts

In the late 1980s, when I was becoming more immersed in graphic design, two contemporary centres of graphic activity galvanised my attention. One, the Netherlands, was a short distance away across the English Channel and easy to visit. The other, California, was halfway around the world, and I had been there only once, a decade earlier, when I had barely heard of graphic design.

In those days, magazines were the only regular means to receive news about what was going on in graphic design, along with the occasional book, although there was much less publishing about the subject back then. I still remember the impact of an article in *I.D.* magazine published in March/April 1988. Written and designed with grid-breaking experimental freedom by Katherine McCoy and David Frej, it was titled "Typography as Discourse", and it was illustrated with small images of graphic projects that looked exhilaratingly avant-garde to my rapidly developing eye for design. Two of these were promotional items by Jeffery Keedy for California Institute of the Arts. There was work by Ed Fella in Valencia and Tom Bonauro in San Francisco, and a page from *Emigre* magazine by Rudy VanderLans. The buzz about *Emigre*, the outsized Californian "culture tab", had reached London, and I would soon get my hands on a copy, issue 9 (1988) – one of those critical moments that both seals and boosts a growing commitment. California seemed like a pulsing nerve centre for the latest ideas in graphic design.

McCoy was the longstanding co-chair of design at Cranbrook Academy of Art and Frej was a notable recent graduate. Fella and Keedy had also gained MFAs at Cranbrook and the article decisively established the tight social and intellectual bonds between Cranbrook and CalArts, where they were both now teaching. As I would soon learn, Keedy and Fella were recruited by Lorraine Wild, another Cranbrook grad, who had become director of the CalArts graphic design program in 1985. They formed a formidable trio and went on to achieve a high profile on the design scene both for the programme and as influential educators and designers. Even before I had seen much else from this new wave of Californian design, Keedy's graphics in *I.D.* – there was also an eccentrically composed postcard for a gallery in LA – served as notice that CalArts offered an educational experience that would challenge many of the norms of contemporary graphic practice and education.

Wild is said to have won the position at CalArts partly because of a paper she wrote, titled "More Than a Few Questions about Graphic Design Education", which appeared in 1983 in *Design Journal*. Graphic design programmes, she argued, were not responding to the growing sophistication of the field.

"If we expect a student to 'make form a meaningful thing'," Wild wrote, "then the student has to understand, in the first place, the importance of meaning, and secondly, the means by which meaning is conveyed." She insisted, "students must see themselves within the historical continuum of visual and verbal communicators." And she ended by suggesting that "innovation and excitement" in graphic design cannot be legislated by the profession. In other words, these benefits will only come about where favourable conditions of openness allow them to thrive. A few years later, at CalArts, Wild and her colleagues created an environment in which innovation and excitement, in pursuit of an expanded conception of graphic meaning, were given free reign.

In 2005, the École des Beaux-Arts in Rennes mounted "Earthquakes & Aftershocks", an exhibition of posters made by students at CalArts since the mid-1980s. An excellent catalogue accompanied the show, with an essay by the French poster designer Michel Bouvet, who describes his encounters with young LA designers on a trip to the city. Where some observers wedded to conventional conceptions of graphic design reacted to CalArts' seemingly outlandish visual investigations with misunderstanding and scorn, Bouvet was highly receptive to what he perceived as their playfulness, though he didn't initially see, he confides, "beyond the fun aspect of the work." Meeting designers such as ReVerb, Keedy, and Michael Worthington – first an MFA student at CalArts and then a teacher – revealed to Bouvet their deep engagement with the profession's history.

"Everything they do is backed up by a great deal of knowledge about graphic design and art in general," he wrote. "The rows and rows of books on European art, photography, and architecture in their studios witnessed to this." Discussing ReVerb's work, he notes the combination of "extreme rigor of composition and type with extreme whimsy in the placement of fonts, often from diverse families and in several different sizes. What appears completely anarchic is in fact thoroughly thought out."

That's a description that could apply to many of the posters collected in the book. Any one of them might serve as a representative example, but let's single out Worthington's Art School Faculty Show poster from 1995. As a base for his typographic manipulations, he sets down a series of nested frames composed of white decorative borders that could be Victorian in origin. The main typographic elements, forming some kind of errant title piece, are similarly anachronistic and whimsical, and he drops them onto the borders in a botched attempt at centring which is, of course, entirely deliberate. The word *Faculty* is drifting to the left and the "w" in *show* has fallen from the line as though it has lost its footing.

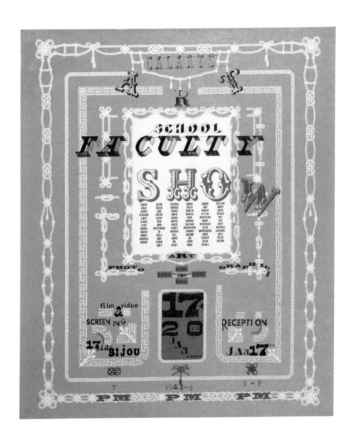

CalArts Art School Faculty Show, poster, California Institute of the Arts, 1995.
Design: Michael Worthington.

If the principal type elements look inebriated, the smaller patches of type in jumbled styles also appear to be woozy and nothing lines up like it should. Only the faculty's names, among them Wild and Keedy, appear resolute in a white box in the middle, although the spindly, dangling columns of the teachers' names look like they have been pressed into service from a completely different style of design.

Most of the CalArts posters, like this one, were created to announce activities at the institute – exhibitions, lectures, concerts and performances – and poster-making as a laboratory for cultivating new strains of graphic and typographic thinking has continued to flourish. The CalArts website has an archive of posters for the REDCAT (Roy and Edna Disney/CalArts Theater), gathering more than 200 works displayed around the school from 2005 to 2015 to encourage students to attend events at the interdisciplinary arts centre in downtown LA.*

The recent posters are even more brazen in their collisions of style, fragmentary construction and eye-baffling complexity than the "Earthquakes & Aftershocks" posters, which once seemed so challenging. The world has caught up and this manner of graphic design can be found in graduate programmes across the planet. Capricious type choices and knowingly misplaced graphic paraphernalia have become a familiar routine. Highly educated designers demonstrate their mastery of old-school graphic convention by violating its tenets and taboos with exquisitely self-conscious bursts of wit. What a pity, though, that experimental form-making still struggles to find expression outside the academy. It's as though anticipation of the wing-clipping to come obliges talented students to let fly while they still have the chance.

I have focused here on CalArts because its work was an exciting entry point for me, but California has a tradition of innovative graphic design spanning the mid-century years, as design programme faculty member

Louise Sandhaus detailed in her magnificent survey *Earthquakes, Mudslides, Fires and Riots* (2014). Alvin Lustig, Saul Bass, April Greiman – these figures were titans. In the book, Sandhaus shows a fine early 1970s piece by Frances Butler. "In my graphic work I've tried to explore new possibilities for communication by isolating and emphasizing different parts of the visual repertoire to make the underlying theoretical emphasis become as important as the recognizable subject matter," Butler writes in her book *Colored Reading* (1979).

That intention could equally well apply to many of the CalArts posters. When Wild and her iconoclastic colleagues arrived a few years later to re-energise the CalArts programme, the graphic climate was already welcoming.

*These posters can now be seen in the CalArts Poster Archive at https://posters.calarts.edu

Flowers in the Forest

The return of decorative design

One of the most striking developments in design since the year 2000 has been the return of ornament and decoration. Yet design commentators, always on the lookout for the latest trends, have taken a surprisingly long time to say much about it. Suddenly, though, the tendency is being noted, delineated and defined. Brooklyn-based design writer Alice Twemlow contributes a perceptive overview to *Eye*, while Unit Editions co-founder Adrian Shaughnessy weighs in with an essay for a special issue of *Graphic* devoted to the subject of the ornate in design.

I can't deny that I have been slow to consider this trend myself. Certainly, the oversight reflects my own ambivalence about this kind of work, a suspicion that graphic design is not so much leading the way here as holding up an uncritical mirror to broader developments in visual culture. Then, whether you like the look of this kind of design or not, there was the inevitable question: why this now? What is the new decorative aesthetic about?

Richly ornamented design has a tangled web of sources. The postmodern digital design of the early to mid-1990s reintroduced the idea of complexity. The images may have been awkward and jarring on occasion and the emphasis was heavily on the type, but these designs were loaded with intricate detail. For those who

The Vanity of Allegory by Douglas Gordon, postcard box, 2005.
Ornamentation and custom type: Marion Bantjes and Matthias Ernstenberg.
Art direction: Stefan Sagmeister.

enjoyed this kind of work, there was much pleasure to be found in allowing the eye to lose itself in such dense visual tapestries.

By the late 1990s, illustration was undergoing an international resurgence and the look of recent decorative design has grown from the elaborately detailed and linear vector styles developed by some illustrators. Where "deconstructive" digital design proved, ultimately, to be limited in its appeal – a bit too obviously rebellious and masculine, perhaps – illustration spoke to a wider audience, attracting fashion people, textile-makers and furniture designers. In 2003, I interviewed Dutch industrial designer Tord Boontje, then living in London. He decorated his chairs, tables and lights with simple images of leaves, branches, flowers and rabbits, a reaction, he said, to the alienating blandness of modernism as it was usually applied to industrial and interior design. Similar imagery could be found in the new decorative design.

I appreciated Boontje's determination to find a new direction, but it didn't really grab me. He was recently a father and it was obvious that his preoccupation with enchanted fairy-tale settings and peaceful woodland groves came from empathising with his child's mental world. (I experienced a similar fascination with the content and mood of fairy tales when my daughter was small.) There will always be a place for such imagery in the nursery, but isn't this taste applied to adult interior décor a little childish and twee?

Looking at *Graphic*'s special issue, that thought kept returning. While there is considerable talent on display, a lot of the imagery is cloying and cute. Popular motifs include petals, foliage, birds, animals, butterflies, insects, wan girls, pouting girls, period clothes, exotic costumed figures and palaces, foaming waves, and swirling, organic lines that express the grandeur of nature and the elements. The basic concerns are no different wherever in the world the imagery originates. *Graphic* asks Birgit Amadori, a German now living in Redondo Beach, California, what her work is about. "Beauty, details, hair, lips, patterns, the ideal Bézier curve," she replies, and the same goes for many of these image-makers.

Amadori was one of 21 young graphic designers, urban artists and illustrators invited in 2005 to embellish the rooms in the Hotel Fox in Copenhagen, a project that stands as an international landmark of the new graphic decoration. In the 61 rooms, the Fox website promises, "You will find flowers, fairy tales, friendly monsters, dreaming creatures, secret vaults …" In room 405, for instance, the nomadic Australian design team Pandarosa take an ornamental line for a walk across the bedspread, floor and walls. This erratic root system culminates in festoons of graphic blossom on the ceiling. Over in room 214, Friends with You, who hail from Miami, surround the bedazzled occupant with a photographic panorama of huge trees inhabited by swans, a llama, an owl and a Yorkshire terrier. Designer Samuel Borkson describes the effect as "a fertility shrine in a magical forest". For her part, in rooms 217, 509 and 510, Amadori conjures up a series of fantasy figures like something out of Hans Christian Andersen, with lavishly patterned robes and writhing locks of hair. And, once again, there's a forest.

It's a little disappointing that the hotel is an elaborate publicity stunt to promote a car – the Volkswagen Fox – rather than a hotelier's independently conceived dream. Even so, the project, put together by Event Labs and Berlin publisher Die Gestalten Verlag, is quite a feat. The Fox is fun and the passionately crafted décor will work for a time for those who are tuned into its fashionable signals. Yet there is still something thin and off-putting about this kind of applied surface prettification. Not all the rooms are so whimsical, but whimsy remains the overriding theme. The images are over-scaled versions of the sort of thing you might see these days in any fashion ad or cool product promotion.

Twemlow and Shaughnessy are surely right when they pinpoint the new decoration as evidence of the return of craft, both as a means to distinguish professional design from amateur efforts and as way of engaging at a deeper level with the process of making. At a certain point in graphic design's development, the designer-as-consultant became more of a director than a doer. Now designers have rediscovered the satisfaction of personally controlling all aspects of the production process. Painstakingly detailed work displays visible signs of the designer's "hand" and can potentially be invested with a high degree of expression and feeling.

As a statement of principle this is fine, but the really interesting thing is what designers and image-makers do with these freedoms. While the new decorative design can be formally inventive, at the level of content it too often opts for juvenile flights of fantasy and cliché. The deep psychological structures of fairy tales can still be mined for meaning, and fiction writers sometimes do this, but fairy-tale imagery reduced to feel-good decorative illustration just looks trite. An attraction to this kind of escapist picture-making may reveal something about our troubled feelings towards present-day reality, but it says nothing especially illuminating about the nature of contemporary experience.

The new decorative design is much more purposeful when it allows this ambivalence to permeate the imagery. Twemlow identifies a current she calls "dystopian". Here, the designer is locked into an ironic, urban way of thinking, even when the imagery takes a day trip into the countryside, as in Geoff McFetridge's "Stoner Forest" fabric pattern, where a lone figure wanders around under a canopy of weirdly distorted trees, oblivious to the quasi-military activities of some nearby hunters with rifles (maybe those guys are stoners, too).

The most convincing recent uses of decoration confirm that, while we don't use the p-word much any more, postmodern ways of thinking continue to influence design. How else to make sense of Marian Bantjes' vector art ornament and titling for the box Stefan Sagmeister designed for "The Vanity of Allegory", an exhibition of artist Douglas Gordon's work? It looks like something found in a gloomy library in an Edward Gorey tale. The design is a kind of paraphrase, referencing the history of book decoration from illuminated manuscripts to ornament-encrusted Victorian title pages, yet the excessive, obsessional quality feels totally contemporary. It's a lot more enjoyable to dwell on than desiccated, risk-averse, neo-modern typography, which has little to offer viewers now.

In the best of the new decoration, we see a love of complexity and a return to ideas about the role of the personal that underpin much of the most significant graphic design of the last two decades. The *Ray Gun* magazine era rejection of basic guidelines for practice left many young designers unsure where to go next. A new generation has solved the problem by reasserting a commitment to craft and skill as the basis of design. With luck, the kindergarten iconography getting so much attention is just a step on the path to something more mature.

Gothic Extra Böld

Heavy metal's extreme aesthetics

In the annals of gratuitously ghoulish album cover design, Slayer's *Reign in Blood* still stands as some kind of perverse classic decades after it first thrilled the teenage thrash metal fans it was aimed at and sent shivers of revulsion through their parents. Three figures, one of them wearing a bishop's mitre, carry a goat-like figure in a chair. There is a decapitated head on a pole and other bodies pierced by spikes hang in the background. What makes it worse is that the painting is really accomplished. The packed composition has been constructed with great skill as a set of shadowy, interlocking forms that drag your eyes into every toxic corner, allowing no escape from this hellhole of the damned.

It might come as a surprise to learn that the designer of this fine piece of epic nastiness is Stephen Byram, celebrated today for his graphically delicate and playful CD covers for the Screwgun jazz label. Heavy metal music graphics are more or less off the radar when it comes to most designers – unless, that is, you happen to be a heavy metal fan yourself. I listened to the founding fathers of heavy metal in my teens – Black Sabbath, Deep Purple, Led Zeppelin – and I would still count myself a rock fan now, but not of this kind of rock. The big hair, the bare chests, the axe-man heroics, the ludicrously overblown song concepts: it all cried out to be ridiculed and, when *This is Spinal Tap* hit the screens in 1984, it was.

Sardonic Wrath by Darkthrone, Peaceville Records, vinyl album cover, 2004.
Cover art: Lorenzo Mariani

But this was an earlier, milder kind of heavy rock. Meanwhile, metal was being retooled and retuned. In the 1980s, it began to splinter into a range of subgenres that even diehard metalheads sometimes have trouble telling apart: speed metal, thrash metal, death metal (and the related grindcore), black metal, groove metal, nu metal. There's even a neo-classical variant of metal. Metal musicians developed the death grunt vocal and perfected the blast-beat drumming style. And, as it evolved, metal became faster, harder, darker and more ferociously extreme, its status as a controversial subculture signalled by the way that big music stores segregate it. Over here, for most of us, is wholesome rock and pop; over there is metal. Sometimes I would flip through the metal album covers, absorbed by the way these images combine to express their own bizarre, unholy, violent and nihilistic view of the world.

No group of musicians has shown greater commitment to the idea of the logo than the metal bands. Motörhead, Anthrax, Slayer, Kreator, Death, Megadeth, Mayhem, Bathory, Burzum and Manowar – they all have them, big, eye-bashing and usually centred at the top. Iron Maiden's band logo, one of the most influential, looks like it was bolted together from angular chunks of, well, iron. Obituary's appears to be forged from glinting scalpel blades. Darkthrone's could be a spidery cluster of branches or lightning bursts; as if following the directions of the most stringent identity manual, the Norwegian band has diligently applied its logo to every release in the past 16 years. Long before it became fashionable among respectable designers to talk about "flexible identities", metal album cover artists were dedicated exponents. Logo colour changes were never a problem. They could drip blood, if the occasion demanded – and, no surprise, it sometimes did – or incorporate the shape of a bat.

These flexible identities were pictorial, too. The British band Motörhead set the standard in 1977 with its Snaggletooth skull sprouting curved boar horns, devised by American artist Joe Petagno and the band's leader, Lemmy. "The inspiration came from just being a naturally pissed-off bastard!" Petagno explained. Elaborate variations on this icon have graced many of Motörhead's covers. Iron Maiden's first album in 1980 featured another painted band mascot, Eddie the 'ead, a murderous-looking skull-head cursed with burning eyes, wizened flesh and hair like straw. Artist Derek Riggs created a never-ending supply of scenes involving Eddie as an axe-wielding psycho killer, as a chained-up madman, as a zombie rising triumphantly from the grave, and became a cult figure in his own right.

Images like these were tacky and tasteless, but they were executed with enormous style and verve, and only a prude could take exception to them. They were no more disturbing, and no more of a threat to the nation's moral fabric, than a fantasy comic book, or a drive-in horror movie meant to give you a pleasant scare. Sometimes they had acidic humour, too. On Edward J. Repka's cover for Megadeth's 1986 *Peace Sells ... But Who's Buying?*, yet another mascot, Vic Rattlehead – a skeleton in a suit with a visor riveted to his eye sockets, metal plugs blocking his ears and staples clamping his mouth shut – leans on a FOR SALE sign as fighter planes swoop over a destroyed building that looks suspiciously like the United Nations. It was a prescient piece of satire, as things have turned out.

"You can call metal many things: stupid, ugly, noisy, violent, and base, and you'd be right," note James Sherry and Neil Aldis in *Heavy Metal Thunder* (2006), a collection of heavy metal covers. "But unlike other genres, metal can laugh at its own absurdities." That's true up to a point. We can only trust that the guys in Manowar, still apparently in love with the idea of muscle-bound warriors waving big swords around, do see the funny side.

In the late 1980s, as death metal became more abrasive in sound and morbid in its lyrical concerns – death, mainly – so did the covers. Most of us would have to work pretty hard to extract a laugh from the grisly goings-on depicted on the painted cover of Cannibal Corpse's *Butchered at Birth* (1991): the title says it all. This was nothing, though, compared to the image decorating Carcass' *Reek of Putrefaction* (1988), a collage hacked into shape from autopsy photographs, which has to be hands-down winner in the "most alarming and offensive record cover of all time" category. Those in the know say that it's a vegetarian polemic against meat-eaters. That didn't stop squeamish record shops from banning it.

Defenders of metal point out its political side and say that the music is about pride, independence and free will. But it was the anti-Christian excesses of black metal that did most to bring the genre into disrepute and force it underground. Bands claiming to be Satanists daubed their faces with corpse paint and emblazoned their covers with the Satanic Baphomet sigil, an inverted pentagram containing a goat's head. Yet even black metal, for all its juvenile compulsion to mortify the faithful, can still produce moments of graphic grandeur. The cover of Darkthrone's *Sardonic Wrath* (2004) is a deftly rendered pencil drawing by Lorenzo Mariani, an Italian art student and metal fan. Taking Gustave Doré's engravings of *The Crowned Virgin* and *Last Judgement* as his models, Mariani pictures bad angels with swords, smiting a chain of naked bodies writhing in the darkness. The Darkthrone logo, thrown into relief by the unearthly light, hangs in the air like a demonic presence, meshing perfectly with the image's monumental symmetry.

Heavy metal's extremity, as a set of aesthetic choices and as a way of life, exerts a continuing fascination for observers that's part admiration, part repulsion. As with other kinds of music, fans grow older but they don't necessarily grow out of it – there are middle-aged metalheads now. Since Deena Weinstein published her scholarly *Heavy Metal: A Cultural Sociology* in 1991, academic researchers have continued to pore over the subculture, and metal offers shiny nuggets for pop anthropologists, too. Canadian artist Steven Shearer uses capitalised song titles and lyric fragments from death metal tracks in white-on-black poster poems exhibited in art galleries and, in summer 2006, on a huge external

wall in Berlin. Literary gems from the Diesel-sponsored project include the lines "Ancestral necrosodomy", "Herpetiform filthgrinder" and "Suck my unholy vomit".

The challenge today for metal's design interpreters is to find ways of referencing the genre's musical and visual heritage without regurgitating imagery that has had all the life chewed out of it. *Nightmares* (2006), an album by a young British metal band called Architects, shows it can be done. Sure, it features a screaming, disembodied head in profile, with orange flames licking around the eyes and mouth. But it's a piece of contemporary digital graphic image-making, not a cartoon-like painted scene. You might almost say it was subtle.

Poems by Steven Shearer, painted wall mural, Berlin Biennale, 2006. Photograph: Uwe Walter.

Photos Lost and Found

Our hunger for unmediated reality

In the picture, an old man in a checked shirt proudly displays a big open-mouthed bass tucked under his arm. Click. Now a small boy wearing a tie stands at attention next to a 1950s-era TV. His eyes seem to pop out of his face like a pair of black marbles. Click. This time we see a couple in the back seat of a car, framed by the rear window. Clouds of white fabric rise into view on both sides – it must be a wedding dress. The photo has a battered edge and there are little nicks and scuff marks all over the image's surface. It looks like something thrown out in the rubbish or found underfoot in the street. Click.

And so it goes on. There are 571 photos, though by the time you read this there may be more. Each click of the "next" button brings up a new snapshot: husbands and wives, mothers and children, friends, family groups, young lovers, pet owners, men in uniform, beach scenes, people in restaurants, people in the countryside, passengers on ships. Most of the pictures are undated and few of them provide any additional details about the people they show. They are celebratory shots, taken with the subject's approval. The rare exceptions are startling: a dark-haired woman leans against a roadside diner weeping; a body lies in an open casket flanked by mourners.

The website, called *Look at Me*, is one of many devoted to found photography.* The man behind it, Frederic Bonn, a creative director at Euro RSCG in New York, started his collection in 1998 with a few photos discovered in a Paris street. The pictures come from the sidewalk, from forgotten boxes at the back of the attic and from old albums acquired at flea markets. Anyone can submit photos, though the images must be at least 25 years old and personal pictures and studio shots don't qualify.

Bonn's approach is rigorous and it pays off: most of the prints have been scanned meticulously, preserving every crease, scratch, crinkled edge and discoloured border, and he presents them one by one at casual angles, as though we were chancing upon them on a table on in a drawer. It is also possible to display all 571 pictures in sequence in a vertical montage. The photos may be amateur efforts, but Bonn directs the site with a delicately professional touch that wrings every nuance of feeling from these discarded mementos.

It's the emotional implications that make found photographs so fascinating. They look much the same as the snapshots that fill our own family albums. Yet cut loose from their points of origin, they become objects of deep mystery. Who are these people? What are the stories behind these ordinary scenes? We have no way of knowing, so we can project any fantasy or speculation we like onto the image. The most obvious mystery is how these private pictures, never intended for general viewing, came to be floating around in the public domain, and the closer they are to the present, the more pressing the question. One of the stranger picture sequences on *Look at Me* shows a middle-aged man photographed in the 1960s and 1970s, usually in swimwear. He looks wealthy, like a bit of a playboy, and he evidently enjoyed his holidays in a variety of locations. Perhaps he is dead now, but how can it be that no one in his family or among his friends cared enough to look after these photos?

The interest in found photography began in the art world. Joachim Schmid, a German artist, has based his career on collecting and organising this kind of material, notably in his "Pictures from the Street" project, which began in the early 1980s. Hungarian artist and filmmaker Sándor Kardos' Horus Archive consists of more than 200,000 amateur photographs.** In a New York bookshop in 2002, American illustrator Jonathon Rosen drew my attention to a copy of Thomas Walter's *Other Pictures* (2000), a collection of amateur snapshots, many from the 1920s and 1930s, and none more recent than around 1960. I bought it immediately. "There is no faking, no strain, no theory here," writes Walther, "only the simplicity and directness of capturing moments of life." The book focuses on images with an inadvertently surreal quality resulting from blurring, odd compositions, negative effects, inexplicable light flares and serendipitous double exposures. Another collection, *Anonymous* (2004), crystallises the genre's growing appeal in its subtitle: *Enigmatic images from unknown photographers.*

The work of unknown photographers of a different kind finds a new audience in the linked genre of vernacular photography. Here, anonymous images first used in corporate literature, product brochures, trade magazines and retail catalogues are plucked from their original contexts and savoured for their unintended implications. The annual magazine *Useful Photography* (founded 2002) compiles shots of shelving systems, women's underwear, racing drivers in crash helmets, socks, protective masks, people hanging wallpaper and model train sets. The editors, who include Erik Kessels of the maverick Dutch design and advertising agency, Kesselskramer, describe this as an "an ode to the photographers we don't know by name but whose work we all know by looking at it daily". They place the captionless, uncredited pictures on a grid, allowing unrelated subjects to form deadpan combinations of these ostensibly utilitarian and, at first sight, seemingly ordinary images.

Useful Photography is as good a sign as any of the way that enthusiasm for found photographs has taken hold in design. The magazine has the matter-of-fact display style of clip art. The photos' "useful" description, as well as noting their original purpose, acts as an encouragement to reuse this imagery in any manner you please. In the same way, designers sometimes ask Frederic Bonn and curators of other notable projects – such as Astrid van Loo, the founder of the *Time Tales* website – for permission to use pictures. Permission is not actually theirs to give, because the display of these images is technically a breach of copyright, though not one likely to be pursued by anyone. At *Found* magazine, created by Davy Rothbart and Jason Bitner in 2001, the finders-keepers philosophy extends from found photos to all kinds of personal flotsam – drawings, bits of writing – collected in public places by readers who send in their peculiar chance discoveries for the editors to share with the world.

One reason for critics' and curators' preoccupation with anonymous forms of photography is the challenge it poses to the idea that only pictures by celebrated photographers deserve study. The unschooled photographer can produce images every bit as engaging, both aesthetically and in content, as anything taken by widely exhibited professionals. More broadly, these unofficial images answer a persistent need to believe that photographs can still capture some essential, unvarnished truth about the subject. Where, even before the digital era, professional photographers were often shown to have manipulated images that might appear to represent actuality, amateur photographers can still be given the benefit of the doubt. Their directness, ineptitude and lack of artifice become signs of reliability. The taste for these pictures is a measure of our enduring hunger to experience unmediated reality.

Perhaps found photographs can sometimes find applications within design projects, but there are obvious pitfalls. Ironic humour might work when applied to garish 1970s sales shots of platefuls of food, or men modelling lumberjack shirts, but it would hardly be appropriate as a way of handling pictures of ordinary people, however amusingly goofy they might appear. These photos were usually taken by family and friends to honour their subjects. The snapping of the picture was a way of declaring: you are important, you matter to me, this moment was significant and we should remember it. But the picture's warm intentions have been undone by events. It has become a relic. Its loss and reappearance in a stranger's collection are reminders of life's fragility. You may be loved today, but sooner than you imagine it might all be gone.

These images can be cruel. The scenes they show are often banal. The people in them don't always look especially good and a snapshot's only virtue, in visual terms, is frequently its awkwardness or inexpressive blankness. This is not much of a memorial. Yet, on the internet, an image never meant for public consumption can receive an unanticipated afterlife as an enigmatic record of an existence about which we know next to nothing. It doesn't get much more poignant than that.

*The *Look at Me* collection can now be found, differently presented, at https://look-at-me.tumblr.com.
**Pictures from the Horus Archive appear in *In Almost Every Picture* 15 (2019), published by KesselsKramer. A woman obliterated images of her husband's former girlfriends from old photographs, but kept the rest of the picture, which showed him.

Cut and Paste Culture

The tenacity of the collage principle

Towards the end of *Collage: The Making of Modern Art*, published in 2004, art historian Brandon Taylor posed a critical question. "Has the Internet," he wondered, "made collage more or less important as an instrument of contemporary aesthetic work?"

At that point, the answer seemed to be that if we apply a rigorous definition of collage as a process of physically cutting and gluing together image fragments to make a new image, then rather less of this was likely to happen in a digital age. If, on the other hand, we interpret the collage principle more liberally, then the evidence, Taylor concluded, already suggested that computer collage would proliferate for as long as software came with "cut" and "paste" commands. Within only a few years of this cautious assessment, collage of every kind – paper-based, digital and all points between – is rampant. Some of this collage-making is finding its way into commercial projects, but there is also plenty of personal work by designers and illustrators who are passionate about collage. *Cutting Edges* (2011), a survey by Gestalten in Berlin, assembles an international art squad of scissor-wielding collage enthusiasts and provides the perfect opportunity to take the measure of the resurgent medium.

The project's coordinator, James Gallagher, a creative director based in Brooklyn, who studied at the School of

Visual Arts in New York, is a compelling collage artist in his own right, as well as being the curator of the "Cutters" series of exhibitions in Brooklyn, Berlin and Cork. Gallagher argues that collage is the perfect medium for coming to terms with a culture saturated in images, both printed and online. "Today's collage artists carve out fragments from this frenzy and force the disparate pieces to become one," he writes. "It is their way of controlling the chaos – or at least pushing the pause button long enough for examination."

Perhaps that explanation sounds too pat, but it does appear to be a primary reason why collage never went away for long and has now returned in force. In his history of collage, Taylor addresses the role the medium played in the development of modern art throughout the 20th century. While he touches on collage's popular uses, which emerge in the 1960s counter-culture and develop through 1970s punk, the wider uptake of collage in popular culture, particularly commercialised popular culture, lies outside his sphere of inquiry. Yet it's here that collage now seems to have found a home in work that, for critical purposes, falls inconveniently into the buffer zone between the increasingly tricky to differentiate camps of art and design.

Oddly, despite assembling an arresting shop window of new projects, *Cutting Edges* does little to put the trend in context. The book's main introduction simply rehearses the art historical development of collage from Cubism and Dadaism, through Surrealism, to Pop, the Situationist International artists, and punk. There is no attempt to connect this to the new work in the book. Nor does the survey structure, with one collage-maker following another in a spectacular, un-signposted parade, make any critical distinctions between different forms of collage. It would be expecting too much for the compilers to venture any evaluative judgments – that's not in the spirit of such enterprises – but the book's presentation of everything on broadly equal terms, though some artists get more pages, certainly prompts the question: is all of this work equally good? With a method this open to all-comers, what qualities make for a good collage?

Almost every collagist in the book loves old imagery: anything photographed or printed before 1960 comes with an instant retro frisson. Any collage using such material is potentially likeable, but that doesn't make it original or cause it to vibrate with commanding inner power. Many of these new generation collagists don't know when to stop. They find source images with potential and bury them in mismatched clutter. A surprising number seem content to float elegant figures of fantasy, fine gentlemen and beautiful ladies, against decorative backgrounds pieced together from colourful snippings. Many compositions amount to little more than mute simulacra of earlier, better collages (Dada, Surrealism, and Pop cast very long shadows). A simple love of old bits of paper is rarely enough to imbue a collage with a feeling of necessity, though Canadian graphic designer Jacob Whibley's intricate constructivist paper abstracts prove it can be done.

The most convincing collagists show an obsessive focus in their image-making. According to an interview in *Elephant* magazine, which ran a survey of 17 collage artists in its winter 2011 issue, Gallagher's preferred sources are, he says, "vintage photo books, sex manuals, clothing catalogs, text books, anything that can be folded into my world". His collages usually feature one or two monochrome figures, their faces always concealed, set against open backgrounds built up from layers of paper to suggest abstracted interior spaces. A restricted palette and sparing use of random lines of type help to define his private graphic world. His aim, he says, is to reveal a zone of hidden behaviour – its beauty, ugliness, solitude, and desire. There is an obvious connection here to the work of Linder Sterling, a British punk-collage pioneer with a debt to Dada, who can make an unforgettable statement about sexual politics by placing an old mono record player over the head of a black-and-white nude torn from a men's magazine.

Ground Control by Julien Pacaud, digital collage, 2014.

Collages by Sergei Sviatchenko (Denmark), Malin Gabriella Nordin (Sweden) and Paul Burgess (UK) share Sterling's and Gallagher's concentration on particular types of imagery and methods of visual treatment. Nordin composes careful arrangements of stone-like precious objects cut from lustrous fabrics; Burgess edits and over-paints bright early 1960s advertising to imply darker relationships and undercurrents; and Sviatchenko, working in three dimensions, positions crude cut-outs of photos from revolutionary Russia against jarring pink and pale blue backdrops.

Brandon Taylor ends his history wondering "whether collage in any of its older senses of displacement and rupture will find other ways of continuity, but by other means." The answer provided by *Cutting Edges* is more straightforward than we might have expected. The bottomless ocean of imagery available on the internet gives collage-makers even greater reserves of ready-made material to filter, borrow, and manipulate, while any paper image can be digitised by scanning. Many of the digital collages that result from these processes look no different from paper collages. The aesthetic stasis in so much contemporary collage expresses an understandable nostalgia for print, even among younger artists, rather than an unqualified embrace of digital collage as a tool for responding to 21st-century modernity.

One of the most distinctive artists in *Elephant* and *Cutting Edges* is Julien Pacaud, a French illustrator who planned to become a filmmaker before discovering collage. Pacaud's use of displacement and rupture is so complete – he only works digitally – that I wonder whether "digital collage" is even the right term for what he does. He blends his source images seamlessly into pictorial scenes that might, as he says, belong to an imaginary film. Whatever the people were doing when he extracted them from their original settings, they become actors in a new hyper-real drama. In one image, an Edwardian lady looks reverently at the grass, while another woman in the distance, holding hands with a companion, points to the sky where two huge planets hang above slender monoliths of light. Pacaud can sometimes overdo the portentous geometry (cubes, pyramids, spheres) but his re-colourised tableaux look like fully contemporary visions and he is in constant demand as an image-maker.

Here, the collage principle is so fully absorbed that these images no longer look like collages.

Throwaway Aesthetics

The transformation of graphic waste

After a lecture, a British artist and publisher named
Tony Hayward approached me with a slender book in
hand, containing some fine sepia photographs of Indian-
made rat traps. In the Hindu faith, the rat is regarded
as a sacred animal and a bringer of good luck, despite
the great health risks posed by rodents. The traps in
the photos were intuitively conceived and beautifully
fashioned by local craftsmen from waste materials. They
mainly used wire, but in a few cases the walls, ramps and
flaps were cut out of old tin containers. The last thing an
inquisitive rat would see before its incarceration would be
promotional graphics for engine parts, Fujicolor film, or
Cuticura talcum powder – a popular brand in India.

There is something immensely satisfying about
objects made from parts and materials that would
otherwise have been thrown away. These gently
subversive inventions intrigue, charm and gladden the
heart. As the great Patti Smith sings in "25th Floor",
"The transformation of waste is perhaps the oldest
preoccupation of man." Even before we started to worry
so much about sustainability, the process represented a
kind of everyday alchemy: the base material of garbage –
spent, downgraded, discarded and unloved – is
ingeniously transmuted into something splendidly
useful. But it's almost always more than that. The new
hand-forged artefact possesses an allure, an artfulness,

a magic and mystery that often makes it far more desirable than the manufactured version, which offers the same, or even superior, function. If I ever find myself in need of a rat trap, I'd much prefer to buy a recycled Indian one.

The strange thing about garbage is that the trick of transformation can be worked irrespective of function. All that's necessary is to extract the detritus from its usual context. When it's underfoot in the street or consigned to the dump, every kind of garbage looks redundant, negligible and impure. Most of the time, we prefer not to look at trash at all, assuming that it is unworthy of our attention. When the trash can overflows and the waste matter breaks out of its allotted area, we want order restored as soon as possible. If dirt is "matter out of place", in the famous anthropological formulation, then garbage out of place is just as likely to cause offence.

Yet put a frame around the trash (implied or actual) and it can become a compelling object of interest. In 2001, a School of Visual Arts student named Justin Gignac began selling garbage for $10–$100 a pop. Gignac wanted to show the importance of packaging in making something – anything at all – impossible to resist, and he started enclosing carefully chosen trash samples "hand-picked from the fertile streets of NY, NY" in clear plastic packages dignified with the legend "Garbage of New York City". The project continues and Gignac, a former advertising man who is now an artist, claims to have sold more than 1,300 of the hygienic little cube sculptures to garbage aficionados in 29 countries.

Although Gignac is clearly onto a good thing, only the scale of the enterprise and the populist price are new. Artists have been reclaiming lowly trash and upgrading it to become collectible gallery art for the last century. One of the purest examples of this tendency (if "pure" isn't a misleading word here) is the 1960s French-born, naturalised American artist known by the single name Arman.

Arman had a genius for reclamation. One piece of his, *Poubelle* (1971), consists of the entire contents of a trash

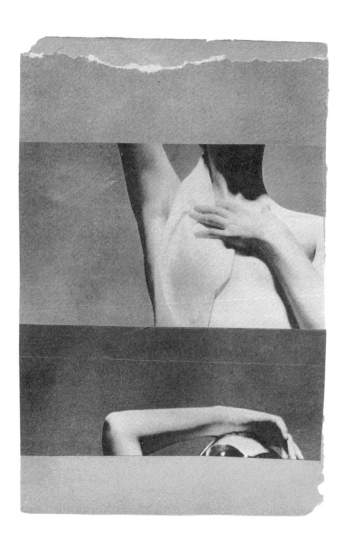

Single Cuts 133 by Katrien De Blauwer, collage, 2018.

can displayed in a vertical glass case like the crushed and half-obscured revelations of some future archaeological dig. He also liked to direct our attention to the distinguishing features of particular kinds of cast-offs. One early Arman consists of nothing but used dentures. Other pieces ask us to consider the insistent, peculiar, utility-stripped "thingness" of watch faces, electric razors, vials, doll hands, squeezed-out toothpaste tubes, gas masks and women's high-heeled shoes (title: *Madison Avenue*, 1962).

Arman's fellow New Realists were just as attracted to waste. Jacques Villeglé built a career out of tearing down the thick layers of tattered street posters that accumulated on Parisian walls, finding in these brutalised surfaces images of beguiling delicacy. His pieces, presented in the gallery like paintings, were a form of collage composed largely by the invisible hand of chance, then given a bit of assistance by the artist. Looking at Villeglé's trash-pictures, which never fail to entrance me, I find myself wondering how something so ripped to shreds could come out looking so good.

For graphic image-makers, collage remains the instrument by which defunct printed matter is reanimated into strange new life. "Cut and paste" is one of the great cultural ideas of the modern era, with applications across all the arts. The history of collage spans the 20th century, and based on present evidence, it looks likely to run through the cultural production of this century, too. The more visual things we make, the more material we have lying around to cut up and reassemble into pleasing and meaningful new shapes. It's hard to imagine a time when the urge to transform this kind of waste would simply wither away. If anything, our increasingly textureless digital existence (could there be a less haptic surface than a touch screen?) has encouraged designers and image-makers to re-engage with the physicality of things. The more we try to limit the use of paper in the coming decades – because we should – the more appealing the substance will look and feel.

The transformation of waste by means of collage, though comparable to the use of bits of old wire and tin to build a trap, is not the same kind of recycling. An Indian rat trap redirects existing materials and puts them to new practical use, and its fabrication requires few resources. However appealing it looks, it exists only to catch unwanted intruders. In a society that regularly built its traps in this way, there would be much less need for manufactured traps that consumed new materials. Although making a collage has the small virtue of being an inexpensive way to construct an image, anyone concerned with paper as a finite resource would do better to collect waste paper and return it for processing so it could be used again.

The impulse to make a collage serves a different purpose. The collagist is usually engaged in the symbolic, rather than actual, rearrangement of reality. Elements of the collage – a hand, a bird, a bicycle, a chair – come from the world we know; we can often identify their provenance and date them to a decade. But their new setting is a kind of proposition in compressed visual form that pictures an idealised or even utopian dimension. In the combinatorial space defined by a collage, colours change, ordinary perspective collapses, the usual scale and relationship between things is inverted (a flower dwarfs a person, a head becomes an eye), different eras in history fold together, and figuration and abstraction merge together on the same visual plane.

The idea of waste matter is intrinsically displeasing. But the collage-maker knows otherwise and refuses to allow waste to go to waste. In plan chests and filing cabinets, lovingly assembled hoards of cut-out pictures and strips of torn paper await their moment. Their chance combinations, as they repose in the drawers, will often suggest new images. By a paradoxical twist, the collage's surface area becomes an arena of intensified aesthetic attention. In a successfully achieved collage, superfluous and otherwise unwanted visual matter – trash by any other name – is transfigured and redeemed, and the garbage comes back to us as a paper jewel.

Strained Relations

Relational aesthetics and relational design

The French curator and writer Nicolas Bourriaud's book *Relational Aesthetics* is the most influential work of art criticism to appear in the past decade. First published in 1998 and translated into English in 2002, it's a fashionable art-world bestseller that can be found in any gallery bookshop. Bourriaud defines "relational aesthetics" as a theory that judges artworks "on the basis of the inter-human relations which they represent, produce or prompt". Relational art, he says, concerns itself with "the whole of human relations and their social context, rather than an independent and private space" – by which he seems to mean the private space of both the artist and the viewer.

The work of Rirkrit Tiravanija, a Thai artist based in New York and Berlin, is often given as an example of relational art. Tiravanija creates events in galleries where he cooks and gives away food (Thai curries, for example) to anyone who wants to join in and eat. The art lies not in the formal or material aspects of the occasion, but in the interactions and relationships that spontaneously occur between the artist and the people who take part. It offers the consolation of "everyday microtopias" where it is possible to find pleasurable moments of sociability free from the manipulations of the highly commercialised public sphere. As Bourriaud writes, "Meetings, encounters, events, various types of collaboration between people, games, festivals, and places of conviviality, in a word all manner of encounter and relational invention thus represent, today, aesthetic objects likely to be looked at as such."

It was only a matter of time before designers and design critics started wondering whether relational aesthetics might be applied in some way to graphic design. In 2006, the British writers Monika Parrinder and Colin Davies, founders of the website *Limited Language*, argued in *Eye* magazine that the central ideas of relational aesthetics can "open up a broader way of thinking about communication and the effects of its dissemination in the world". It was a brave attempt, but not entirely convincing. While it is possible to find graphic design projects that offer some degree of interactivity or draw people into a relationship with a space, projects that promote social relationships between people are rare. Parrinder and Davies cite a room at Tate Britain in London – designed by the studio A2/SW/HK – where visitors to the annual Turner Prize exhibition could write their comments about the art on cards and hang them on the wall. They claim that this is "more than a simple method of feedback; it is about meeting and creating a live community." Fascinating as these cards were to read, I saw no evidence that they had the power to cause complete strangers to break into debate about art or anything else.

Relational aesthetics is at root a political idea – Bourriaud describes how the relationship between people is "symbolised by goods or replaced by them, and signposted by logos". Clearly, this is a world shaped by design. Today, he suggests, we are presented with the "illusion of an interactive democracy in more or less truncated channels of communication". Thus, you can write your opinion on the wall at Tate Britain, but it has no influence on the selection process for the prize, or the jury's decision about the winner. Participation is an illusion. The system, controlled by the curators, continues much as it always did.

Difficulties also arise in a *Design Observer* blog post by Andrew Blauvelt, head of design at the Walker Art Center in Minneapolis. Blauvelt argues ambitiously that, after design's formal and semantic phases, we are now in a third phase of modern design history, which is relationally based and contextually specific. Blauvelt must have known that his title, "Towards Relational Design", would immediately bring to mind Bourriaud's relational aesthetics for some readers (Parrinder and Davies imply the term, but don't use it), but nowhere in his article does he explain the connections or differences. When questioned about this in a comment, Blauvelt replied that although he is very aware of relational aesthetics, he "chose not to 'go there' because it doesn't offer a comprehensive enough theory that could possibly bridge the divide between contemporary art culture and specific design practices."

In that case, we might ask, why use the term "relational" at all, especially when this new usage also risks confusion with relational database design, a well-established term in computing? In fact, Blauvelt's rather abstract description of relational design – the most detailed example in his post concerns vacuum cleaners rather than graphics – does suggest areas of thinking in common with Bourriaud. Blauvelt, too, is for real-world settings rather than unattainable utopias. Noting the influence of digital developments such as interactivity, open source collaboration and social networking, he focuses on design's performative and participatory aspects and its "ability to facilitate social interactions".

The art writer Claire Bishop, a critic of relational aesthetics, has pointed out its supporters' tendency to assume that any encounter that permits social interaction, regardless of its content, must be inherently democratic, without showing how these encounters are valuable. "If relational art produces human relations," she writes, "then the next logical question to ask is what types of relations are being produced, for whom, and why?"

That question is even more trenchant and pressing when it comes to graphic design as a medium of public communication, for the reasons Bourriaud indicates. Yet Blauvelt doesn't address these essentially political issues, preferring upbeat but vague allusions to "open-ended rather than closed systems" and "connected ecologies", even as he acknowledges that the public is viewed instrumentally (by commercial organisations) as a social entity to be "exhaustively data-mined and geodemographically profiled". Here, "relational" starts to sound like a euphemism for ever more subtle forms of social monitoring and control. If this is the era of relational design and if graphic design really is a part of it, then Bishop's clear-sighted question – what types of relations, for whom and why? – remains the one we need to answer.

Critical Omissions

The origins of critical graphic design

The term "critical design" has been gaining currency in design circles for several years and, in 2007, it went public in the titles of three imaginative exhibitions. Two of these shows, in the UK and Belgium, dealt with three-dimensional design. The exhibition that concerns me here was the first I know of to apply the term to graphic design. "Forms of Inquiry: The Architecture of Critical Graphic Design" took place at the Architectural Association in London, a private school with a huge international reputation (former students include Rem Koolhaas, Richard Rogers and Zaha Hadid). The exhibition's two young curators were Mark Owens, an American designer, writer, and filmmaker, and the AA's art director, Zak Kyes, a Swiss-American.

As a term, "critical design" has plenty going for it: it sounds sharp, analytical, engaged and urgent. It also raises some questions, since its existence as a special category implies that regular design is, by contrast, *not* critical. Our view of this does, of course, depend on what we expect design to be doing. But if the implicit aim is simply to help clients sell more doodads, then all that matters is how effectively design achieves this goal. Design that lacks critical awareness of the situations in which it operates can only be a compromised activity. Critical design suggests aims and methods that are different in some fundamental ways from the norm.

Even if we allow that most design is not in any deep sense critical, it surely can't be the case that there has never been any critical design until now. Yet proponents of "critical graphic design" tend to present it as though it had arrived fully formed with no precedents. In a section of the *Forms of Inquiry* book devoted to modes of production, Kyes and Owens ask: "But what happens when the designer assumes the role of editor, publisher, and distributor outside the constraints of the familiar client/designer relationship? Taking such a position challenges the [...] service-based model of graphic design, reliant as it is on supplied content, external requests, and the division of work-flow into discrete specialisations."

These are good points, and a few graphic designers have been making them with great self-awareness and no little controversy for 20 years, if not longer. To give just one example, *Emigre* magazine was a self-initiated venture that debated such questions at length while demonstrating by its own independent example exactly what it was talking about. In the 1990s, these critical discussions were usually conducted under the banner of "the designer as author" and sometimes, especially in the Netherlands, "the designer as editor", but the similarities to contemporary critical design are clear enough. In a discussion about critical design exhibitions on *Design Observer*, design educator Steven McCarthy, co-organiser of the 1996 exhibition "Designer as Author: Voices and Visions", expressed concern that the initial post by design critic Alice Twemlow didn't "acknowledge that much of the philosophical foundation of 'critical design' resides in the theories of graphic design authorship advanced over ten years ago." This omission certainly reflected the self-positioning of many of the critical designers, who seem to want to distance themselves from these earlier debates.

In reality, some of the older graphic designers associated with critical design and featured in "Forms of Inquiry" – Paul Elliman, Armand Mevis and Linda van Deursen, and Stuart Bailey of Dexter Sinister and *Dot Dot Dot* magazine – were in the early stages of their careers as the concept of the designer as author took hold. No well-informed designer could have failed to notice these debates – Bailey even contributed to *Emigre*. At CalArts, where Kyes earned a BFA, instructors such as Lorraine Wild (who taught design history), Louise Sandhaus and Gail Swanlund were all associated with *Emigre*, and Michael Worthington was invited by Kyes and Owens to participate in "Forms of Inquiry". Jeffery Keedy and Ed Fella, central to the authorship discussion, were also influential figures at the school.

More than anything, the reluctance to acknowledge recent precedents is probably just a new generation's desire to establish its own identity, combined with a cyclic swing in graphic taste. Where the 1990s was a decade of thickly encrusted visual overload, the critical designers can't get enough don't-sweat-it typography and fastidious conceptual restraint. Their shyness about origins does seem short-sighted, though; it's just the latest example of graphic design's endemic lack of faith in its own worthiness. Art and architecture, conspicuous sources of envy among the new critical designers – many of their projects are for artists – would never make this mistake. Critical design can only gain from an explicit acceptance and conscious interrogation of its own evolving history.

There are, nevertheless, some differences of emphasis. While the new critical designers take their own agency for granted, just as post-feminists took the feminists' hard-won gains for granted, they are less concerned with what Owens, writing in *Dot Dot Dot*, calls the "market value of 'the designer as author'". They tend, at least in graphic terms, to be humbler than their predecessors. They stress their role as participants and collaborators, proclaim the value of process over final product, and rethink the means of distribution, favouring the idea of "just in time" production – a manufacturing term – to avoid needless waste. "In my graphic design practice, leaving things as found, or even taking things away, can be just as valid a design decision as making something new," says James Goggin. (It's also worth noting how tight-knit this group of like-minded colleagues appears to be. As one of the selectors for Phaidon's *Area 2* compendium, Goggin chose to include Dexter Sinister, Owens and Will Holder, who was also in "Forms of Inquiry".)

To make critical design's recent history and usage more complicated for graphic designers, the term was first applied to industrial design. Anthony Dunne and Fiona Raby devote a section to it in their 2001 book *Design Noir*, and anyone using it now should consult their discussion.* "Critical design, or design that asks carefully crafted questions and makes us think, is just as difficult and just as important as design that solves problems or finds answers," write Dunne and Raby. "Its purpose is to stimulate discussion and debate amongst designers, industry, and the public. [...] Critical design takes as its medium social, psychological, cultural, technical, and economic values in an effort to push the limits of lived experience, not the medium."

Dunne and Raby are absolutely clear about the political nature of critical design. Its task, as they see it, based on their own practice, is to develop design proposals in the form of models, publications and exhibitions that challenge conventional values. They caution that designers must avoid the pitfalls of earlier attempts at critical design and develop strategies that link it to everyday experience and engage the viewer.

Kyes and Owens don't mention Dunne and Raby in their *Forms of Inquiry* book, but the most carefully thought-out, fully realised and convincing example of critical design they present is strikingly close to Dunne and Raby's precepts. Metahaven, headed by Daniel van der Velden, Vinca Kruk, and Gon Zifroni in Amsterdam and Brussels, is a kind of graphic design think tank that uses models, proposals, essays and lectures to discover how design might facilitate new forms of critical investigation. One Metahaven project focused on the identity of the Principality of Sealand, a former Second World War anti-aircraft tower off the coast of Britain, which became a "micro-nation" in 1967 when a broadcaster declared it a sovereign state. The team's contribution to "Forms of Inquiry" dealt with the destruction of 7 World Trade Center during the afternoon of the September 11 attacks. The building's collapse was announced by BBC television 26 minutes before it happened, an event that became the focus of conspiracy theories. Metahaven's graphic report for the exhibition was a double-sided poster carrying a dense grid of data about the building.

"We as designers want to step out of the ideological deadlock offered by current politics," they write, "and explore the possibilities of design re-engaged with the imagination and the political." In their democratic view, designers are, first of all, citizens. This is energising talk, but again, the idea of the "citizen designer" has a history that shouldn't be forgotten. If critical graphic design is more than an aloof intellectual pose, it should spend less time hanging out with artists, turn its intelligence outward and communicate with the public about issues and ideas that matter now.

*Now regarded as a classic design book, *Design Noir: The Secret Life of Electronic Objects* was reissued by Bloomsbury, London, in 2021.

Critical Practice

A Swedish perspective on critique

There is an old saying that every new generation thinks it has invented sex. That is also how it sometimes seems with graphic designers and critical practice. The old-timers just didn't get it – bless them! – but now, thanks to a mysterious sudden enlightenment, the new guard sees the situation of being a graphic designer more clearly, and more critically, than anyone ever managed to see it in the past.

There is an element of this wishful thinking in *The Reader*, a thick volume published in Swedish and English, which forms part of The Iaspis Forum on Design and Critical Practice initiated in Stockholm. The forum's other components were an international seminar and a travelling exhibition, "Forms of Inquiry: The Architecture of Critical Graphic Design", first shown in 2007 at the Architectural Association in London, which inspired the whole project. I read this timely book with great interest when it appeared and I recommend it to anyone preoccupied by the question of where graphic design is now. *The Reader* contains plenty of astute observation, sharp comment and useful wisdom. It also displays signs of confusion, compounded by moments of naive self-regard, which could have been avoided if some participants had taken a more accurately historical view of even the recent past, never mind the past 100 years of graphic design.

The Reader is based on four conversations between designers, supplemented by other interviews and texts. Designers always like to add something to the brief, sometimes to the point of ignoring it entirely, and this is the case here. The proposed dialogue between Abäke and the eminent Swedish designer H.C. Ericson never happens. Instead, the designers present a meandering, ultimately pointless transcript of a car journey chat and a studio visit. This is probably meant to be charming, but it wasn't worth publishing. An email exchange between Will Holder and Samuel Nyholm is also vague and indulgent. Experimental Jetset declined to engage in a dialogue with Nille Svensson, proposing that they separately answered the same questions from the editors, allowing readers to compare their answers. Here, "rewriting the brief" pays off: these are two of the book's most absorbing and insightful texts. The dialogue between James Goggin of Practise and the four-person team Europa, which was conducted as requested, is also rewarding.

All of these individuals are designers. This is deliberate but it is also *The Reader*'s weakness. Magnus Ericsson, one of the editors, says the book is an "attempt to let these voices be heard instead of others on the outside doing the interpreting." This assertion might refer to some aspect of the situation in Sweden of which I am unaware. Another editor notes that there were "virtually no graphic design agencies" in Sweden 15 years ago, which suggests the design scene is still in formation. The reality elsewhere is that graphic designers are almost the only people talking about graphic design. In countless lectures, conferences, blogs, magazine articles and books, what discussion there is represents the designer's perspective and agenda. A critical forum would have been the perfect place to open up the discussion to other voices and other points of view.

Without this external perspective, *The Reader* falls into some highly familiar refrains. On the one hand, graphic designers declare themselves to be ideally positioned and apparently uniquely gifted to be able to become involved in every kind of endeavour. According to Goggin, the designer's "invisibility makes it easier for graphic design to infiltrate and use the systems of other disciplines (art, architecture, literature) by stealth." Mark Owens, who worked with curator Zak Kyes on "Forms of Inquiry", discerns an even more sweeping sense of entitlement among some practitioners: "being a graphic designer is more like having a passport that allows you to trespass in multiple domains, whether it be filmmaking, art, writing, publishing, curating, fashion, or even architecture."

No one pauses to question why any of these fields, already occupied by highly competent practitioners, might need "trespassing" designers to help them do the job, or what it is about graphic design education that would qualify a designer to intervene in such a range of disciplines. (If we are merely talking about carrying out graphic design tasks for these clients, then this is just business as usual.) Leaving aside the designer's understandable desire to try new things – everyone would like to do that – what does the audience have to gain from an "expanded" interpretation of graphic design's role? Also, does this new mobility work both ways? Could curators, architects, writers and fashion people start doing graphic design? Would they even want to?

This self-aggrandising vision of what graphic design could be is accompanied by plaintive expressions of doubt that have also been heard many times before. "Maybe graphic design suffers from a kind of inferiority complex and a desire to be more intellectually challenging," says Svensson. Perhaps its status is too low, he suggests, for it to be the starting point for more demanding kinds of expression. "Maybe the problem is graphic designers in general are incompetent," says Holder. "We have the theory we deserve, or at least the one we can generally understand." He wonders whether it wouldn't be best to leave others, outside graphic design, to talk about the discipline. This would be just as counterproductive as a situation where only designers talk about design.

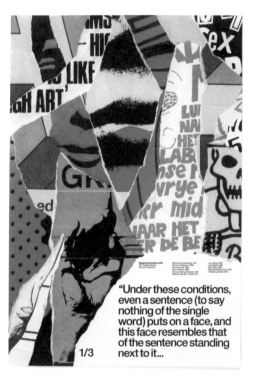

Statement and Counter-Statement by Experimental Jetset, poster project for
Graphic Design: Now in Production exhibition, Walker Art Center, Minneapolis, 2011.

3/3

"Truth becomes
something living;
it lives solely in the
rhythm by which
statement and
counter-statement
displace each
other, in order to
think each other."
—W. Benjamin

The issue of authorship lies at the heart of the dilemma glimpsed in these mutually cancelling sentiments. Authorship became a matter for discussion in the 1990s, among an earlier generation of critically minded designers, because there can be no significant expansion of the discipline, no greater visibility or enhanced status for graphic designers, without it. It is highly visible authorship in the adjacent fields that designers envy and aspire to enter (art, writing, film, fashion, architecture) that gives these fields their social, professional and cultural capital. Goggin, however, sees the "designer as author" debates as "digressive" and suggests that we should forget about the concept. Owens regards graphic authorship as an example of graphic design's use of second-hand terminology – more graphic design self-doubt – that ended up morphing "into a shorthand for a kind of market-savvy, entrepreneurial form of self-promotion". (This debatable claim is a good example of why critical discussion of graphic design needs to be more sensitive to context. What Owens says might be true of the US, though he provides no examples, but it wasn't the case in Britain, where design authorship was much slower to be discussed and never widely accepted as a concept.)

Other participants in *The Reader* take a more pragmatic and strategic view of authorship, though this way of thinking has also been visible in the practice for decades. Stuart Bailey, who co-founded *Dot Dot Dot* magazine in 2000, reports that the "relative scarcity of 'good work'" from clients provided him and his collaborators with the impetus to create outlets for themselves in their own projects. "I'm convinced that my success as a designer is mainly due to the fact that one can sense the author in my design, a personal 'voice'," says Svensson. This, too, makes sense. Why should I, as a viewer, be attracted to and convinced by visual messages in which the author is invisible? Who, in the absence of any apparent author, is speaking through the work? One could argue that a key problem that bedevils contemporary visual communication today is the impersonal tone, off-the-shelf visual language, prosaic corporate voice and nakedly manipulative instrumentality of so many communications. Fully authored graphic design is often much richer, as the history of graphic design has repeatedly shown. If graphic designers give up on these possibilities, beaten into submission by the reductive notion of "everyone as author" (Goggin's phrase), the practice will wither and the irrepressible urge to create open, complex visual messages that say something deeply felt and meaningful about our experiences will emerge elsewhere.

The Reader does offer a handful of examples of what a more sophisticated way of talking about graphic design can sound like. Is it only a coincidence that two of these contributions come from Dutch designers? Where many graphic designers, even those who aspire to be critical, lack the theoretical tools needed to fully understand their position, both Experimental Jetset and Metahaven seek to incorporate insights gained from regular wide reading into their philosophies and working methods. In an interview with the editors, Experimental Jetset cite Karl Marx, Jacques Derrida, Guy Debord's *The Society of the Spectacle* (an early influence), Herbert Marcuse's *The Aesthetic Dimension*, and an essay about socialism and print by Régis Debray published in the journal *New Left Review*. This isn't just name-dropping. They discuss these sources in clear, unpretentious language and show why they are important for the team's conception of design. They argue that making is a form of thinking, that ideology is a product of design and that every designer is an ideologist, whether he or she realises it or not.

With a bravura flourish that is almost enough to make one believe graphic design really does have the potential to be the bedrock of civilised, social democratic visual expression, Experimental Jetset apply Marcuse's idea that "aesthetics is a form of radical political praxis in itself" to their task as designers, declaring that "the true political potential of a designed object is foremost located in its aesthetic dimension." By "aesthetics" they mean not only the composition of formal elements in the work, but also the composition of ideas and allusions. They believe, as I do, that the solution to the condition of social alienation described by Marx lies, at least in part, in the "de-alienating power" of aesthetics, and they profess an unswerving modernist faith in the transformative, utopian potential of free aesthetic form.

If this sounds strange in the context of contemporary graphic design, and perhaps even suspect, it is because we so rarely hear design discussed in anything other than commercial and professional terms. Most graphic design is totally depoliticised, relentlessly middlebrow and proud of it. It isn't going to change in essence, though it may well get worse, since, as Metahaven rightly observe, "Our discipline has already become fully instrumentalized." The designers featured in *The Reader* stand, with varying degrees of acuity, for an alternative. Experimental Jetset assert their commitment to "strong, almost hermetic ideas" realised through form. Why shouldn't at least some graphic design offer communication as personal, challenging and involving to the viewer as literature, film or art? Worrying about whether or not design is trying to be art is a red herring. Most of the designers here want their work to be accepted on equal terms, but no one claims that art and design are the same.

Strangely, it is the project's initiators, Kyes and Owens, who seem most anxious to argue with opponents who aren't cited and might not even exist. They insist on a distinction between "Critical Design" (capitalised), as a "categorical or polemical designation", and "critical practices" (lowercase), as explored in their exhibition. They seem curiously affronted by any attempt to link the two terms, despite the fact that (a) critical design (its originators don't capitalise it) began as a method of critical practice and the terms are increasingly likely to be used interchangeably; (b) they use the term "critical graphic design" in their exhibition subtitle; and (c) the key word in both coinages is, in any case, "critical". Kyes and

Owen's defence of the imagined purity of their curatorial concept, which is merely a launch pad in the book for broader discussion, hinders them from recognising committed fellow travellers in the search for critical modes of designing, whatever form this might happen to take.

After all, as design researcher Ramia Mazé writes in her concluding essay, the crucial question we must ask is "critical of what?" and the crucial part of the question – as Experimental Jetset and Metahaven show every sign of thinking – concerns design's political relation with society. It's a shame this clarion call was placed at the end of the book: it ought to have been the editors' starting point. Clearly, though, there is great scope, in Sweden and elsewhere, for further exploration of the aims and methods of critical practice, ideally involving a broader mix of voices next time. If it is to succeed, critical practice must bring with it clients, collaborators, critical viewers and other believers in the vital social and cultural need for a "graphosphere" (Debray's term). So let's involve them in the conversation.

At the heart of any future debate, we would also do well to focus on one of the most telling ideas in *The Reader*, an issue that even critical graphic designers are inclined to neglect because they take what they do for granted. Once you step out of the circle, though, and look at the discipline with detachment, this is the essential challenge. "If graphic design wants to move from being an applied art to becoming an autonomous form of expression," suggests Svensson, "it has to do so by demonstrating its unique worth – that there are methods with which graphic design can communicate in a way that other disciplines cannot." What exactly, then, is graphic design's unique worth?

Critical Condition

Critical design's unfulfilled promise

In 2008, I wrote a column about a phenomenon labeled "critical graphic design", which at that point appeared to be emerging. My essay (see page 272) focused on the catalogue to an exhibition titled "Forms of Inquiry: The Architecture of Critical Graphic Design". This was the first use of the term in connection with a public manifestation or event and the show went on to travel to art schools and similar venues for a few years. The catalogue's editors, Mark Owens and Zak Kyes, weren't pleased by my comments and we had a brief exchange, published on *Print*'s website.

In the years since, I have written about critical graphic design from time to time, but the tendency has never seemed adequately debated, never quite real, as a Google search soon confirms.* In the absence of a widely used definition, we could adapt the wording of Anthony Dunne and Fiona Raby's definition of critical design as it applies to products, and say that critical graphic design "uses speculative design proposals to challenge narrow assumptions, preconceptions and givens about the role graphic communication plays in everyday life."

If something significant for professional practice had been going on – I'm using "professional" in the widest sense – then one would have expected to see many articles discussing it in the design press, yet the subject has been greeted largely by indifference. To my knowledge, *Eye* has never published a critical report on critical graphic design,

June 10, 2008
Meseburg, Germany

June 5, 2010
Meseberg, Germany

June 11, 2008
Meseberg, Germany

August 25, 2010
Berlin, Germany

August 26, 2009
Berlin, Germany

June 28, 2011
Berlin, Germany

May 22, 2012
Berlin, Germany

July 8, 2009
l'Aquila, Italy

January 9, 2012
Berlin, Germany

July 15, 2008
Berlin, Germany

February 2, 2012
Beijing, China

November 19, 2010
Berlin, Gemany

February 12, 2008
Berlin, Germany

April 28, 2010
Berlin, Germany

March 15, 2011
Berlin, Germany

June 9, 2011
Berlin, Germany

February 9, 2009
Berlin, Germany

September 28, 2009
Berlin, Germany

October 27, 2009
Berlin, Germany

June 1, 2012
Berlin, Germany

September 9, 2008
Berlin, Germany

June 17, 2011
Berlin, Germany

July 18, 2008
Nuremberg, Germany

April 3, 2009
Baden Baden, Germany

October 29, 2010
Muninch, Germany

June 16, 2011
Berlin, Germany

June 20, 2011
Frankfurt, Germany

February 17, 2012
Berlin, Germany

May 15, 2012
Berlin, Germany

July 8, 2008
Toyako, Japan

February 23, 2011
Berlin, Germany

February 5, 2011
Munich, Germany

October 1, 2008
Berlin, Germany

March 31, 2009
Berlin, Germany

June 1, 2008
Berlin, Germany

November 14, 2011
Leipzig, Germany

Pantone Merkel, The Spectacle of the Tragedy by Noortje van Eekelen,
research project, 2012.

and nor has *Print*. Despite the list of "Forms of Inquiry" participants hailing from the artier end of design, one would struggle to name even five designers who have since the exhibition proven to be publicly and strongly committed to the concept and what it might represent. The one salient exception is the research-led Dutch design team Metahaven, author of the books *Uncorporate Identity* (2010) and *Black Transparency* (2015). If there were plenty of designers operating at the same level of ambition and impact, then critical graphic design would by now be a force to be taken seriously and a topic for wide discussion.

Regardless of its low visibility in the professional mainstream, critical graphic design has persisted – as term, idea and design mode – within graphic design education, particularly at MFA level. Anyone studying over the last few years at institutions such as Yale University or Rhode Island School of Design in the US, or at the Sandberg Institute or Werkplaats Typografie in the Netherlands, will be familiar with "Forms of Inquiry" and its milieu. Some impressive student projects can be found online, though they aren't necessarily classified as critical graphic design, and only insiders, or people who follow the output of particular design schools, are likely to see them. Something of the flavour of this educational culture can be gleaned from a Tumblr started two years ago, titled "Critical Graphic Design". Its tone is humorous and satirical, suggesting an engagement with the theme that is ambivalent, if not sometimes hostile.

A poem on the Tumblr, titled "Love. Of Critical Graphic Design", begins: "I want to fuck you/in front of/works of critical graphic design/in front of installations/ [...] performances/video graphic design/at a graphic design gallery/or at a graphic design auction/while people call out lot numbers/and bang gavels." And so it goes on for many lines. I thought it was hilarious until I realised it was a steal from a poem on the *n+1* literary website. The words "contemporary art" repeated like a mantra, have been changed throughout to "critical graphic design".

In the wickedly accurate "Critical Graphic Design Song" (2013) by Michael Oswell, who worked at Metahaven for a while, Oswell intones the names of Zak Kyes and Czech type designer Radim Peško, who featured in "Forms of Inquiry", to the point of absurdity in a cod-threatening mid-European accent over an ominous techno beat. These are obviously household names to the critical design crowd.

In a rare article about critical graphic design posted on *Design Observer*, Francisco Laranjo, a doctoral candidate at the London College of Communication, draws attention to the Critical Graphic Design Tumblr and laments the way that graphic jokes and parodies have become substitutes for more formal critiques of critical graphic design projects. He gives some compelling examples of this kind of initiative, including *Taxodus* by Femke Herregraven, *Drone Survival Guide* by Ruben Pater, and *The Spectacle of the Tragedy* by Noortje van Eekelen, which can all be found online.

But Laranjo, who is situated within design education, tends to overestimate the interest of student work for external observers.** Students of history or literature often produce accomplished writing, but we don't expect the outside world to pore over their school essays. We wait for noteworthy public contributions from these individuals in their subsequent careers. We want to see existing channels occupied and transformed. At a time when graphic design criticism appears to be in general decline, it isn't so surprising that student projects have failed to inspire a detailed public critical response. It's equally unsurprising that students don't publish formal critiques of each other's projects. Even if they were to do so, how would this connect to a wider critical discourse, if that's what we still hope for from critical graphic design?

In any consideration of the issue, it is always worth going back to Dunne and Raby's concept of critical design – introduced in Dunne's book *Hertzian Tales: Electronic Products, Aesthetic Experience and Critical Design* (1999). Dunne and Raby told me that the initial uptake was slow and that, by around 2005, they had more or less stopped using the term. Then, in 2006, MIT Press reissued the book, giving it international distribution, and critical design is now established as a stance in the experimental industrial design and interactive design communities, though its use is complicated by the emergence of related concepts such as "speculative design" and "design fiction". The same thing is happening in graphic design. The "All Possible Futures" exhibition (2014), curated by Jon Sueda at the SOMArts Cultural Center in San Francisco, focused on speculative design. Sueda was a participant in "Forms of Inquiry" and included ten of the 19 designers or design teams in his show, as well as Zak Kyes' studio, Zak Group.

Despite my occasional critical remarks about the vagueness of critical graphic design, I have always argued for and supported the idea of using design for more critical purposes. Laranjo believes that critical graphic design's moment (not that it has been much of a moment) may be passing and that newer, more fashionable terms will supersede it, although the ideas and methods they represent may not be so different. Recent attempts by student thesis writers to summarise criticality in design display a regrettable tendency to look inward. "Critical practice is more about expressing disciplinary issues or concerns in ways that help define and strengthen the graphic design discipline," writes Amanda Thomas, who studied MFA Communication Design at Texas State University, on the Walker Art Center blog.

If critical graphic design were to become a consolidated, fully evolved mode of practice, then it's highly likely that it would strengthen graphic design as a profession by deepening its thinking, enhancing its reputation, and extending its influence. But this cannot be the sole or even main motivation for undertaking such projects. The primary aim should be to produce work that addresses and interrogates communication needs and issues – not the meta-problems of being a designer – and that proves itself to be beneficial to society in some way.

"I worry that critical design is only preaching to the choir," observed Susan Yelavich, associate professor at The New School for Design, in a debate about non-graphic critical design on the Museum of Modern Art's website. "Work like this needs to move into the space of editorials and essays that are read outside of the design community." This is surely true. Dunne and Raby said as much from the start. Yet the argument has not been made with conviction – looking outwards beyond graphic design's borders – by practitioners willing to identify themselves as critical graphic designers. Whatever we are going to call the activity, it remains the case that the world needs more critically engaged graphic communicators.

*In three-dimensional design, critical design has been taken more seriously as a developing branch of practice. See Matt Malpass' *Critical Design in Context: History, Theory, and Practices*, Bloomsbury, London, 2019.
**The Spectacle of the Tragedy* was a spectacular exception, attracting media interest from *The Guardian*, *Daily Mail*, *Le Monde*, *La Repubblica* and *Die Zeit*.

The Not So New Ugly

The fake rebellion of impure design

An article by *Creative Review*'s editor Patrick Burgoyne, published in 2007, bore the arresting title "The New Ugly". The possibility that ugliness in graphic design had once again become a burning issue grabbed my attention, but I wasn't convinced that his examples – the London 2012 Olympics logo and a couple of magazines, *Super Super* and *032c* – amounted to a significant or compelling trend. (We'll pass over the enduring mystery of why the Games' organisers felt it useful to saddle an event supercharged with international goodwill with a graphic device of such grotesquely unlovable ineptness.)

Something curious and misshapen was stirring in the undergrowth, though, and the publication by Gestalten in Berlin of *Pretty Ugly: Visual Rebellion in Design* (2012) confirms that a tendency that would once have caused dismayed design industry leaders to throw around epithets like "garbage" is now well entrenched in parts of Europe. The book has a sprinkling of Anglo-American designs, but most of the evidence comes from France, Belgium, the Netherlands, Germany, the Czech Republic, Poland and Bulgaria, and most of the work was created in the last few years by studios founded as recently as 2007 and 2008. Few of the names – Helmo, Antoine + Manuel, Jurgen Maelfeyt, Cox and Grusenmeyer, Bureau Mirko Borsche, Anymade Studio, Noviki, Poststudio – are widely known.

For anyone who remembers the last great splurge of "ugly" design in the 1980s and early 1990s, none of the work in *Pretty Ugly* will come as much of a surprise; nor is it likely to cause the same kind of controversy. There will be no Randian outpourings of scorn this time, no paroxysms of head shaking, finger wagging and sighs of "What are we coming to?" in response to this collection. Whichever way you read the title – as "fairly ugly" or "attractively ugly" – the wording freely admits that this is a more tractable and agreeable kind of unsightliness, while the subtitle's claim that this work is a "visual rebellion" is sweetly disingenuous. The real rebellion of the contemporary era happened a long time ago in graphic design inspired by the 1960s counterculture, by 1970s punk and politics, by 1980s deconstruction, by 1990s grunge. Today's graphic design culture, an enlightened play space in which a book like *Pretty Ugly* is not remotely disquieting, is the beneficiary and product of all of these rebellious influences, and aesthetic pluralism has been our "condition" for years. Whether designers choose to exploit this openness is up to them – many don't and from the mid-1990s, plenty retreated into neo-modernist visual certainties – but even so, anything is now theoretically possible, on a stylistic level, in graphic design.

In 1993, when Steven Heller wrote his notorious essay "Cult of the Ugly" for *Eye*, we had not come so far. Many of the big challenges to design-business sobriety, from psychedelia to punk and the new wave, had happened in areas of musical subculture that were marginal to mainstream design. A shared sense of what decorous professional graphic design should be still existed and Heller was determined to defend it. As then-editor of *Eye*, I was happy to run his piece in the interest of provoking debate, though I admired and had published a lot of the design under attack. Heller's argument required something of a balancing act. He knew that dissonant forms could be powerful devices – from Futurism and Dada to 1960s newsstand magazines and Swiss Punk. "When Art Chantry uses naive or ugly design elements he

Endangered Ghost, poster, TIC Gallery, Prague, 2011. Design: Anymade Studio.

transforms them into viable tools," Heller wrote. What Heller objected to was what he saw as visual chaos born of self-indulgent excess and he feared that this hip "style" would be applied without discrimination.

In Heller's definition, "ugly design, as opposed to classical design (where adherence to the golden mean and a preference for balance and harmony serve as the foundation for even the most unconventional compositions) is the layering of unharmonious graphic forms in a way that results in confusing messages."

Heller misread some designers he later came to appreciate (notably Ed Fella) and his essay ignited a firestorm of complaints. There was truth in his predictions, though, and a vast amount of poorly conceived ugly design ensued. Recently, I went through a box of samples in my attic that designers around the world sent me at the time. I threw almost all of them away because I knew I could never do anything with them, and they weren't worth keeping any more. Clearly, as Heller maintained, there is a vital difference between "good ugly" and "bad ugly", and that difference must lie in qualities of formal resolution – the presence of an underlying order, even within work that might appear "confused" to the uninitiated – as well as in a design's integrity of conception and purpose.

One of the most interesting issues Heller raises in "Cult of the Ugly" is just as relevant to the design in *Pretty Ugly*: do the social and cultural conditions of our time involve the kind of upheaval that can often lead to "critical ugliness"? In the case of 1990s design, Heller felt that the work lacked sufficient justification. This conclusion was inevitable if one applied the yardstick of historical crisis, such as war. But 1990s ugly design was still a response to its time. It first anticipated, and then gained added impetus from, a new technological freedom that gave designers much greater control of production and, with it, the possibility of experimenting more easily with form. It also reflected wider trends in postmodern culture under late capitalism: an ever-increasing emphasis on the visual realm, a relentless questioning of old ideas and assumptions, and a defiant assertion of new forms of identity.

The compilers of *Pretty Ugly* – the book is weirdly attributed to their website, TwoPoints.Net, in a tiny credit line inside – make no reference to the history of ugly design or to postmodernism in their ultra-minimal text. But it's hard not to see the work as bearing many of the same characteristics. Just consider the section titles: "Deviant", "Mundane", "De-constructed", "Impure", "Mishmash", "Deformed", and "Neo-artisanal". If we take the most obviously secondhand of these, "De-constructed", the editors explain this as, "De-constructing [sic] our cultural heritage: breaking it down to its basic elements until it can be constructed as something new." This kind of knowing appropriation and repurposing is the essence of the postmodern design method applied and critically elucidated 20 years ago. The same could be said of the impurity that comes through mixing disparate sources, or of the "mishmash" effect of allowing several narratives to exist simultaneously in a design.

The complexity and awkwardness of form is a means of projecting the authentic human element in design work, and though this might seem too mild an aim (when compared to full-blown activism) to deserve the word "rebellion", it is certainly a vital gesture of defiance against the curbed ambitions and conformity of so much market-led design. "For us it's clear that we don't use these kind of elements to shock people," the Belgian designers Ines Cox and Lauren Grusenmeyer say in the book. "In most cases it's rather a natural visual outcome of an idea. We use certain aesthetics because they communicate an idea in a certain way. It is intentional, yes, but we don't measure according to 'good' or 'bad'."

However ungainly the examples in *Pretty Ugly* might look to some eyes, this is a perfectly standard and unimpeachable rationale for communication design. I can imagine there are still plenty of Swiss-loving gridniks who would find this work not to their taste, and it will probably be a bit too retinal for conceptual minimalists, although the uglies share the same background and influences – people like Armand Mevis and Linda van Deursen, Experimental Jetset, Julia Born, and Jop van Bennekom. I would lay money that this is one of those exercises in catchy naming where the participants don't especially like their designation and don't see themselves as being engaged in "ugly design" at all. I enjoy a lot of the work and embrace its visual energy and willingness to use graphic form. At this point, though, "ugly" is just a red herring. That was yesterday's battle and it doesn't need to be fought again.

The End of Graphic Design
as We Know It?

The social necessity of
visual communication

"I'm worried about graphic design. It's at a critical turning point. The window of opportunity is about to close." The speaker is Richard Buchanan, distinguished American design professor and co-founder of the journal *Design Issues*. The place is the London College of Communication, where the "New Views 2: Conversations and Dialogues in Graphic Design" conference – organised by Teal Triggs of LCC and Laurene Vaughan of RMIT University in Melbourne – is drawing to an end. Buchanan's role, as invited observer and *éminence grise*, is to sum up what has taken place during the last two days.

It is an impossible task and Buchanan tells us straight away that he intends to do no such thing. I can see his point. In its programme, structure and insistence that everyone attending take part in the dialogue, this has been the most unorthodox conference I have ever attended. I went along as an observer, intending to review the event, and wound up becoming a participant myself. The official speakers submitted abstracts of the papers they hoped to deliver in the usual way – these texts could be read in the conference handbook – but then all of this personal research was, figuratively speaking, thrown out of the window. Instead of presenting their work, speakers were assigned to one of six thematic groups. Each team's task was to spend two days in a room together pondering the challenges facing graphic design and the way forward. At the end, they delivered their conclusions to the rest of the conference.

Rather than attempting to summarise all this – you can't be in six places at once – Buchanan treated us to some general observations about the state of graphic design. The conference's agenda-setting ambitions, as he pointed out, were hardly new. Graphic designers and design educators have been worrying for years about where the discipline is heading, though as he noted, graphic design remains more of a "field" than a true discipline. As Buchanan sees it, the news for graphic designers is mostly troubling. The practice is at a fragile moment, he says, and may not make it through the window. Other people can do what graphic designers do for less money and the interest graphic design generated 15 or 20 years ago, at the height of its professional confidence, is moving on to other subjects now. Graphic designers have been too insular and egocentric. Graphic design still fails to register as a necessary activity on the radar in key areas of society, even in business. For government (Buchanan presumably means the US government) graphic design just doesn't figure.

Even worse, Buchanan thinks the time is fast approaching when a critical public will start to ask what graphic designers have actually accomplished. As with marketing before it, the visibility of graphic design will bring accountability. "That's going to be the basis of the attack," he warns, "that we have filled more dumps and landfills than any other profession."

Buchanan was also clear that whatever graphic design becomes, "graphic design" is not the term that will be used to describe it – "Why name a field after a printing process?" While he was no longer interested in what he called the grammar and logic of graphic design, he did offer some grounds for optimism. The window of opportunity was still open so long as designers could articulate a new kind of practice, and this practice – like

"New Views 2" – would have to be based on conversation. In Buchanan's view, genuine conversation, which is to say the free exchange of ideas, has been missing in recent years from both graphic design conference halls and the territory of practice. The main conversation designers need to have now is with their clients.

It was a brilliantly assured performance. Buchanan, a specialist in these conference perorations, has perfected the gently commanding tone of the sage, dispensing the unsettling wisdom of his insights to the crowd. "The truth begins with two," he told us more than once – another allusion to the power of conversation. For half an hour or so, it all sounded pretty unarguable. Buchanan took the conference premise that design is changing quite a lot and trumped it by suggesting that none of the groups reporting back on their findings – the interdisciplinarity team, the research/innovation and new critical thinking team, and so on – had gone far enough. The interdisciplinarians, who wanted to banish graphic design in favour of simply "design" – "Graphic design should become illegal. It should not be used as a term" – were still too cautious for him. Buchanan demanded that (graphic) designers learn the language of everything from nursing to economics.

Later, though, away from the charisma of delivery, not all of this seemed quite so convincing. From educators, industry commentators and even students, we constantly hear that graphic design as we know it is somehow over, as though it were no longer possible for designers to do what they once did. My first response to such apocalyptic talk is always simply to look around, and my senses invariably tell me exactly the opposite. There is more graphic communication going on than ever. Yes, there are more platforms for design now, making the activity more complicated as a professional undertaking (and creating, one might think, more opportunities) but there appears to be no obvious diminution in output, even in traditional print areas such as books, magazines, newspapers, packaging, billboards, and every kind of promotional graphic. Whether these forms of design are as good as the best examples used to be is open to discussion. Still, there is no lack of material. "Good" graphic design was, in any case, always the exception. Most city streets are graphically wild places and they probably always will be. Many people just don't care about graphic design that much.

So, if there is as much graphic communication going on as ever, is there likely to be less need for it in future? Short of catastrophe, the answer is surely no. Is it likely, then, that the continuing or increasing need for graphic communication can be entirely met by untrained amateur designers? Here, again, no seems the most plausible answer. This is clearly the real point of contention and cause for concern in any discussion of graphic design's future framed, as this was, within the institutions of design education. The issue for them is not so much graphic communication – an activity fundamental to modern societies – as the future of graphic designers as a specially educated, tuition-fee-paying group, with an established professional identity and aspirations to a career.

Nevertheless, the uneasiness about the term "graphic design" – not a new concern – is entirely justified. Since the mid-1990s, I have preferred to describe my own sphere of interest as "visual communication", putting the emphasis on the visual outcome rather than the technical procedures involved in getting there. "Graphic design" is a pallid, unengaging description of the activity for anyone outside the design field and it has done little to stimulate public interest in graphic communication. Nor is visual communication the exclusive province of graphic designers as a professional group. One has only to look at graphic phenomena coming from other directions – fine artists, comic book artists, amateurs, vernacular sources – to find compelling alternative currents that suggest the inherent limitations of design industry-determined modes and standards of practice. I value graphic communication in all its variety more than I value the perpetuation of the graphic designer's professional class and status.

Here, an observation by Buchanan seemed especially germane. "Maybe we [designers] have been the victims of a social construction," he suggested. What I take this to mean is that professional identity, with all its institutionalised concerns and assumptions, can become a cage that restricts the occupant's view of what else might be possible outside. Craft is a good example. Certainly, graphic designers' hard-won skills and careful attention to typographic detail are important, but too many graphic designers seem obsessed with finesse at the expense of understanding the social role and meaning of their work, and then thinking through their position in the cycle of visual production. If the work is meaningless noise bound for the landfill, who cares about its typographic refinement?

Another point that struck me forcefully at "New Views 2" – ostensibly a graphic design conference – is how little sign there was that speakers cared that much about visual communication. (Getting the chance to see the fruits of people's research might have changed that impression.) While it is certainly necessary to rebalance graphic design along the lines just indicated, without a concern for the visual there won't be much left. It is true that what Buchanan called "the sharp division among the disciplines of design" has been limiting, especially for the "social construction" of graphic design, which is often seen by practitioners and theorists of three-dimensional design as a lesser activity, pushed off to the margins in its own publications and organisations. Graphic design, if we continue to call it that for now, can only benefit from being regarded as a branch of design like any other, and many of its practitioners do have the ability to think about design in non-graphic ways. (Some have been proving it for decades, from Will Burtin's science exhibits to Abram Games' Cona coffee-maker.) Yet the essential purpose of graphic design is still to shape graphic form.

Buchanan and others at "New Views 2" no longer seem very interested in this task. But if it isn't graphic design that these academic discontents want graphic design to do, then what is it they want it to do? Buchanan, who has just taken up a post in the business school at Case Western Reserve University in Cleveland, Ohio, enthused about the opening keynote lecture by Chris Downs, founding partner of Live/Work, a service design company. "Who is stealing design from the designers? And why is this the best thing that can possibly happen to the discipline?" asked Downs. (To which one possible answer is: "be careful what you wish for, Chris.") Services we encounter as customers should, of course, be planned properly, with their users in mind, and this might sometimes involve a graphic element. If they haven't been "designed" well until now, this is a failure of human awareness and common sense that must be laid squarely at the door of business, not designers. The fashionable focus on service design seen at "New Views 2" doesn't change the fact that life is richer, more interesting, more aesthetically stimulating and more efficient with visual communication carried out at the highest levels of creative intelligence.

So, sure, it's good to talk. By all means involve the client – hasn't a good client relationship always been the goal of sensitive designers? Yes, the discipline needs to be more reflective – designers have said that for years. But, please, design educators: less masochism. There is still a graphic task out there that cries out to be done.

The Place Formerly Known as Graphic Design

Design as an expanded transmedia discipline

I am in a darkened room queuing behind other people at the back of a building that was once an air-raid shelter in Amsterdam's Vondelpark. We have been instructed to pick up a torch from a basket and look around, but there are so many people pressed into the small space that all the torches have already been taken. I can see sheets of paper on the wall with mysterious rectilinear markings and I'm brushing against clothes on hangers suspended from the ceiling. At the back, there is a laptop showing pages from a book – it's hard to read at a distance in the gloom. Some kind of street protest is playing on a video monitor behind me near the entrance. I have no idea what to make of all this, and even if I had a torch and could linger, I'm not sure it would make much difference.

This multimedia installation, which took place in July 2011, was part of the graduation show for the Sandberg Institute's MFA design course. Annelys de Vet, a Dutch designer, heads the programme, and Daniel van der Velden of Metahaven is a tutor on the course. Seven designers were graduating, all women, and each student had put together a display.

The darkened room was devised by Anja Groten, a German student, and it represented a group of activists she called the Invisible Operators. We had been warned that these anonymous figures might be present among us in the room, though they wouldn't make themselves known. It was only the next day, in the student presentations, that it became fully clear that the project was about squatting in empty buildings in Amsterdam, which was made illegal in October 2010 after years of tolerance by the authorities. The enigmatic markings, to be inscribed by hand on the cement between bricks, were a secret code by which the clandestine "operators" broadcast messages, bypassing phones, email, social media and other traceable forms of digital communication.

I single out this event because I happened to take part in it – I was invited to join the graduation jury – but in many ways Groten's challenging installation was no more than one might now expect from an MFA course in graphic design, or a graduation show. Graphic design stopped looking like graphic design, as we once knew it, several years ago. Of course, one can still find posters and pieces of print to admire, but no self-respecting student at master's level pays hefty tuition fees and prolongs her education to end up looking like a throwback; graphic communication, as it once was, is no longer the inevitable focus of designers' thinking or concerns.

In a previous article, I questioned many graphic designers' apparent lack of interest in visual form, arguing that design without a concern for the "graphic" is cutting off its nose to spite its face, and risks ending up with not much of an identity at all. But this complaint takes it for granted that since the field once existed as a clearly defined activity (and identity), it should continue to exist in that form. Let's not forget, too, that even in its heyday, with a secure professional identity and consistent visual outcomes, graphic design always struggled to achieve external recognition of what it was and why it was significant. The point was often made in rueful anecdotes from designers who found themselves at a loss to explain to a doubtful relative quite what they did for a living.

The other students' projects in the Vondelpark were equally broad in their interpretation of graphic design. One took the form of a performance by an actor pretending to be the president of the Chimerican Union, a notional marriage of China and the US. He addressed us from the podium in tones of extravagant satire while a couple of women in nurses' uniforms – one of them the student, Lauren Grusenmeyer – shouted support and tried to inflame the crowd. The banners and placards were certainly graphic but secondary to the symbolic concept and writing. Later, Janneke de Rooij, a student concerned with the public's stereotypical views of Africa, attempted to subcontract the design problem by encouraging the audience to workshop graphic messages using texts and supplied pictures. A third student, Maartje Smits, showed documentaries. Her charming onscreen presence, entertaining writing and compelling voice-over suggested she might have the makings of a future Miranda July: writer, storyteller, visualiser and filmmaker.

The next day, at the presentations, Smits was introduced as a poet, which she also is, and she openly stated her plan to be an artist. Afterwards, in a jury meeting with the MFA tutors, I asked what any of this had to do with graphic design, posing the question from the perspective of the old, fixed view of the discipline – it is, nevertheless, the natural thing to ask. Rob Schröder, a tutor and a former member of the radical design team Wild Plakken, argued that students such as Smits, a graduate of the Rietveld Academy's "Language and Image" course, are perfectly suited to the design MFA. (It's worth noting that Schröder's career spans graphic design and documentaries.) He wasn't specific, perhaps because he is too fully immersed to separate the elements anymore, but I can understand his point of view. I have met many people in graphic design who might just as easily have studied art, photography, digital media or film and whose interests span all these activities – as mine do – without drawing strong distinctions between them.

More than anything, these distinctions are devices of disciplinary convenience. There was a period from the 1930s to the 1990s when the idea of the "graphic designer" as a term of professional self-definition and identity took hold and flourished. This required graphic designers to argue, often vehemently, that design was something quite different from art. Strong as the case might be, it was never entirely convincing because many designers continued to produce work that couldn't be so neatly classified. Even so, the legacy of this drive to construct graphic design as a discipline can be seen in the ubiquitous support structure of professional organisations, competitions, magazines, history books and conferences, and the vast number of degree courses offering instruction in how to become a graphic designer. Plenty of designers still do something recognisable as this job description, but everyone's workload is broader now, and design's vanguard has moved to a more open and less definable location – a place that looks more like what we see going on at the Sandberg Institute.

It was hard, though, to imagine any of these graduates ever choosing to work in packaging or branding. In their final essays, which I had the chance to read, they showed an intellectual grasp of critical issues in contemporary culture that better suits them to a future engaging in research, initiating their own projects, teaching, curating exhibitions, and creating hybrid forms of communication that draw on their skills as writers, editors, conceptualisers and form-givers. Yes, it does sound close to art, since artists engage in similar activities and the design MFA explicitly sets out to develop individuals with a strong personal position and voice. As design evolves, there is a need throughout higher education to rethink some no longer black-and-white aspects of the art/design relationship.

As an observer and writer, I naturally find myself in the same volatile and ambiguous position as those I study, and so, like some of the people formerly known as graphic designers, I cast about for a more protean term to describe my interests. "Visual communication", "visual culture", "communication art", and even "language and image" are closer to the nub, though old-school "graphic design" might sometimes still be part of the visual mix, or the glue that bonds everything together. Graphic design was always a place where interdisciplinary interests could find a home and one can view recent developments as an inevitable fulfilment of the field's implicit potential. For this kind of work, though, "graphic design" has become an outmoded and even misleading term. We need a sharp new name to convey the purpose, contribution and identity of an expanded, integrative, transmedia discipline of communication and expression.

Image credits

Publication credits

Essays marked * were originally published under different, or slightly different, titles.

"The Soul of Design", *Icon*, no. 38, August 2006
"Down with Innovation", *I.D.*, May 2008
"Being Somewhere"*, *Print*, January/February 2005
"Design as Dictator", *Print*, October 2010
"Stuck in the Middle"*, *Print*, November/December 2005
"Raging Bullshit"*, *Print*, September/October 2005
"Empty Buzzwords"*, *Print*, December 2014
"Agency or Studio?", *Dutch Design Yearbook*, NAi Publishers, 2010
"Counter Points", *Print*, August 2008
"The Death of Form", *Print*, April 2011
"The Takeaway Effect", *Print*, February 2013
"Thinking Outside Ourselves"*, *Print*, July/August 2005
"Power by Design", *Print*, February 2012
"Singular Sensations", *Print*, May/June 2004
"Loaded Choices"*, *Print*, July/August, 2002
"Absolutely the 'Worst'", *Eye*, no. 68, 2008
"The Death of the Critic", *Icon*, no. 33, March 2006
"Designers Need Critics", *Frame*, no. 77, November/December 2010
"Standing Still", *Print*, September/October 2007
"Sexy Nextness", *Print*, April 2008
"Stars in Our Eyes"*, *Print*, Spring 2016
"Between the Lines" *Print*, Fall 2015
"A Delicate Relationship"*, *Print*, June 2013
"One Week in Pictures", *Eye*, no. 73, 2009
"Typographic Selfies", *Print*, Summer 2017
"Revise, Reform, Rebuild"*, *Print*, August 2011
"Future of the Past"*, *Print*, Spring 2015
"Show and Tell", *Print*, June 2010
"Illustrators Illuminated"*, *Print*, Summer 2016
"Questions of Authorship", *Creative Review*, February 2001
"Art's Little Brother", *Icon*, no. 23, May 2006
"Kissing Cousins", *Print*, March/April 2005
"Where is Art Now?", *Elephant*, no. 4, Autumn 2010
"Rigorous Anarchy"*, *Print*, Spring 2017
"Flowers in the Forest"*, *Print*, May/June 2006
"Gothic Extra Böld", *Print*, September/October 2006
"Photos Lost and Found"*, *Print*, March/April 2006
"Cut and Paste Culture"*, *Print*, June 2011
"Throwaway Aesthetics"*, *Print*, August 2012
"Strained Relations", *Print*, April 2009
"Critical Omissions", *Print*, October 2008
"Critical Practice"*, *Tecknaren*, no. 3, 2010
"Critical Condition"*, *Print*, October 2014
"The Not So New Ugly"*, *Print*, October 2012
"The End of Graphic Design as We Know It?"*, *Eye*, no. 63, August 2008
"The Place Formerly Known as Graphic Design"*, *Print*, October 2011

Index

Biography

Rick Poynor is Professor of Design and Visual Culture at the University of Reading. He is the author of three other essay collections, *Design Without Boundaries* (1998), *Obey the Giant: Life in the Image World* (2001) and *Designing Pornotopia* (2006). A public champion of critical design writing for three decades, he was the founding editor of *Eye* magazine and a co-founder of the *Design Observer* website. He has taught critical writing at the Royal College of Art, London, and the School of Visual Arts, New York. His other books include *No More Rules: Graphic Design and Postmodernism* (2003), *Communicate: Independent British Graphic Design since the Sixties* (2004), *Jan van Toorn: Critical Practice* (2008) and *David King: Designer, Activist, Visual Historian* (2020).

Rick Poynor

Why Graphic Culture Matters

Copy editing: Marc Sinclair
Proofreading: Antony Hudek
Picture research: Jane Poynor
Design: Sara De Bondt
Design assistance: Leroy Meyer
Printing: die Keure
Typefaces: Maax, Mule and Muoto

Published by Occasional Papers
occasionalpapers.org

ISBN: 978-1-9196277-1-7